The
Reference Shelf®

Representative American Speeches 2016-2017

The Reference Shelf
Volume 89 • Number 6
H.W. Wilson
A Division of EBSCO Information Services, Inc.

Published by
GREY HOUSE PUBLISHING
Amenia, New York
2017

The Reference Shelf

The books in this series contain reprints of articles, excerpts from books, addresses on current issues, and studies of social trends in the United States and other countries. There are six separately bound numbers in each volume, all of which are usually published in the same calendar year. Numbers one through five are each devoted to a single subject, providing background information and discussion from various points of view and concluding with an index and comprehensive bibliography that lists books, pamphlets, and articles on the subject. The final number of each volume is a collection of recent speeches. Books in the series may be purchased individually or on subscription.

Publisher's Cataloging-In-Publication Data
(Prepared by The Donohue Group, Inc.)

Names: H.W. Wilson Company, compiler.
Title: Representative American speeches, 2016-2017 / [compiled by] H. W. Wilson, a division of EBSCO Information Services.
Other Titles: Reference shelf ; v. 89, no. 6.
Description: [First edition]. | Amenia, New York : Grey House Publishing, 2017. | Includes index.
Identifiers: ISBN 9781682174562 (v.89, no.6) | ISBN 9781682174500 (volume set)
Subjects: LCSH: Speeches, addresses, etc., American--21st century. | United States--Politics and government--2009---Sources. | Civil rights--United States--Sources. | United States--Emigration and immigration--Sources. | Social action--United States--History--21st century--Sources.
Classification: LCC PS661 .R46 2017 | DDC 815/.608--dc23

Contents

3

The Year In Review

4

Resistance and Persistence 2017

5

Free Speech on Campus

6

DREAMers and DACA

Preface

Wisdom from the Divided Republic—Speeches of 2017

Feminist pioneer Susan B. Anthony was arrested in 1872 for casting an illegal vote in the presidential election. Ordered to pay a $100 fine, Anthony refused and, instead, traveled around the country delivering a series of now famous speeches in which she passionately argued, "It was we, the people; not we the white male citizens...who formed the Union." It took nearly another half century for women to gain the right to vote and Anthony died before seeing her dream become a reality, and yet her speeches endured because the ideas that Anthony fought for—that all persons, whatever their gender, background, or race, deserved equal access to the rights of citizenship—gradually came to be seen as fundamental *American* values, despite, for many years, having been seen as little more than fringe activism. Had women never gained the right to vote, it is possible that Anthony's speeches might have been entirely forgotten or might now be remembered only as a reflection of an archaic movement.

Consider, for instance, that the speeches of Adolf Hitler are now typically remembered only when considering the dangers of xenophobia, nationalism, racism, and fascism, despite the fact that Hitler's attitudes about race were not uncommon among white males of the era. Hitler's Nazi Party not only lost the Second World War, but also lost the war of ideas and it is this struggle, the ideological debate that underlies all cultural evolution, that determines whose ideas—and the speeches, articles, and essays used to present them—will be celebrated by future generations. While a great speech might therefore have impact in the moment, the full significance of the ideas within can only be assessed in reflection, against the progress of cultural evolution.

The United States in 2017 was a nation fractured along deep cultural and political lines. The polarization of American society is part of a global trend resulting from the gradual erosion, distillation, and radicalization of conservative and traditionalist ideology. In 2016, with Democrat voters divided between radical (Sanders) and moderate (Clinton) versions of political progressivism, Republicans succeeded in electing businessman outsider Donald Trump to serve as president of the United States. Trump's election was one of many global events fueled by a surge of conservative antimodernism; defined as the belief that the modern world (or some portion of the world) has become dysfunctional or is, in some way, worse off than in some real or imagined past era. Trump explicitly supported this reading of American culture, arguing that an incompetent, corrupt liberal political machine, allegedly aided by a conspiratorial press and higher education system, had essentially led the nation down the wrong path and that it was therefore necessary to rebuild the nation in an effort to "Make America Great *Again*."

The major issues of the year—race relations, immigration, healthcare, foreign policy, and domestic security—and the speeches, essays, and policies proposed to cope with the nation's challenges can therefore be seen as volleys in this ongoing ideological struggle. It remains to be seen, for instance, whether Trump's inaugural address will be remembered as the beginning of a new conservative direction for the nation, or will be resurrected only to call attention to the failures and faults of his worldview, or whether his speech will be largely forgotten by the next generation (like most presidents' inaugural addresses). While the fate of the various world-views remains uncertain, the many passionate speakers who explored, criticized, celebrated, and dissected the issues of the year help to define a narrative, not only for the year, but for the era and ultimately for the entire history of American society.

Speaking to the Future: Commencement and the Shifting Political Landscape

Each year, colleges and universities invite public figures—often graduates of the same institution or individuals seen as having had a significant social or cultural impact on society—to address the year's graduating classes. Colleges and universities have long served as an important forum for political discourse and it is within the nation's universities and colleges that future leaders hone the skills that make them great leaders and innovators. Recognizing this, commencement speakers typically express hope for the graduates of the year and for the future world that they will help to shape and, in many cases, such speeches impart personal and professional lessons to help illuminate the paths that might be taken towards the goal of personal and professional fulfillment.

Some of the year's essential speakers shared personal stories of their professional journeys as a way to inspire and inform the year's graduates. Comedian Will Ferrell's comedic address at the University of Southern California and author Anna Quindlen's speech to Washington University students provide examples, with both encouraging the graduates of the year to seek out and follow their own unique path and identity. Other speakers took a more directly political approach, like Kamala Harris who, speaking to students at historically Black Howard University, encouraged those in attendance stand strong against social, cultural, and racial injustice while Senator Bernie Sanders used his address at Brooklyn College to explore the economic injustice of America's market-driven system in which less than 1 percent of the population controls more than 90 percent of the nation's wealth. Some, like journalist Sheryl Sandberg and Senator Cory Booker, both reacting in different ways to the polarized political environment of the year, spoke about reaching across the lines that divide individuals and groups, encouraging the year's graduates to use love, resilience, and recognition to help those who are suffering and to find collective meaning and identity.

From the stages of America's institutions of higher learning to the public podiums of the era's political establishment, the year was also about transition, with the administration of Donald Trump, and the ideology of antimodernist conservatism, replacing the moderate progressivism of the Barack Obama era. Speeches in this category are also about the future, drawing a close to one era while providing the first glimpses of what life might be like in the coming years. In his farewell address, former President Obama argued that, "…the long sweep of America has been defined by forward motion, a constant widening of our founding creed to embrace all, and not just some." By contrast, Trump, in his inaugural address, blamed foreign powers and corrupt democratic politicians for the problems faced by the American people and argued that "protectionism" and an "America first" agenda would pave the way to a more prosperous future. From the contentious election through the first year of Trump's presidency, critics and supporters alike have been struggling to understand how the America first agenda would translate to policy, as the President, seemingly unable to marshal the support of his own political party, the public, or the nation's industry and social leaders, struggled to enact the changes he promised in his historically controversial campaign.

Speaking to the Moment: Political Activism, Social Justice, and the Annual Review

Each year, some of those asked to deliver speeches or public addresses concentrate on the year at hand, speaking about the issues occurring in the moment that define current and future debate. One of the most contentious issues of the year was the ongoing controversy over the revelation that Russia interfered in the 2016 US elections to support the candidacy of Donald Trump. Dozens of speeches were delivered on the issue, with Trump and allies maintaining that allegations of Russian interference had been exaggerated and claiming that a conspiracy, potentially involving foreign agents, the Federal Bureau of Investigation (FBI), and the Democratic Party, was attempting to delegitimize his administration. The Russian election controversy was part of a broader debate over the legitimacy of the press and "fake news," the use of misinformation presented as legitimate news in an effort to sway public opinion on a specific issue. The controversy forced agents of the press, as well as the chief executive officers (CEOs) of the nation's dominant social media outlets, to reconsider their policies in an effort to balance the right to free speech with the responsibility of encouraging legitimate debate and discourse in an era unfortunately marred by information manipulation.

While race relations have been among the most contentious issues for several years, 2017 saw a renewed controversy over one small aspect of the broader issue; proposals to remove Confederate monuments from public property on the basis that such monuments symbolize white nationalism, white supremacy, and support for slavery. Donald Trump sided with the white nationalist groups who have gathered to protest the removal of the monuments, arguing that Confederate monuments are not symbolic of racism or slavery and that the removal of Confederate monuments might lead to a slippery slope in which the legitimacy of any and all monuments of American leaders might be seen as "offensive" or "inappropriate" for public display. The issue came to a head in Charlottesville, Virginia, when a white nationalist protesting the removal of a statue of General Robert E. Lee from a public park drove a car through a crowd, killing one young woman and injuring many others before being arrested. Trump drew criticism for failing to specifically condemn racism and white nationalism, but was also praised by white nationalist leaders who felt the president's decision not to specifically denounce the alt-right was a form of implicit support for their agenda.

Finally, the Trump administration's polarizing approach to politics has inspired an unprecedented level of activism from the American people. To understand why Trump has been the target of such frequent and passionate criticism, it is important to note that Trump did not win the popular vote, and so began his presidency without a popular mandate. Over the course of the year, many of America's most well-known activists and political figures gave speeches criticizing the Trump administration's policies and ideals as well as Trump's personal and professional behavior. While feminist activists Angela Davis and Gloria Steinem called on the women of the nation to stand up to Trump's misogynistic professional and personal behavior, others blasted the administration, and Trump, for helping to foster racism and xenophobia. Other public figures spoke out about the administration's decision to back out of international climate change agreements and called upon Americans to fight for environmental protection even while living with an administration that has embraced the common though thoroughly disproven belief that climate change is a myth.

Speaking to the World: Immigration and the Nature of Citizenship

Of all the difficult issues that emerged over the course of the year, the Trump administration's proposals on immigration reform were perhaps the most controversial and contentious. First, the Trump administration's attempts to enact a travel ban excluding individuals from several Muslim majority countries drew widespread criticism and two efforts to push through a ban failed legal challenges on constitutional grounds. Further, Trump's promise to build a border wall along the Mexican/US border failed to gain support among US legislators, some of whom objected to the projected cost of the project, while others believed that the wall, even if completed, would not be effective. Mexican President Enrique Nieto's repeated public statements that Mexico would not fund the wall, a promise the Trump repeatedly made during his campaign, further eroded faith in the plausibility of the administration's immigration policy.

In September, the Trump administration announced that it was going to end the Deferred Action for Childhood Arrivals (DACA) program created by an executive order from President Obama. DACA provides a streamlined path to citizenship for undocumented individuals who were brought to the United States as children (16 or under), have no criminal record, and agree to either attend college or to serve in the military. The idea that became DACA started as a bipartisan legislative effort known as the DREAM Act, and the population that this ultimately failed legislation sought to protect, have since been known as DREAMers. Though immigration is a perennially contentious issue and though immigrants have been blamed, largely without evidence, for the decline of the American working class and for high crime rates, a significant majority of Americans support allowing the DREAMers to become citizens, rather than consigning them to deportation.

The reasons for Trump's decision became clear in October when the White House announced that congress would have an opportunity to "save" the DACA program, and by extension, the 800,000 DREAMers themselves, by approving Trump's $21 billion plan to build a wall along the Mexican border, in addition to supporting a number of other unpopular and controversial immigration proposals. Attorney General Jeff Sessions summed up the executive order with the statement "We can't admit everyone," and argued that Obama's executive order violated constitutional law and thus that Trump, in canceling the order, was only upholding the constitution. Among the many speeches and articles written on the issue was a solemn and forthright rebuttal from former President Obama, who asked, "What if our kid's science teacher, or our friendly neighbor turns out to be a Dreamer? Where are we supposed to send her? To a country she doesn't know or remember, with a language she may not even speak?"

Speaking to the Nation: Reconciliation and Free Speech

Many thinkers, writers, journalists, and public figures have espoused the idea that the US population, in 2017, was deeply divided, but there were, however, a few moments in which intellectuals who might otherwise disagree on many central issues were able to set their differences aside in support of a common goal. One such issue involved free speech on college campuses, and emerged from a number of high profile incidents in which left-wing agitators prevented universities from allowing right-wing figures to speak on university grounds. This phenomenon, though most likely a product of youthful exuberance and the highly charged political climate, brought criticism from both sides. In one example of cross-ideological concord, progressive author Cornel West and conservative scholar Robert P. George issued a joint statement asking the nation's students to reach across the ideological divide and to recognize that informed debate, rather than rhetoric, is the key to a functioning democracy.

In a year when reconciliation seemed rare, the debate on free speech in America's colleges demonstrates that individuals on both sides can and will come together to defend and protect the fundamental values of American society. There is, however, no consensus on what those fundamental values should be. Whether the promises of a new political guard or the passionate protests of an ongoing human rights struggle, these words of wisdom, from within the divided republic, point the way towards some of the nation's many possible futures, and also demonstrate the passion, humor, fear, kindness, and cruelty of the American people.

Micah L. Issitt

1

To the Graduating Class

Photo by Marvin Joseph/*The Washington Post* via Getty Images

US Senator Kamala D. Harris (D-CA) gave the convocation oration for The 2017 Howard University Commencement Ceremony in Washington, DC on May, 13, 2017.

Commencement Speech to the University of Southern California Class of 2017

By Will Ferrell

Celebrated comedian Will Ferrell, graduate of University of Southern California (1990) delivers the commencement address to the 2017 undergraduate class of USC. Ferrell, who starred on the comedy program Saturday Night Live *from 1995 to 2002, and went on to star in a list of successful films, speaks about his time at USC working on his undergraduate degree in sports information and about the early experiences that led to his decision to pursue a comedy career. Ferrell encourages USC graduates to experiment with new fields and interests as they struggle to define themselves and their goals after graduation.*

We are SC We are [SC]. We are [SC]. We are [SC]. Thank you. Thank you.

It is such an honor to deliver this year's commencement address to the University of Southern California's graduating class of 2017.

I would like to say thank you, graduates, for that warm welcome. I would also like to apologize to all the parents who are sitting there, saying, "Will Ferrell? Why will Ferrell? I hate Will Ferrell. I hate him. I hate his movies. He's gross. Although he's much better-looking in person. Has he lost weight?"

By the way, that discussion is happening out there right now.

Today I have also received an honorary doctorate, for which I would like to give my thanks to President Max Nikias. I would also like to recognize my esteemed fellow honorary doctorates, Suzanne Dworak-Peck, a great humanitarian and visionary in the field of social work. Dr. Gary Michelson, whose innovation as one of the country's leading orthopedic spinal surgeons has revolutionized this field. Mark Ridley Thomas, a pillar of local and state government for over 25 years. David Ho whose work in AIDS research led him to be *Time* magazine's Man of the Year for 1996. And one of the great actors of our time, Academy-Award winning actress Dame Helen Mirren.

And then there's me. Will Ferrell, whose achievements include running naked through the city of Montrose in *Old School*. Montrose in the house, alright. Running around in my underwear and racing helmet, thinking that I'm on fire as Ricky Bobby in *Talladega Nights*. Running around in Elf tights eating gum off the ground and playing cowbell. I think my fellow doctorates would agree based on our achievements we are all on equal footing.

Delivered on May 12, 2017 at the University of Southern California, Los Angeles, CA.

I want the university to know that I do not take this prestigious honor lightly. I've already instructed my wife and my children, from this point on, they have to address me as Dr. Ferrell. There will be no exceptions. Especially at our children's various school functions and when opening Christmas presents. "Yay, we got the new Xbox, thank you Dad! I mean, Dr. Ferrell."

I've been informed that I can now perform minimally invasive surgery at any time or any place, even if people don't want it. In fact, I am legally obligated to perform minor surgery at the end of today's ceremonies, or my doctor's degree will be revoked. So if anyone has a sore tooth that needs to be removed or wants hernia surgery, please meet me at the "surgery center"—by "surgery center" I mean a windowless van I have parked over by the Coliseum.

The next time I'm flying and they ask if there's a doctor on board, I can now confidently leap to my feet and scream, "I'm a doctor, what can I do? Yes, no problem, I can absolutely deliver that baby." Hopefully it will be on United Airlines, in which I will be immediately be subdued and dragged off the aircraft, which we all know will be recorded on someone's iPhone and put on YouTube. You will hear me say, "Call Max Nikias, President of USC. He told me I'm a doctor." Rest assured, President Nikias, I will use my powers wisely.

Although this is my first commencement address I have delivered to an actual university, this is not my first commencement speech. The institutions to which I have spoken at previously include Bryman School of Nursing, DeVry Technical School, Debbie Dudeson School of Trucking, University of Phoenix, Hollywood DJ Academy and Trump University. I am still waiting to get paid from Trump University. In fact, it turns out I owe Trump University money for the honor to speak at Trump University.

You are the graduating class of 2017. And by every statistical analysis you are collectively considered the strongest class ever to graduate from this university. All of you have excelled in various courses of study. All of you, except for four students. And you know exactly who you are. If you would care to stand and reveal yourself right now, that would be great, those four students. There's one. Two. Three, four, five, six, eight, more like 20. Very honest of you.

It is incredibly surreal, one might even say unbelievable, that I get to deliver this address to you. As a freshman in the fall of 1986, if you were to come up to me and say that in the year 2017 you, Will Ferrell, will be delivering the commencement address for USC, I would have hugged you with tears in my eyes.

I then would have asked this person from the future, "Does that mean I graduated?"

"Yes, you did," says the person from the future.

"What else can you tell me about the future?"

Future person turns to me and says, "I can tell you that you will become one of the most famous alumni in this university, mentioned in the same breath as John Wayne, Neil Armstrong and Rob Kardashian. You will be referenced in rap songs from Kanye West, to Little Wayne to Drake." Nas will say, "Get me real bonkers like Will Ferrell on cat tranquilizer."

"Is that it?" I would ask.

"Yes, that sums it up. Except one other thing—in the future there will be something called Shake Shack. It will start in New York and then come to LA and people will wait hours for a milkshake that is definitely good but not that good that you should wait two hours."

So yes, if I had heard all of that I would have been incredulous at best. But it turns out I did graduate in 1990 with a degree in Sports Information. Yes. You heard me, Sports Information. A program so difficult, so arduous, that they discontinued the major eight years after I left. Those of us with Sports Information degrees are an elite group. We are like the Navy Seals of USC graduates. There are very few of us and there was a high dropout rate.

So I graduate and I immediately get a job right out of college working for ESPN, right? Wrong. No, I moved right back home. Back home to the mean streets of Irvine, California. Yes. Irvine always gets that response. Pretty great success story, right? Yeah, I moved back home for a solid two years, I might add. And I was lucky, actually. Lucky that I had a very supportive and understanding mother, who is sitting out there in the crowd, who let me move back home. And she recognized that while I had an interest in pursuing sportscasting, my gut was telling me that I really wanted to pursue something else. And that something else was comedy.

For you see, the seeds for this journey were planted right here on this campus. This campus was a theater or testing lab if you will. I was always trying to make my friends laugh whenever I could find a moment. I had a work-study job at the humanities audiovisual department that would allow me to take off from time to time. By allow me, I mean I would just leave and they didn't notice. So I would literally leave my job if I knew friends were attending class close by and crash a lecture while in character. My good buddy Emil, who's also here today—Emil, in the house—Emil told me one day that I should crash his Thematic Options literature class one day. So I cobbled together a janitor's outfit complete with work gloves, safety goggles, a dangling lit cigarette, and a bucket full of cleaning supplies. And then I proceeded to walk into the class, interrupting the lecture, informing the professor that I'd just been sent from Physical Plant to clean up a student's vomit. True story.

What Emil neglected to tell me was that the professor of his class was Ronald Gottesman, a professor who co-edited the *Norton Anthology of American Literature.* Needless to say a big-time guy. A month after visiting my friend's class as a janitor, I was walking through the campus when someone grabbed me by the shoulder and it was Ron Gottesman. I thought for sure he was going to tell me to never do that again. Instead what he told me was that he loved my barging in on his class and that he thought it was one of the funniest things he'd ever seen and would I please do it again? So on invitation from Professor Gottesman I would barge in on his lecture class from time to time as the guy from Physical Plant coming by to check on things, and the professor would joyfully play along.

One time I got my hands on a power drill and I just stood outside the classroom door operating the drill for a good minute. Unbeknownst to me, Professor Gottesman was wondering aloud to his class, "I wonder if we're about to get a visit from our Physical Plant guy?" I then walked in as if on cue and the whole class erupted in laughter. After leaving, Professor Gottesman then weaved the surprise visit into his lecture on Walt Whitman and the *Leaves of Grass*. Moments like these encouraged me to think maybe I was funny to whole groups of people who didn't know me, and this wonderful professor had no idea how his encouragement of me—to come and interrupt his class no less—was enough to give myself permission to be silly and weird.

My senior year I would discover a comedy and improv troupe called the Groundlings located on Melrose Avenue. This was the theater company and school that gave the starts to Laraine Newman, Phil Hartman, John Lovitz, Pee Wee Herman, Conan O'Brien, Lisa Kudrow to name a few. Later it would become my home where I would meet the likes of Chris Kattan, CheriOteri, Ana Gasteyer, Chris Parnell, Maya Rudolph, Will Forte and Kristin Wiig. I went to one of their shows during the spring semester of my senior year and in fact got pulled up onstage during an audience participation sketch. I was so afraid and awestruck at what the actors were doing that I didn't utter a word. And even in this moment of abject fear and total failure I found it to be thrilling to be on that stage. I then knew I wanted to be a comedic actor.

So starting in the fall of 1991, for the next three and a half years I was taking classes and performing in various shows at the Groundlings and around Los Angeles. I was even trying my hand at stand-up comedy. Not great stand-up, mind you, but enough material to get myself up in front of strangers. I would work the phones to invite all my SC friends to places like Nino's Italian Restaurant in Long Beach, the San Juan Depot in San Juan, Capistrano, and the Cannery in Newport Beach. And those members of my Trojan family would always show up. My stand-up act was based mostly on material derived from watching old episodes of *Star Trek*. My opening joke was to sing the opening theme to *Star Trek*. [Sings]

Thank you. Not even funny, just weird. But I didn't care, I was just trying to throw as many darts at the dartboard, hoping that one would eventually stick. Now don't get me wrong, I wasn't extremely confident that I would succeed during this time period, and after moving back to LA there were many a night where in my LA apartment, I would sit down to a meal of spaghetti topped with mustard, with only $20 in my checking account and I would think to myself, "Oh well I can always be a substitute schoolteacher." And yes, I was afraid. You're never not afraid. I'm still afraid. I was afraid to write this speech. And now, I'm just realizing how many people are watching me right now, and it's scary. Can you please look away while I deliver the rest of the speech?

But my fear of failure never approached in magnitude my fear of what if. What if I never tried at all?

By the spring of 1995 producers from *Saturday Night Live* had come to see the current show at the Groundlings. After two harrowing auditions and two meetings with executive producer Lorne Michaels, which all took place over the course of six weeks, I got the word I was hired to the cast of *Saturday Night Live* for the '95-'96 season.

I couldn't believe it. And even though I went on to enjoy seven seasons on the show, it was a rocky beginning for me. After my first show, one reviewer referred to me as "the most annoying newcomer of the new cast." Someone showed this to me and I promptly put it up on the wall in my office, reminding myself that to some people I will be annoying. Some people will not think I'm funny, and that that's okay. One woman wrote to me and said she hated my portrayal of George W. Bush. It was mean-spirited, not funny and besides you have a fat face. I wrote her back and I said, I appreciate your letter and she was entitled to her opinion, but that my job as a comedian especially on a show like *Saturday Night Live* was to hold up a mirror to our political leaders and engage from time to time in satirical reflection. As for my fat face, you are 100% right. I'm trying to work on that. Please don't hesitate to write me again if you feel like I've lost some weight in my face.

The venerable television critic for the *Washington Post* Tom Shales came up to me during my last season of the show. He told me congratulations on my time at the show and then he apologized for things he had written about me in some of his early reviews of my work. I paused for a second before I spoke, and then I said, "How dare you, you son of a bitch?" I could tell this startled him, and then I told him I was kidding, and that I'd never read any of his reviews. It was true, I hadn't read his reviews. In fact I didn't read any reviews because once again, I was too busy throwing darts at the dartboard, all the while facing my fears.

Even as I left *SNL*, none of the studios were willing to take a chance on me as a comedy star. It took us three years of shopping *Anchorman* around before anyone would make it. When I left *SNL* all I really had was a movie called *Old School* that wouldn't be released for another year, and a sub-par script that needed a huge re-write about a man raised by elves at the North Pole.

Even now I still lose out on parts that I want so desperately. My most painful example was losing the role of Queen Elizabeth in the film *The Queen*. Apparently it came down to two actors, myself and Helen Mirren. The rest is history. Dame Helen Mirren, you stole my Oscar!

Now one may look at me as having great success, which I have in the strictest sense of the word, and don't get me wrong, I love what I do and I feel so fortunate to get to entertain people. But to me, my definition of success is my 16-and-a-half-year marriage to my beautiful and talented wife, Vivica. Success are my three amazing sons, Magnus, 13, Matthias, 10 and Axel age 7. Right there, stand up guys, take a bow, there you go.

Success to me is my involvement in the charity Cancer for College, which gives college scholarships to cancer survivors, started by my great friend and SC alum Craig Pollard, a two-time cancer survivor himself, who thought of the charity while we were fraternity brothers at the Delt house, up on West Adams. Craig was also one of the members of my Trojan family sitting front-and-center at my bad stand-up comedy shows, cheering me on.

No matter how cliché it may sound you will never truly be successful until you learn to give beyond yourself. Empathy and kindness are the true signs of emotional intelligence, and that's what Viv and I try to teach our boys. Hey Matthias, get your hands of Axel right now! Stop it. I can see you. Okay? Dr. Ferrell's watching you.

To those of you graduates sitting out there who have a pretty good idea of what you'd like to do with your life, congratulations. For many of you who maybe don't have it all figured out, it's okay. That's the same chair that I sat in. Enjoy the process of your search without succumbing to the pressure of the result. Trust your gut, keep throwing darts at the dartboard. Don't listen to the critics and you will figure it out.

Class of 2017, I just want you to know you will never be alone on whatever path you may choose. If you do have a moment where you feel a little down just think of the support you have from this great Trojan family and imagine me, literally picture my face, singing this song gently into your ear: *If I should stay, I would only be in your way. So I'll go, but I know, I'll think of you every step of the way. And I will always love you, will always love you, will always love you, Class of 2017. And I will always love you.*

Thank you, fight on!

Print Citations

CMS: Ferrell, Will. "Commencement Speech to the University of Southern California Class of 2017." May, 2016. Speech presented at the University of Southern California Class of 2017 Commencement, Los Angeles, CA, May, 2017. In *The Reference Shelf: Representative American Speeches 2016-2017*, edited by Betsy Maury, 3-8. Ipswich, MA: H.W. Wilson, 2017.

MLA: Ferrell, Will. "Commencement Speech to the University of Southern California Class of 2017." University of Southern California Class of 2017 Commencement. Los Angeles, CA. May, 2017. Presentation. *The Reference Shelf: Representative American Speeches 2016-2017*. Ed. Betsy Maury. Ipswich: Salem Press, 2017. 3-8. Print.

APA: Ferrell, W. (2017). Commencement speech to the University of California class of 2017. [Presentation]. *Speech presented at the University of Southern California class of 2017 commencement*. Los Angeles, CA. In Betsy Maury (Ed.), *The reference shelf: Representative American speeches 2016-2017* (pp. 3-8). Ipswich, MA: H.W. Wilson. (Original work published 2017)

Remarks to the Howard University Class of 2017

By Kamala D. Harris

US Senator Kamala Harris of California delivers the 2017 commencement address to the students of Howard University, one of the nation's oldest historically black universities, established in 1867. Harris, a former district attorney for San Francisco who was elected in 2016 to fill the seat previously held by Senator Barbara Boxer, has built a reputation as a fierce critic of the Donald Trump administration and a passionate advocate of the contemporary civil rights movement. Harris encourages Howard's 2017 graduating class to stand strong and "speak truth" when faced with racial prejudice, fascism, and xenophobia. She also speaks about the importance of political action and community service.

Greetings, Bisons! It is so great to be back home. President Frederick… members of the Board… distinguished faculty—thank you for this incredible honor. And to the Class of 2017—congratulations!

And to your families and friends who encouraged you and held you up—thank you for all you did. Let's hear it for them!

I've had the honor of speaking at many commencements. But this one is particularly special for me. Because decades ago, I sat just where you sit now, feeling the embrace of my Howard family. Our Howard family.

And a family, at its best, shares common values and aspirations. A family shares hardships and a connected history. A family looks for ways to support and inspire one another.

Our family includes a young woman who worked her way through school and is graduating as a published poet—Angel Dye. It includes the fourth Rhodes Scholar in Howard's history—Cameron Clarke. It includes a woman who got elected to an Advisory Neighborhood Commission at 18 years old, the youngest elected official in D.C. history. And she is your HUSA President—Allyson Carpenter.

And our family also includes those who came before you.

Thurgood Marshall and Zora Neale Hurston… Shirley Franklin and Doctor LaSalle Leffall… Mr. Vernon Jordan and Ta-Nahesi Coates… Elijah Cummings and Mayor Kasim Reed. And now, graduates, you are ready to join the ranks.

You are finally at your Commencement. So look around. Capture this moment. Hold it in your heart and hold it in your mind. You're looking at people you will read

Delivered on May 13, 2017, at Howard University, Washington, DC.

about for the trailblazing work they will do. You're looking at the faces of friends who one day will ask you to Godparent their children.

You may even be looking at someone you'll grow your family with—even if one or both of you doesn't fully know that right now.

And graduates, also look back on the experiences you've already had.

Remember—those first days on the Yard. Moving into the Quad and Drew. Learning how to navigate the "Howard Runaround" so you could get that dorm room or sign up for a class.

Remember—or maybe even try to forget—all those late nights at Founders… and those other nights at the Punchout or El Rey.

Above all, remember that you are blessed. Wherever you came from, you now have the gift—the great gift—of a Howard University education.

And you are also part of a legacy that has now endured and thrived for 150 years.

Endured when the doors of higher education were closed to Black students. Endured when segregation and discrimination were the law of the land. Endured when few recognized the potential and capacity of young Black men and women to be leaders.

But over the last 150 years, Howard has endured and thrived. Generations of students have been nurtured and challenged here—and provided with the tools and confidence to soar.

Since this school was founded, in 1867, Howard has awarded more than 120,000 degrees.

It has prepared and produced thousands of Black lawyers and doctors, and artists and writers… dentists and pharmacists… social workers and engineers. And most recently, Howard has partnered with Google to bring more Black students into the tech industry.

It prepared me for a career in public service, starting with my first-ever political race—for freshman class representative on what was then called the Liberal Arts Student Council.

So at this moment, when voices at the highest level of our government seem confused about the significance and even the constitutionality of supporting HB-CUs, I say look over here at Howard University!

So now you are all official members of what I call the "Role Model Club."

And it's a pretty exclusive club. It includes my distinguished fellow Commencement honorees.

It includes members of the Class of 1967, who today celebrate their 50th anniversary, and who marched and fought for justice when Jim Crow was still the law of the land.

And it includes people like Charles Hamilton Houston and Thurgood Marshall, who were among my inspirations for going to law school.

History has proved that each generation of Howard graduates will forge the way forward for our country and our world.

And now, it is your turn. And let's look at the world you are now entering.

You are graduating into a very different time than it was when you arrived a few short years ago.

You are graduating into a time when we see a revival of the failed War on Drugs and a renewed reliance on mandatory minimum prison sentences.

A time when young people who were brought to America as children fear a midnight knock on the door.

A time when throwing millions of working people off their health insurance to give tax breaks to the top 1% is considered a victory to some.

A time when we worry that a late-night tweet could start a war.

A time when we no longer believe the words of some of our leaders, and where the very integrity of our justice system has been called into question.

Graduates, indeed we have a fight ahead. And it's not a fight between Democrats and Republicans. It's not rich versus poor or urban versus rural.

It's a fight to define what kind of country we are.

It's a fight to determine what kind of country we will be.

And it's a fight to determine whether we are willing to stand up for our deepest values.

Because let's be clear—we are better than this.

And you know what I'm talking about.

From the time you arrived on this campus, you participated in the 50th anniversary of the March on Washington, and you students have joined that fight for justice.

You've protested. From the streets of Ferguson to the halls of the United States Congress.

You have lived the words of James Baldwin: "There is never time in the future in which we will work out our salvation. The challenge is in the moment; the time is always now."

Indeed, the time is always now. And because you are a Howard graduate, the bar is high.

Which means you must be at the front of the line. You must be the first to raise your hand. You must lead.

The motto of this university is: "Veritas et Utilitas." Truth and Service.

And I know sometimes we're afraid of falling short. It's not that we don't know what we should do. It's that the bar can sometimes feel too high. It takes so much time and effort to reach it, so much sweat and so many tears. And being human, we sometimes fall short. And that's OK.

But because you went to Howard University, you have a responsibility to keep reaching for that bar. To keep serving.

So, Class of 2017, proud members of the Role Model Club, in these unprecedented times, you must ask: How will I serve? How will I lead?

Well, I've got three pieces of advice on how to answer that question. Reject false choices. Speak truth. And, you don't think you need a big title to make a big difference.

So let's talk about each of these.

First, to lead and thrive you must reject false choices. Howard taught me, as it has taught you, that you can do anything and you can do everything.

At Howard, you can be a football player and a valedictorian. You can be a budding computer scientist and a poet. You can have a 4.0, intern on the Hill, and still find time to "darty" on the weekend.

Back in the day, I'd go down to the National Mall to protest the United States' investment in apartheid South Africa. And I interned in the United States Senate.

I chaired the economics society and was on the Howard debate team. And I pledged my dear sorority, Alpha Kappa Alpha. (In fact, several of my line sisters came here to be with me today.)

So the notion of rejecting false choices that Howard taught us has carried me throughout my career—as the District Attorney of San Francisco, as the Attorney General of California, and now as a United States Senator.

And in my career, the conventional wisdom was that people were either soft on crime or tough on crime. But I knew we should be smart on crime.

I was told prosecutors don't need to focus on recidivism—people said, "that's not your job, just keep locking folks up." But as DA, I launched an initiative to help first-time offenders re-enter society and not go back to prison.

I was told prosecutors shouldn't focus on the needs of children. But we created a Bureau of Children's Justice, that took on elementary school truancy.

So, graduates, I share all of this with you to make the point that there is no limit to what you can do when you detect and reject false choices.

You can advocate for Environmental justice, and you can be the CEO who commits to cutting your company's carbon footprint.

You can march for workers on a picket line, and you can be their voice inside the Department of Labor.

You can call for greater diversity in the arts and entertainment, and you can be like Howard's own Taraji P. Henson on the screen, bringing to life those "hidden figures."

You can march for Black lives on the street, and you can ensure law enforcement accountability by serving as a prosecutor or on a police commission.

The reality is on most matters, somebody is going to make the decision—so why not let it be you?

Because, if we're going to make progress anywhere, we need you everywhere.

And, sometimes to make change you've got to change how change is made.

So do not be constrained by tradition.

Do not listen when they say it can't be done.

And do not be burdened by what has been when you can create what should be.

Like Baldwin said, the time is always now. So no false choices.

My second piece of advice is that you must speak truth.

And let me be clear, speaking the truth is different from telling the truth. Telling the truth means separating fact from fiction.

The earth is round. The sky is blue. Howard University is the REAL H-U.

But unlike telling the truth, speaking the truth means you must speak up and speak out. Even when you're not being asked, and even when it's uncomfortable or inconvenient.

Let me give you an example. Just a few years after I left Howard, I was working as a prosecutor during the crack epidemic in the 1990s. It was the height of gang violence in LA, and California had passed what were known as gang enhancement laws, which meant longer sentences if a person was affiliated with a gang. And because these laws were new, prosecutors were trying to figure out how to prove these cases in court.

So one day I was in my office at the courthouse, and I heard my coworkers talking outside my door. They were talking about how they'd prove certain people were gang-affiliated.

So they mentioned the neighborhood where the arrest had occurred—the way the people were dressed, the kind of music they were listening to.

And hearing this conversation, well you know I had to poke my head outside my door. And I looked at them and I said: "Hey, guys. You know that corner you were talking about? Well, I know people who live there."

"You know the clothes you were talking about? I have family members who dress that way."

"And that music?"—and now I'm about to date myself—"Well, I have a tape of that music in my car."

And in case you all are wondering, that tape was of Oakland's own Too Short.

So they looked up, a little embarrassed. And needless to say, they realized they needed to think differently about who does what and where.

So Howard encourages us—expects us—to use our voice.

And I promise you, as you leave this place, you will often find that you're the only one in the room who looks like you, or who has had the same experience as you. And you're going to feel very alone.

But wherever you are—whether you're in a courtroom, a board room, or a tech incubator, whether you're in Washington or Wichita—you must remember: you are never alone.

Your entire Howard family, past and present—everyone here—will be in that room with you, cheering you on, as you speak up and speak out.

The time is always now. Speak truth.

Here's my third piece of advice and final story. You don't need a big title to make a big difference.

So after my second year of law school, I was a summer intern at the Alameda County DA's office, and there had been a big drug bust. And working on the case, I realized that among those arrested was an innocent bystander.

But it was late on a Friday afternoon, and most people had gone home. Which meant the case wouldn't get called until Monday. Meaning this innocent bystander would have been held all weekend. And then I learned she had young children.

Now, no innocent person should spend a weekend in jail. And I knew what it would mean if she couldn't get home, including that she could even lose her children. So I sat right there in the courtroom and I waited. And waited. And waited.

I told the clerk we had to call the case. I pleaded for the judge to come back. I wouldn't leave until the judge finally gave in. And when that happened, with the swipe of a pen, this woman got to go home to her children.

It would be years before I would run a major prosecutor's office… before I would create policies and write legislation that would be adopted at the state and national level.

And I didn't realize it at the time. But that Friday afternoon in that courtroom, in Oakland, California, that woman taught me that when you see something in front of you that's wrong, you can just go ahead and do what you know is right. And it will make a difference. Even if nobody but you and she knows.

The time is always now. You don't need a big title to make a big difference.

So, graduates, as you begin this next phase of your life, I have one request of you. When you get your diploma later, take a good look at it. Remember what's on it? "Veritas" and "Utilitas." Truth and Service.

That is your duty—the duty of your degree. That is the charge of a Howard graduate.

So whatever you plan to do next—whether you want to design the latest app or cure cancer or run a business. Whether you're going to be a dentist, a lawyer, a teacher, or an accountant—let your guiding principle be truth and service.

At a time when there are Americans—disproportionately Black and brown men—trapped in a broken system of mass incarceration…Speak truth—and serve.

At a time when men, women, and children have been detained at airports in our country simply because of the God they worship…Speak truth—and serve.

At a time when immigrants have been taken from their families in front of schools and outside courthouses… Speak truth—and serve.

And at a time of incredible scientific and technological advances as well…when we're dreaming of a mission to Mars…and unraveling the mysteries of the brain… and entrepreneurs in my home state of California are even starting to test flying cars…Speak truth—and serve.

We need you. Our country needs you. The world needs you.

Allyson, your HUSA President, said to me, "Boy, we can't wait until we're in charge." Well, guess what—I can't wait either. And neither can our world. So get out there.

And your Howard family will be with you every step of the way.

Congratulations!

Print Citations

CMS: Harris, Kamala D. "Remarks to the Howard University Class of 2017." Speech presented at the Howard University Class of 2017 Commencement, Washington, DC, May, 2017. In *The Reference Shelf: Representative American Speeches 2016-2017*, edited by Betsy Maury, 9-15. Ipswich, MA: H.W. Wilson, 2017.

MLA: Harris, Kamala D. "Remarks to the Howard University Class of 2017." Howard University Class of 2017 Commencement. Washington, DC. May, 2017. Presentation. *The Reference Shelf: Representative American Speeches 2016-2017.* Ed. Betsy Maury. Ipswich: H.W. Wilson, 2017. 9-15. Print.

APA: Harris, K.D. (2017). Remarks to the Howard University class of 2017. [Presentation]. *Speech presented at the Howard University class of 2017 commencement.* Washington, DC. In Betsy Maury (Ed.), *The reference shelf: Representative American speeches 2016-2017* (pp. 9-15). Ipswich, MA: H.W. Wilson. (Original work published 2017)

Building Collective Resistance

By Sheryl Sandberg

Sheryl Sandberg, an executive, author, and activist famous for her 2013 book Lean In *and the Leaninfoundation that emerged from her work as a feminist activist, delivered an address to the 2017 class at her alma mater, Virginia Tech. Sandberg, offering personal reflections on her life and coping with loss, discusses the concept of "resilience" on both a personal and a community level and offers advice on how to develop resilience in one's own life as well as in helping others develop the ability to cope with the challenges and transformations in their lives.*

Hello Hokies!

President Sands, esteemed faculty, proud parents, devoted friends, wet siblings…congratulations to all of you. But most importantly, congratulations to the Virginia Tech class of 2017!

I am honored to be with you and this San Francisco summer day feels just like home, just like it does with anything with "Tech" in its name.

I'm so delighted to be here with my friend, Regina Dugan. As you just heard, Regina used to run DARPA—for real!—and now she is developing breakthrough technologies at Facebook. In Hokie terms, she's our Bruce Smith. And she is just one of so many alums doing amazing things around the world.

Today, class of 2017, you join them. And I'm thrilled for you. And thrilled for all of the people who are here supporting you—the people who have pushed you, dried your tears and laughed with you from your first day to this day. Let's show them all of our thanks.

Commencement speeches can be pretty one-sided. The speaker—that's me—imparts her hardearned wisdom…or at least tries to. The graduates—that's you—you sit in the rain today and listen like the thoughtful people you are. Then you hurl your caps in the air, hug your friends, let your parents take lots pictures of you—(post them on Instagram, just one idea)—and head off into your amazing lives…maybe swinging by Sharkey's for one last plate of wings before you go.

Today's going to be a little bit different because I'm not going to talk about something I know and you don't. I want to talk about something the Virginia Tech community knows all too well.

Today, I want to talk about resilience.

This university is known for so many things. Your kindness and decency… your

---

Delivered on May 12, 2017 at Virginia Tech, Blacksburg, VA.

academic excellence…your deeply-felt school spirit. I've spent time at a lot of time at colleges—yes for work, but also because I might want to relive my 20s just a little.

Few people talk about their school the way Hokies talk about Virginia Tech. There is so much pride and unity here—such a deep sense of identity, and I am going to prove it by asking you one simple question:

What's a Hokie? [I am!]

That's it! What you might not realize is that that Hokie spirit has made all of you more resilient. I've spent the last two years studying resilience because something happened in my life that demanded more of it than I ever would have thought possible.

Two years and eleven days ago, I lost my husband Dave suddenly and unexpectedly. Sometimes I still have a hard time saying the words because I can't quite believe it actually happened. I woke up on what I thought would be a totally normal day. And my world just changed forever.

I know, important day—it's raining, and I'm up here talking about death. But I promise you there's a reason—and even one that's not even sad.

Because what I've learned since losing Dave has fundamentally changed how I view this world and how I live in it. And I want to share it with you, on this day because I think it's going to help you lead happier, healthier, and more joyful lives. and you deserve all of that.

Each of you walked a very unique path to reach this day. Some of you faced real trauma. All of you faced challenges. Disappointment, heartache, loss, illness—all of these are so personal when they strike—but they are also so universal.

And then there are the shared losses. The Virginia Tech community knows this. You've stopped for a quiet moment by the 32 Hokie stones on the Drillfield, as I did with President Sands just this morning. You've joined your friends for the "Run in Remembrance." You know that life can turn in an instant. And you know what it means to come together, to pull together, to grieve together, but, ultimately, to overcome together.

After Dave died, I did something I've done at other hard times in my life: I hit the books. With my friend Adam Grant, a psychologist who studies how we find meaning in our lives, I dove into the research on resilience and recovery.

The most important thing I learned is that we are not born with a certain amount of resilience. It is a muscle, and that means we can build it.

We build resilience into ourselves. We build resilience into the people we love. And we build it together, as a community. That's called "collective resilience." It's an incredibly powerful force—and it's one that our country and our world need a lot more of right about now. It is in our relationships with each other that we find our will to live, our capacity to love, and our ability to bring change into this world.

Class of 2017, you are particularly suited to the task of building collective resilience because you are graduating from Virginia Tech. Communities like this don't just happen. They are formed and strengthened by people coming together in very specific ways. You've been part of that here, whether you knew it or not. As you go off and become leaders—and yes, you will lead, you are destined to lead—you can make the communities you join—and the communities you form—stronger.

Here's where you start.

You can build collective resilience through shared experiences. You've had lots of those: jumping to "Enter Sandman,"—I saw that this morning, it's incredible. Enduring the walk across the Drillfield in the winter (kind of like Jon Snow at the Wall), finding new loves and then NEW new loves, being there for each other through triumph and through disappointment. Every class, every meal, every all nighter has added another strand to a vast web that connects you to each other and to Hokies everywhere.

These ties do more than connect—they support. Nearly 30 years ago, a very talented young man made it from a very underprivileged background all the way to college, but then he didn't finish. And when he dropped out, he said, "If only I had my posse with me, I would have graduated." That insight led an amazing woman named Deborah Bial to create the Posse Foundation, which recruits high-potential students in teams of 10 to go from the same city to the same college. Posse kids have a 90 percent graduation rate from some of the best schools in the country.

We all need our posses—especially when life puts the obstacles in our path. Out there in the world, when you leave Virginia Tech, you're going to have to build your own posse—and sometimes that's going to mean asking for help.

This was never easy for me. Before Dave died, I tried to bother people as little as possible—and yes, "bothering people" is what I thought it was. But then my life changed and I needed my friends and family and colleagues more than I ever could have thought I would. My mom—who along with my dad is here with me today just like yours are here with you—stayed with me for the very first month, literally holding me as I cried myself to sleep. I had never felt weaker. But I learned that it takes strength to rely on others. There are times to lean in and there are times to lean on.

Building a posse also means acknowledging our friends' challenges. Before I lost Dave, if a friend was going through something hard, I would usually say I am sorry—once. And then I wouldn't bring it up again because I didn't want to remind them of their pain. Losing my husband taught me how absurd that was—you can't remind me I lost Dave. But like I had done with others, when people failed to mention it, it felt like there was a big, old elephant following me around everywhere I went.

It's not only death that ushers in the elephant. You want to completely silence a room? Say you have cancer, that your father went to jail, that you just lost your job. We retreat into silence just when we need each other the most. Now, not everyone is going to want to talk about everything all the time. But saying to a friend, "I know you are suffering and I am here with you" can kick a very ugly elephant out of any room.

If you are in someone's posse, don't just offer to help in a generic way. Before I lost Dave, when a friend was in need, I would say, "Is there anything I can do?" And I meant it kindly—the problem is, that question kind of shifts the burden to the person in need. And when people asked me, I didn't know how to answer the question. "Can you make Father's Day go away?" Here's a different approach. When my friend Dan Levy's son was sick in the hospital, a friend texted him and said, "What do you not want on a burger?" Another friend texted from the lobby and said "I'm in the lobby of the hospital for a hug for the next hour whether you come down or not."

You don't have to do something huge. You don't have to wait for someone to tell you exactly what they need. And you do not have to be someone's best friend from the first grade to show up. If you are there for your friends, and let them be there for you—if you laugh together until your sides ache, if you hold each other as you cry, and maybe even bring them a burger with the wrong toppings before they ask—that won't just make you more resilient, it will help you lead a deeper and more meaningful life.

We also build collective resilience through shared narratives. That might sound light—how important can a story be? But stories are vital. They're how we explain our past and they are how we set expectations for our future. And they help us build the common understanding that creates a community in the first place.

Every time your friends tell their favorite tales—like, I don't know, when Tech beat UVA in double overtime—you strengthen your bonds to each other.

Shared narratives are critical for fighting injustice and creating social change. A few years ago, we started LeanIn.Org to help work towards gender equality—helping women and men form Lean In circles—small groups that support each other's ambitions. There are now more than 33,000 Circles in 150 countries. But It wasn't until I lost Dave that I understood why Circles are thriving—it's because they build collective resilience.

Not long ago, I was in Beijing and I had a chance to meet with women from Lean In circles across China. Like in a lot of places, it's not always easy to be a woman in China. If you're unmarried past age 27, you're called sheng nu—a "leftover woman." And I thought the word "widow" was bad! The stigma that comes from being a leftover woman can be intense. One woman—a 36-year-old economics professor—was rejected by 15 men because—wait for it—she was—too educated. After that, her father forbade her younger sister from going to graduate school.

But more than 80,000 women have come together in Lean In Circles to create a new narrative. One Circle created a play, *The Leftover Monologues*, which celebrates being "leftover" and tackles the topics too often unspoken, like sexual harassment, date rape, and homophobia. The world told them what their stories should be, and they said, actually, we're writing a different story for ourselves. We are not leftover. We are strong and we will write our own story together.

Building collective resilience also means trying to understand how the world looks to those who have experienced it differently—because they are a different race, come from a different country, have an economic background unlike yours. We each have our own story but we can write new ones together—and that means seeing the values in each other's points of view and looking for common ground.

Anyone here a little bit anxious about your future? Not sure where the future is taking you? Sometimes me too. And you know what helps you combat that fear? A very big idea captured in a very tiny word: hope.

There are many kinds of hope. There's the hope that she wouldn't swipe left. Sorry. There's the hope that as you sit here your stuff will magically pack itself. Sorry. There's the hope that it would stop raining. Double sorry. But my favorite kind of hope is called grounded hope—the understanding that if you take action you can make things better.

We normally think of hope as something that's held in individual people. But hope—like resilience—is something we grow and nurture together. Just two days ago, I visited Mother Emanuel church in Charleston. We all know about the shooting that took place there just two years ago, claiming the lives of a pastor and eight worshippers. What happened afterwards was extraordinary. Instead of being consumed by hatred, the community came together to stand against racism and violence. As a local pastor Jermaine Watkins beautifully put it: "To hatred, we say no way, not today. To division, we say no way, not today. And to loss of hope, we say no way, not today."

That was the theme of maybe the most touching Facebook post I've ever read—and let's face it, I've read a lot of Facebook posts. This one was written by Antoine Leiris, a journalist in Paris whose wife Hélène was killed in the 2015 Paris attacks. Two days later—two days—he wrote an open letter to his wife's killers. "On Friday night, you stole the life of an exceptional being, the love of my life, the mother of my son. But you will not have my hate. My 17-month-old son will play as we do every day, and all his life this little boy will defy you by being happy and free. Because you will not have his hate either."

Strength like that makes all of us who see it stronger. Hope like that makes all of us more hopeful. That's how collective resilience works—we lift each other up. This might seem very intuitive to you Hokies because these qualities of collective resilience—shared experiences, shared narratives, and shared hope—shine forth from every corner of this university. You are a testament to courage, faith and love—and that's been true, not just for these past 10 years, but for over a century before then. This university means a lot to you, graduates…but it also means a lot to America and to the world. So many of us look to you as an example of how to stay strong and brave and true.

This is your legacy, Class of 2017. You will carry it with you—that capacity for finding strength in yourselves and building strength in the people around you.

Virginia Tech has given you a purpose, reflected in your motto, "That I May Serve." An important way you can serve and lead is by helping build resilience in the world. We have a responsibility to help families and communities become more resilient—because none of us get through anything alone. We get through it together.

As you leave this beautiful campus and set out into the world, build resilience in yourselves. When tragedy or disappointment strike, know that deep inside you, you have the ability to get through anything. I promise you do. As the saying goes, we are more vulnerable than we ever thought, but we are stronger than we ever imagined.

Build resilient organizations. Speak up when you see injustice. Lend your time and your passion to the causes that matter. My favorite poster at Facebook reads, "Nothing at Facebook is someone else's problem." When you see something that's broken and there is a lot that is broken out there, go fix it. Your motto demands that you do.

Build resilient communities. Virginia Tech founded the Global Forum on Resilience four years ago, and it's doing outstanding work in this field. Be there for your friends and family. And I mean in person—not just in a message with a heart emoji. Even though those are pretty great too. Be there for your neighbors; it's a divided time in our country, and we need you to help us heal. Lift each other up and celebrate each and every moment of joy. Because one of the most important ways you can build resilience is by cultivating gratitude.

Two years ago, if someone had told me that I would lose the love of my life and become more grateful, I would have never have believed them. But that's what happened. Because today I am more grateful now than I ever was before—for my family and especially my children. For my friends. For my work. For life itself.

A few months ago, my cousin Laura turned 50. Graduates, you may not appreciate that turning 50 happens soon and feels old—but your parents do. I called her that morning and I said, "Happy Birthday, Laura. But I am also calling to say in case you woke up this morning with that 'oh my God, I'm 50' thing. Don't do that. This is the year Dave doesn't turn 50." Either we get older, or we don't. No more jokes about growing old. Every year—every—even in the pouring rain—is an absolute gift.

You don't have to wait for special occasions—like graduation—to feel and show your gratitude to your family, your friends, your professors, your baristas—everyone. Counting your blessings increases them. People who take the time to focus on the things they are grateful for are happier and healthier.

My New Year's resolution last year was to write down three moments of joy before I went to bed each night. This very simple thing has changed my life. Because I realize I used to go to bed every night thinking about what I did wrong and what I was going to do wrong the next day. Now I go to sleep thinking of what went right. And when those moments of joy happen throughout the day, I notice them more because I know they'll make the notebook. Try it. Start tonight, on this day full of happy memories—but maybe before you hit Big Al's.

Graduates, on the path before you, you will have good days and you will have hard days. Go through all of them together. Seek shared experiences with all kinds of people. Write shared narratives that create the world you want to live in. Build shared hope in the communities you join and the communities you form. And above all, find gratitude for the gift of life itself and the opportunities it provides for meaning, for joy, and for love.

Tonight, when I write down my three moments of joy, I will write about this. About the hope and the amazing resilience of this community. And maybe you'll write that I finally stopped talking.

You have the whole world in front of you. I cannot wait to see what you do with it.

Congratulations and go Hokies!

Print Citations

CMS: Sandberg, Sheryl. "Building Collective Resilience." Speech presented at the Virginia Tech Class of 2017 Commencement, Blacksburg, VA, May, 2017. In *The Reference Shelf: Representative American Speeches 2016-2017*, edited by Betsy Maury, 16-22. Ipswich, MA: H.W. Wilson, 2017.

MLA: Sandberg, Sheryl. "Building Collective Resilience." Virginia Tech Class of 2017 Commencement. Blacksburg, VA. May, 2017. Presentation. *The Reference Shelf: Representative American Speeches 2016-2017*. Ed. Betsy Maury. Ipswich: H.W. Wilson, 2017. 16-22. Print.

APA: Sandberg, S. (2017). Building collective resilience. [Presentation]. *Speech presented at the Virginia Tech class of 2017 commencement*. Blacksburg, VA. In Betsy Maury (Ed.), *The reference shelf: Representative American speeches 2016-2017* (pp. 16-22). Ipswich, MA: H.W. Wilson. (Original work published 2017)

I See You, I Love You

By Cory Booker

New Jersey Senator Cory Booker delivers a speech to the 2017 graduating class of the University of Pennsylvania. Booker, a graduate of Stanford University and Yale Law School was a former Newark City councilor before serving as mayor of Newark between 2006 and 2013. Since 2013, Booker has served as senator of New Jersey, becoming the first African American elected to the Senate from the state. Booker speaks about the struggle of developing identity and the need to try and recognize and understand one another, as well as the importance of love in dealing with one's friends and enemies.

Thank you very much. It is incredible to be here and I want to thank you all for inviting me to be a part of this day of history in your lives, I want to thank you for allowing me to be a small part of this extraordinary community. I want to congratulate the graduates, and I want to thank everyone who helped to make this possible and when I say everyone, it took so many people to make this day possible. I want to thank the parents and the grandparents, and the family members. I want to thank everyone from the incredible president and astounding provost, all the way up to those people who cleaned floors and manicured lawns and served food to contribute to this community.

And so I confessed to you, when I was graduating from college, I felt like I knew a lot and now that I'm about twice your age, I'm not as confident in what I know. In fact, I am a person who believes I am in struggle, as we all are. The beautiful thing that I've realized is that we're all in this struggle together. We perceive that there are differences between us, gaps and gulfs, but we are far more united, far more indivisible, far more involved in a larger common struggle than we know. And so what I'd like to do very briefly today, is confess to you two things I struggle with and it's really two stories, one from someone from history who I've come to admire and the other one is perhaps one of my greatest mentors ever.

The person from history, it's a short story, I don't even know if it's apocryphal or not, but it's made a point that I struggle with and it's a story about Mahatma Gandhi. Gandhi was said to be rushing on busy days, running from point to point but now he was said to be running for a train to leap into the third class section that he's travelled in, people were there to grab him and help him to get on to the train but one of his sandals fell off and everybody watched with disappointment that Mahatma Gandhi had lost his sandal, but before people could settle into their thoughts of disappointment or consolation, or problem solving about how they were going

Delivered on May 15, 2017 at the University of Pennsylvania, Philadelphia, PA.

to deal with this one sandaled man, Gandhi reached down, really quickly, grabbed his other sandal and threw it onto the tracks. People were curious, "Mahatma, why would you throw your other sandal out there?" and he looked like it was a confusing and bemusing question. He said, "I threw the other sandal because whoever finds that first sandal, wouldn't it be nice if they found the other one as well?" I heard that story when I was about your age and I was astounded by the moral imagination of Gandhi in that story. To literally see people who are not there but yet still expand his love, to touch those folks we would never even see, it was the most creative compassion and I wanted to try to live my life in that way. I knew, and I experience now, the same rush of chasing after dreams, of racing around a day, of moving from there to there, but I realized a simple lesson the older I get, that how we live our days, is how we live our lives. And as we're chasing after our destinations, our goals and our dreams, it actually is those small things we do every single day that define us. In fact, in truth, more than a big speech than you've prepared for, more than a big goal or a big dream, more than the big fight, more than our race, more than our religion, it is our actions every day that define who we are, they define us. I've begun to learn in my life that perhaps the biggest thing you could in a given day is really just a small act of kindness, of decency, of love, an exhibition of moral imagination, or creative compassion.

I wonder about this when we miss our opportunities every single day with just the people around us while we talk big about changing the world or about what's wrong with other people, but we forget that we have so much power to make a difference. Now look, I say I struggle with this because I don't always get it right. Let me give you an example. I had been elected as a United States' Senator, I still live in the central ward of Newark. We're not the wealthiest community there in my neighborhood, the median income is about $14,000 per household but my community is rich with spirit, rich with energy, rich with compassion.

But one day as I was driving home, I felt a little bit like Odysseus, because as I passed this fast food restaurant, I began to hear the Siren call. Now look, I'm a vegan, and listen to these people because how do you know if someone is a vegan? Don't worry they'll tell you. And so I'm a vegan and I knew that in my neighborhood, folk know me but I couldn't resist the call to this fast food restaurant. It was a call in a language that I don't even speak any of them, it was French and it was French fries that were calling to me and I don't speak any French but I could swear I heard that song, "Voulez-vous coucher avec French fry" now. And as I told my driver, an incredible officer named Kevin Batts, retired from the Newark Police Department, joined my staff because of our friendship and our bond, I said to him "Kev, we're almost home but do you mind? We have to swing through the drive-thru." Now, Kevin, he didn't say a word but he smirked, he was mocking me and my weakness and we drove around to the drive-thru, I sunk down in the seat, I didn't want anyone to see me, the person said to me, "May I take your order?" and I used a falsetto voice, I ordered two of the most super-sized French fries I could, we pulled around to pick up the fries, I was still leaning down low, and then they handed these fries into my window and I'm telling you, I'm a Senator now so maybe I could change this, because these French fries could be a schedule 1 or schedule 2 narcotic, I mean they must sprinkle a narcotic on these fries because as soon as they got in I felt this joy and this anticipation, I cuddled my fries like I was from *Lord of the Rings*, my precious, and we began to move but then I see a guy at the end of the drive way there, a young white man in a garbage, rooting around and I slowed down and I told Kevin to roll down the window and he rolled down the window and I said, "Hey man, anything I can do to help you? Are you OK?" And he turns around and he looks at me and he says, "No I'm OK I don't need anything" and I go, "Are you sure?" and he goes, "well I'm hungry." Now I don't know what religion you all pray to, if you do at all, but I swear Jesus said something like, "If I have two McDonald French fries and my neighbor has none..." And so I reached in my bag as the aroma hit me, I shook as a grabbed that large fries and I reached to him and I swear he put his hand on it to take it from me and I resisted for just a moment. And then he pulled the fries to him, he was happy and I felt some sense of, ok I did the right thing. And then he was about to leave and he turned around and now his face went from appreciation to anguish, almost as if he was in pain and he says to me, "hey man do you have any socks? I need some socks." And it was a strange question but I knew it must speak to something he was dealing with, some pain, some hurt and I look at him, I wish that I could help him but I don't carry any spare socks in my car and I said, "I'm sorry I can't help you," and he began to leave but then this retired police detective, born in Newark, raised in the projects, threw the car in park, reached down between his legs, kicked off his shoes, pulled off his socks and handed them through the window. I sat back and I realized—wait a minute—I'm a few blocks away from my house, I have so many socks I don't even wear that my mother gave me on some birthday or special occasion but yet I was not living with that moral imagination, that creative compassion.

I've come to learn in my life that we have such power that we do not use as we go about our big challenges, our big goals, our desire to make big differences, we forget the power we have right now, we have a choice in every moment if we just look around us, and the choice that we often surrender and fail to make is to accept things as they are or to take responsibility for changing them. And no you may not be able to end homelessness, maybe you're not going to be able to end hungry but we can never allow our inability to do everything to undermine our determination to do something. We—as great as every one of us are, as much as I spent my life trying to change the world, we cannot forget that our real power is not necessarily to change the world, but to make a world of change to the people we encounter every day, a smile, creative and a kind word, finding a way to throw a sandal onto the track—that is the power we have today and every day. It was Desmond Tutu who said, "Do a little bit of good where you are. It's those little bits of good, put together, that overwhelm the world." We're not here because of the people we read about, history books, yes, that's part of the story, but we're here because of little bits of good, of sacrifice, of decency, of mercy and of love. Let me tell you about two Ralphs. And when I was in college, to ralph meant something completely different so let me be more specific. It was Emerson who said very simply, to paraphrase him, "...that only what we within, can we see without, if we see no angels, it's because we harbor none." Now I worry because I still see now the words of Ralph Ellison be so true, he said, "I am an invisible man, because people refuse to see me." I believe that there are so many people we encounter every day that we just don't see. But what is even worse than that, and I am compelled by that, it is what drives me every day to try to make this nation one more of justice and mercy and decency, but I'm telling you now that I'm in a professional world, I've come to worry about a different type of invisibility that actually can't be best described as invisibility, but maybe it is how we, every single day, reduce people, strip them from their layers of their humanity down to a label or a presumption.

I love the flowing words of Martin Luther King Jr. when he talked about repentance, he says we will have to repent in this day and age, not just for the victory of the violent words and actions of the bad people, but also the appalling silence and inaction of the good people. Well, I'll tell you, I am compelled to try to motivate and inspire through my action good people to get off the sidelines to realize that this democracy is not a spectator sport, but I also worry about those folks who we assign labels like vitriolic words and we assign conclusions about their souls that they are bad people. We do this in ways we don't even realize, I remember as a young guy, living in the projects in Newark, I was in New York trying to chase down money for a non-profit, and I was scuttling through, on an awful day, sleet and snow and every street seemed to have curbs of slush and as I walked to this one curbs, I saw what amounted to one of the great lakes of slush and I worried about my shoes, how was I going to get around it, and then I saw an elderly African-American woman, amongst all the hustle and bustle of this fancy New York street, she was carrying a cart, one of those metal carts with wheels, trying to make it across a busy street, with the light about to change, heading towards the ocean of slush, my mama raised me right, I began to dart over to her, but before I could, some guy cut me off. I was angry about it. He was dressed like a Wall Street guy in a coat that was probably worth more than my car. He had fancy shoes on and I looked at this white man, cutting in front of me, just holding back for a second, it's like he didn't see me, but suddenly, he does what I don't expect—he goes through the great lake of slush in his fancy shoes, grabs the woman's cart, lifts it up, pulls it to the sidewalk, goes back through the slush to grab the woman and take her all the way around, putting his hand up to traffic to get the woman on the curb. Before my implicit biases about this man because of the color of his skin or because of what he was wearing, could fully settle in, he shocked me to the consciousness. I didn't render him invisible, but I stripped away his humanity because I did not see him. The question we have to ask ourselves about the importance of being good and decent and loving, morally creative, is that do we extend those feelings and those emotions just to people we like, or just to people we deem worthy or just to people who agree with us or just to people who think like us. I don't understand, and it hurts me that we're becoming a society, that just because someone has different views, we tend to strip them from their humanity.

I want to talk about us and our daily lives, but let me use the public stage for one moment. One of my lowest points during the Presidential elections, was when I was sitting at home watching the Republican debate. And it was one of those strange moments where I knew a lot of folks, I mean heck, half the America was running for the nomination for the Republican Party at that point, and there was my Governor. Now, I could write a dissertation on my disagreements—we literally fought over policy issues, yet he and I had forged a friendship, we knew that he was the Governor of the state, I was the Mayor of the largest city, we had to put aside the 60, 70, 80% of things we disagreed on because I represented a struggling city in a recession and when the country has a recession, inner cities face depressions. I had to seek the common ground with him to try to find a way to make some difference for my community and as I sat there during a Presidential election, I could not believe my eyes when these other nominees were castigating Chris Christie for hugging Barack Obama. Now let me tell you about this hug. It was after hurricane Sandy. The President flew into the state of New Jersey. So many people died, thousands of people lost their homes. And here is the President of the United States, coming down the steps to meet the Governor and the two of them at the bottom of the steps, they hugged. And I want to tell you something, I'm a hugger, and it wasn't really a good hug either—it was one of those awkward guy hugs. But what have we become in a society where we are vilifying people so much so that to hug someone of a different party, that thinks different, is a sin! Where have we come as a nation?

But that's the national stage, I want to tell you. I was just a few weeks ago at a Humane Society banquet dinner. And it's the humane society, treatment of animals, did I tell you I'm a vegan? And here we are talking about compassion and kindness and treatment of animals and someone comes up to me and says, "Senator Booker, I so appreciate what you're doing, thank you for being in the fight. Hey, let me show you what I tweeted just now," and they showed me a tweet to Paul Ryan and it was probably one of the most troll-y, vile, angry tweets I'd ever seen! And the incongruency of the moment really struck me. So this is the challenge—can we be a nation that can disagree but still find common ground? But that's the country, can you be a person whose love is so great that you love those people you disagree with, you love those people who curse you, you love those people who you see even as an obstacle to justice. Now, I'm not asking folks to do what my heroes did like Mandela did in prison who found a way to love his captors and eventually forgive them or Gandhi with the oppressive, imperialistic regime, but still found a way to love his enemy, or Martin Luther King who literally got on his knees and prayed for white supremacists, no. I'm just asking you, hey, can you sit down with somebody that's wearing a red "Make American Great Again" hat and have a conversation. And, by the way, one of the best pieces of advice I've ever been given, was simply this, "Talk to the person, but you don't have to attend every argument you've invited to." You could look for other common ground.

But that brings me to the last person and who I want to end on. Because this was my mentor who lived these lessons that I am struggling to embody. This man's name was Frank Hutchins and he was a legend. By the time I was a law student, coming to Newark, the stories of him as a tenant activist and a tenant organizer were legendary. He literally was responsible for the longest rent strike in Newark's history against the worst of slum lords, the Federal Government and Newark Housing Authority. And he won. By the time I met him, we were organizing these neighborhoods that had high-rise buildings that had some of the most difficult slum lords imaginable, people that were caricatures of slum lords. But I'll never forget this guy, when we would sit in negotiations and I would be angry and be fit to fight and yet he still found a way to look at them with grace and even mercy. He seemed to understand that you don't have to be mean to be tough, you don't have to be cruel to be strong, that you don't have to curse the person who curses you. I saw Frank now in tenant meetings where we would sit up and have to take people's complaints, to try to write it down, to fight these battles and it was amazing to me how Frank would sit in the tenant meeting that would go on for hours and hours, I would get restless as another person would get up and tell their whole life story but he never seemed to falter at looking at those people, teaching me that perhaps the most valuable thing you can give someone in your life, is your attention. As he sat there, I talked to him after the meeting and I said, "God that was too long, people went on..." and he goes, "Cory, it's important that we heal those buildings from the crisis that they're in but people too need healing, we're all fighting hard battles, pay attention to people, see them."

Well I would become a councilman and a Mayor and Frank and I would still work together. And yet, he got older and older and then he started getting sick. His disease took his eyesight from him and I would still take him out to restaurants and I would still take him shopping and he would demand that I still take him to the movies and I was like, "Frank you can't see man!" And he would say, "No, no take me there I want to listen, I want to listen." By the time Frank's health became failing, they put him in hospice but I would still go visit and I confess to you, I was frustrated at times that the hospice room wasn't full of people. Here's a guy that thousands and thousands of people relied on, I was frustrated that he was alone. And I'll still always remember the last day I saw him alive. This is my hero. And I walked into the hospital room after the nurse told me that he wouldn't last long and I could see his breath was faltering. Now, when Frank's eyesight started going we started a little joke, I would see him before I would take him out to dinner and I'd say, "Hey Frank, it's Cory" and he'd push me off and he'd say, "I see you Cory, I see you." Well it became our thing, hey Frank it's Cory, and I see you. But now in this hospital room, his voice is not there, his breath is rapid and I said, "Frank, its Cory." I saw him with such effort, he labored and he said to me, "I see you." I walked to the side of his bed and I held his hand and I talked to him and as I sat there I felt this peace and I still saw his light and I realized that he was trying to teach me that, Cory I am here and I've lived a good life. I felt like he was trying to teach me that ultimately, life is not about celebrity, it's about significance; life is not about popularity, it's about purpose; life is not how many people show up when you're dead but about how many people you show up for while you are alive. I sat with him for as long as I could, I felt such love for this man and I knew this would be our last time. He said no words except for that when I entered, "I see you." Then I had to go, I told him I was leaving, I stood up and I leaned over and I kissed him on the forehead, I put my hand on the side of his face and I said with all of my heart, I said, "Frank, I love you." And then as I was beginning to pull away, he wanted to say something again, I lean close to his bed and he repeated my words, he looked at me and with short breaths, he forced out, "I love you." I walked out of his room, I closed the door, I started crying, I knew it would soon be over and it was, he would die there soon after.

So class of 2017, I got to leave you with those six words that Frank said, "I see you. I love you." I see you. I love you. I see you! I love you! Class of 2017, you're going to go out for the big challenges, the big fights, I see you, I love you. You're going to have tough days, you're going to fall, you're going to fail but I see you and I love you. May your vision and your love not just change the world but make a world of change for everyone that you can. God bless you.

Print Citations

CMS: Booker, Cory. "I See You, I Love You." Speech presented at the University of Pennsylvania Class of 2017 Commencement, Philadelphia, PA, May, 2017. In *The Reference Shelf: Representative American Speeches 2016-2017*, edited by Betsy Maury, 23-29. Ipswich, MA: H.W. Wilson, 2017.

MLA: Booker, Cory. "I See You, I Love You." The University of Pennsylvania Class of 2017 Commencement. Philadelphia, PA. May, 2017. Presentation. *The Reference Shelf: Representative American Speeches 2016-2017*. Ed. Betsy Maury. Ipswich: H.W. Wilson, 2017. 23-29. Print.

APA: Booker, C. (2017). I see you, I love you. [Presentation]. *Speech presented at the University of Pennsylvania class of 2017 commencement*. Philadelphia, PA. In Betsy Maury (Ed.), *The reference shelf: Representative American speeches 2016-2017* (pp. 23-29). Ipswich, MA: H.W. Wilson. (Original work published 2017)

Address to the Harvard University Class of 2017 on Success, Failure, and Entrepreneurship

By Mark Zuckerberg

Mark Zuckerberg, co-creator of the popular social media site Facebook and celebrated entrepreneur, gives a graduation speech to the 2017 graduating class of Harvard University. Zuckerberg, who attended but did not graduate from Harvard University, speaks to students about his life, marriage, Harvard culture, and about the process of finding purpose in his professional and personal life. Zuckerberg proposes the idea that the fundamental challenge for the millennial generation is building a world in which every individual has a sense of purpose as a potential solution to the disconnection and depression experienced by many struggling in American society.

President Faust, Board of Overseers, faculty, alumni, friends, proud parents, members of the ad board and graduates of the greatest university in the world...

I'm honored to be with you today, because let's face it, you accomplished something I never could. If I get through this speech, it'll be the first time I actually finish something at Harvard. Class of 2017, congratulations!

I'm an unlikely speaker, not just because I dropped out, but because we're technically in the same generation. We walked this yard less than a decade apart, studied the same ideas and slept through the same Ec10 lectures. We may have taken different paths to get here, especially if you came all the way from the Quad, but today I want to share what I've learned about our generation and the world we're building together.

But first, the last couple of days have brought back a lot of good memories.

How many of you remember exactly what you were doing when you got that email telling you that you got into Harvard? I was playing "Civilization" and I ran downstairs, got my dad, and for some reason, his reaction was to video me opening the email. That could have been a really sad video. I swear, getting into Harvard is still the thing my parents are most proud of me for.

What about your first lecture at Harvard? Mine was Computer Science 121 with the incredible Harry Lewis. I was late, so I threw on a t-shirt and didn't realize until afterwards it was inside out and backwards with my tag sticking out the front. I couldn't figure out why no one would talk to me—except one guy, KX Jin, he just

Delivered on May 25, 2017 at Harvard University, Cambridge, MA.

went with it. We ended up doing our problem sets together, and now he runs a big part of Facebook. And that, Class of 2017, is why you should be nice to people.

But my best memory from Harvard was meeting Priscilla. I had just launched this prank website Facemash, and the ad board wanted to "see me." Everyone thought I was going to get kicked out. My parents came to help me pack. My friends threw me a going away party. As luck would have it, Priscilla was at that party with her friend. We met in line for the bathroom in the Pfoho Belltower, and in what must be one of the all-time romantic lines, I said: "I'm going to get kicked out in three days, so we need to go on a date quickly."

Actually, any of you graduating can use that line.

I didn't end up getting kicked out—I did that to myself. Priscilla and I started dating. And you know, that movie made it seem like Facemash was so important to creating Facebook. It wasn't. But without Facemash I wouldn't have met Priscilla, and she's the most important person in my life, so you could say it was the most important thing I built in my time here.

We've all started lifelong friendships here, and some of us even families. That's why I'm so grateful to this place. Thanks, Harvard.

Today I want to talk about purpose. But I'm not here to give you the standard commencement about finding your purpose. We're millennials. We'll try to do that instinctively. Instead, I'm here to tell you finding your purpose isn't enough. The challenge for our generation is creating a world where everyone has a sense of purpose.

One of my favorite stories is when John F. Kennedy visited the NASA space center, he saw a janitor carrying a broom and he walked over and asked what he was doing. The janitor responded: "Mr. President, I'm helping put a man on the moon."

Purpose is that sense that we are part of something bigger than ourselves, that we are needed, that we have something better ahead to work for. Purpose is what creates true happiness.

You're graduating at a time when this is especially important. When our parents graduated, purpose reliably came from your job, your church, your community. But today, technology and automation are eliminating many jobs. Membership in communities is declining. Many people feel disconnected and depressed and are trying to fill a void.

As I've traveled around, I've sat with children in juvenile detention and opioid addicts, who told me their lives could have turned out differently if they just had something to do, an after school program or somewhere to go. I've met factory workers who know their old jobs aren't coming back and are trying to find their place.

To keep our society moving forward, we have a generational challenge—to not only create new jobs, but create a renewed sense of purpose.

I remember the night I launched Facebook from my little dorm in Kirkland House. I went to Noch's with my friend KX. I remember telling him I was excited to connect the Harvard community, but one day someone would connect the whole world.

The thing is, it never even occurred to me that someone might be us. We were just college kids. We didn't know anything about that. There were all these big technology companies with resources. I just assumed one of them would do it. But this idea was so clear to us—that all people want to connect. So we just kept moving forward, day by day.

I know a lot of you will have your own stories just like this. A change in the world that seems so clear, you're sure someone else will do it. But they won't. You will.

But it's not enough to have purpose yourself. You have to create a sense of purpose for others.

I found that out the hard way. You see, my hope was never to build a company, but to make an impact. And as all these people started joining us, I just assumed that's what they cared about too, so I never explained what I hoped we'd build.

A couple years in, some big companies wanted to buy us. I didn't want to sell. I wanted to see if we could connect more people. We were building the first News Feed, and I thought if we could just launch this, it could change how we learn about the world.

Nearly everyone else wanted to sell. Without a sense of higher purpose, this was the startup dream come true. It tore our company apart. After one tense argument, an advisor told me if I didn't agree to sell, I would regret the decision for the rest of my life. Relationships were so frayed that within a year or so, every single person on the management team was gone.

That was my hardest time leading Facebook. I believed in what we were doing, but I felt alone. And worse, it was my fault. I wondered if I was just wrong, an impostor, a 22-year-old kid who had no idea how the world worked.

Now, years later, I understand that is how things work with no sense of higher purpose. It's up to us to create it, so we can all keep moving forward together.

Today I want to talk about three ways to create a world where everyone has a sense of purpose: by taking on big meaningful projects together, by redefining equality so everyone has the freedom to pursue purpose and by building community across the world.

First, let's take on big meaningful projects.

Our generation will have to deal with tens of millions of jobs replaced by automation like self-driving cars and trucks. But we have the potential to do so much more together.

Every generation has its defining works. More than 300,000 people worked to put a man on the moon—including that janitor. Millions of volunteers immunized children around the world against polio. Millions of more people built the Hoover dam and other great projects.

These projects didn't just provide purpose for the people doing those jobs, they gave our whole country a sense of pride that we could do great things.

Now it's our turn to do great things. I know, you're probably thinking: I don't know how to build a dam, or get a million people involved in anything.

But let me tell you a secret: no one does when they begin. Ideas don't come out fully formed. They only become clear as you work on them. You just have to get started.

If I had to understand everything about connecting people before I began, I never would have started Facebook.

Movies and pop culture get this all wrong. The idea of a single eureka moment is a dangerous lie. It makes us feel inadequate since we haven't had ours. It prevents people with seeds of good ideas from getting started. Oh, you know what else movies get wrong about innovation? No one writes math formulas on glass. That's not a thing.

It's good to be idealistic. But be prepared to be misunderstood. Anyone working on a big vision will get called crazy, even if you end up right. Anyone working on a complex problem will get blamed for not fully understanding the challenge, even though it's impossible to know everything upfront. Anyone taking initiative will get criticized for moving too fast, because there's always someone who wants to slow you down.

In our society, we often don't do big things because we're so afraid of making mistakes that we ignore all the things wrong today if we do nothing. The reality is, anything we do will have issues in the future. But that can't keep us from starting.

So what are we waiting for? It's time for our generation-defining public works. How about stopping climate change before we destroy the planet and getting millions of people involved manufacturing and installing solar panels? How about curing all diseases and asking volunteers to track their health data and share their genomes? Today we spend 50 times more treating people who are sick than we spend finding cures so people don't get sick in the first place. That makes no sense. We can fix this. How about modernizing democracy so everyone can vote online, and personalizing education so everyone can learn?

These achievements are within our reach. Let's do them all in a way that gives everyone in our society a role. Let's do big things, not only to create progress, but to create purpose.

So taking on big meaningful projects is the first thing we can do to create a world where everyone has a sense of purpose.

The second is redefining equality to give everyone the freedom they need to pursue purpose.

Many of our parents had stable jobs throughout their careers. Now we're all entrepreneurial, whether we're starting projects or finding or role. And that's great. Our culture of entrepreneurship is how we create so much progress.

Now, an entrepreneurial culture thrives when it's easy to try lots of new ideas. Facebook wasn't the first thing I built. I also built games, chat systems, study tools and music players. I'm not alone. J.K. Rowling got rejected 12 times before publishing *Harry Potter*. Even Beyoncé had to make hundreds of songs to get "Halo." The greatest successes come from having the freedom to fail.

But today, we have a level of wealth inequality that hurts everyone. When you don't have the freedom to take your idea and turn it into a historic enterprise, we all lose. Right now our society is way over-indexed on rewarding success and we don't do nearly enough to make it easy for everyone to take lots of shots.

Let's face it: There is something wrong with our system when I can leave here and make billions of dollars in 10 years, while millions of students can't afford to pay off their loans, let alone start a business.

Look, I know a lot of entrepreneurs, and I don't know a single person who gave up on starting a business because they might not make enough money. But I know lots of people who haven't pursued dreams because they didn't have a cushion to fall back on if they failed.

We all know we don't succeed just by having a good idea or working hard. We succeed by being lucky too. If I had to support my family growing up instead of having time to code, if I didn't know I'd be fine if Facebook didn't work out, I wouldn't be standing here today. If we're honest, we all know how much luck we've had.

Every generation expands its definition of equality. Previous generations fought for the vote and civil rights. They had the New Deal and Great Society. Now it's our time to define a new social contract for our generation.

We should have a society that measures progress not just by economic metrics like GDP, but by how many of us have a role we find meaningful. We should explore ideas like universal basic income to give everyone a cushion to try new things. We're going to change jobs many times, so we need affordable childcare to get to work and healthcare that aren't tied to one company. We're all going to make mistakes, so we need a society that focuses less on locking us up or stigmatizing us. And as technology keeps changing, we need to focus more on continuous education throughout our lives.

And yes, giving everyone the freedom to pursue purpose isn't free. People like me should pay for it. Many of you will do well and you should too.

That's why Priscilla and I started the Chan Zuckerberg Initiative and committed our wealth to promoting equal opportunity. These are the values of our generation. It was never a question of if we were going to do this. The only question was when.

Millennials are already one of the most charitable generations in history. In one year, three of four U.S. millennials made a donation and seven out of 10 raised money for charity.

But it's not just about money. You can also give time. I promise you, if you take an hour or two a week—that's all it takes to give someone a hand, to help them reach their potential.

Maybe you think that's too much time. I used to. When Priscilla graduated from Harvard she became a teacher, and before she'd do education work with me, she told me I needed to teach a class. I complained: "Well, I'm kind of busy. I'm running this company." But she insisted, so I taught a middle school program on entrepreneurship at the local Boys and Girls Club.

I taught them lessons on product development and marketing, and they taught me what it's like feeling targeted for your race and having a family member in prison. I shared stories from my time in school, and they shared their hope of one day going to college too. For five years now, I've been having dinner with those kids every month. One of them threw me and Priscilla our first baby shower. And next year they're going to college. Every one of them. First in their families.

We can all make time to give someone a hand. Let's give everyone the freedom to pursue their purpose—not only because it's the right thing to do, but because when more people can turn their dreams into something great, we're all better for it.

Purpose doesn't only come from work. The third way we can create a sense of purpose for everyone is by building community. And when our generation says "everyone," we mean everyone in the world.

Quick show of hands: How many of you are from another country? Now, how many of you are friends with one of these folks? Now we're talking. We have grown up connected.

In a survey asking millennials around the world what defines our identity, the most popular answer wasn't nationality, religion or ethnicity, it was "citizen of the world." That's a big deal.

Every generation expands the circle of people we consider "one of us." For us, it now encompasses the entire world.

We understand the great arc of human history bends towards people coming together in ever greater numbers—from tribes to cities to nations—to achieve things we couldn't on our own.

We get that our greatest opportunities are now global—we can be the generation that ends poverty, that ends disease. We get that our greatest challenges need global responses too—no country can fight climate change alone or prevent pandemics. Progress now requires coming together not just as cities or nations, but also as a global community.

But we live in an unstable time. There are people left behind by globalization across the world. It's hard to care about people in other places if we don't feel good about our lives here at home. There's pressure to turn inwards.

This is the struggle of our time. The forces of freedom, openness and global community against the forces of authoritarianism, isolationism and nationalism. Forces for the flow of knowledge, trade and immigration against those who would slow them down. This is not a battle of nations, it's a battle of ideas. There are people in every country for global connection and good people against it.

This isn't going to be decided at the U.N. either. It's going to happen at the local level, when enough of us feel a sense of purpose and stability in our own lives that we can open up and start caring about everyone. The best way to do that is to start building local communities right now. We all get meaning from our communities. Whether our communities are houses or sports teams, churches or music groups, they give us that sense we are part of something bigger, that we are not alone; they give us the strength to expand our horizons.

That's why it's so striking that for decades, membership in all kinds of groups has declined as much as one-quarter. That's a lot of people who now need to find purpose somewhere else.

But I know we can rebuild our communities and start new ones because many of you already are.

I met Agnes Igoye, who's graduating today. Where are you, Agnes? She spent her childhood navigating conflict zones in Uganda, and now she trains thousands of law enforcement officers to keep communities safe.

I met Kayla Oakley and Niha Jain, graduating today too. Stand up. Kayla and Niha started a non-profit that connects people suffering from illnesses with people in their communities willing to help.

I met David Razu Aznar, graduating from the Kennedy School today. David, stand up. He's a former city councilor who successfully led the battle to make Mexico City the first Latin American city to pass marriage equality—even before San Francisco.

This is my story too. A student in a dorm room, connecting one community at a time, and keeping at it until one day we connect the whole world.

Change starts local. Even global changes start small—with people like us. In our generation, the struggle of whether we connect more, whether we achieve our biggest opportunities, comes down to this—your ability to build communities and create a world where every single person has a sense of purpose.

Class of 2017, you are graduating into a world that needs purpose. It's up to you to create it.

Now, you may be thinking: can I really do this?

Remember when I told you about that class I taught at the Boys and Girls Club? One day after class I was talking to them about college, and one of my top students raised his hand and said he wasn't sure he could go because he's undocumented. He didn't know if they'd let him in.

Last year I took him out to breakfast for his birthday. I wanted to get him a present, so I asked him and he started talking about students he saw struggling and said "You know, I'd really just like a book on social justice."

I was blown away. Here's a young guy who has every reason to be cynical. He didn't know if the country he calls home—the only one he's known—would deny him his dream of going to college. But he wasn't feeling sorry for himself. He wasn't even thinking of himself. He has a greater sense of purpose, and he's going to bring people along with him.

It says something about our current situation that I can't even say his name because I don't want to put him at risk. But if a high school senior who doesn't know what the future holds can do his part to move the world forward, then we owe it to the world to do our part too.

Before you walk out those gates one last time, as we sit in front of Memorial Church, I am reminded of a prayer, Mi Shebeirach, that I say whenever I face a challenge, that I sing to my daughter thinking about her future when I tuck her into bed. It goes: "May the source of strength, who blessed the ones before us, help us 'find the courage' to make our lives a blessing."

I hope you find the courage to make your life a blessing.

Congratulations, Class of '17! Good luck out there.

Print Citations

CMS: Zuckerberg, Mark. "Address to the Harvard University Class of 2017 on Success, Failure, and Entrepreneurship." Speech presented at the Harvard University Class of 2017 Commencement, Cambridge, MA, May, 2017. In *The Reference Shelf: Representative American Speeches 2016-2017*, edited by Betsy Maury, 30-37. Ipswich, MA: H.W. Wilson, 2017.

MLA: Zuckerberg, Mark. "Address to the Harvard University Class of 2017 on Success, Failure, and Entrepreneurship." Harvard University Class of 2017 Commencement. Cambridge, MA. May, 2017. Presentation. *The Reference Shelf: Representative American Speeches 2016-2017*. Ed. Betsy Maury. Ipswich: H.W. Wilson, 2017. 30-37. Print.

APA: Zuckerberg, M. (2017). Address to the Harvard University class of 2017 on success, failure, and entrepreneurship. [Presentation]. *Speech presented at the Harvard University class of 2017 commencement.* Cambridge, MA. In Betsy Maury (Ed.), *The reference shelf: Representative American speeches 2016-2017* (pp. 30-37). Ipswich, MA: H.W. Wilson. (Original work published 2017)

Remarks to the Brooklyn College Class of 2017

By Bernie Sanders

Vermont Senator Bernie Sanders, whose controversial 2016 presidential campaign demonstrated the birth of a rising populist progressive movement in the United States, speaks to students of Brooklyn College. Sanders, who was born in New York and grew up in Brooklyn, became a political activist in college, participating in the emerging civil rights and socialist movements in American cities. After serving as mayor of Burlington Vermont from 1981 to 1989, Sanders won election to the US House of Representatives, representing Vermont from 1991 to 2007, before winning election to the Senate. Addressing students at Brooklyn College, Sanders speaks about income inequality and the economic elite class in the United States, of which Trump is a member and leader, that conspires to maintain the economic hierarchy at the expense of America's middle- and working-class families.

Brothers and sisters,

Let me begin by congratulating the graduating class of 2017. Today is an important day in your lives, something that you've worked hard to attain, and I want to wish all of you the very best of luck in your future endeavors. May you all live healthy and happy lives, doing the work you enjoy and surrounded in love by family and friends.

Let me thank president Michelle Anderson, Nicole Haas, the Brooklyn College Administration, faculty and staff and all of you for inviting my wife, Jane, and me back to Brooklyn, where we were both born and raised. I am greatly appreciative of the honorary degree which you bestow on me today.

I grew up in Flatbush and graduated from James Madison High School. Jane was raised in Flatbush and Bed-Sty, and graduated from St. Savior's High School a few miles away from here.

In 1959, I attended Brooklyn College for a year—a year which had a major impact in my life. Thank you, Brooklyn College. After that year I left for the University of Chicago, where I eventually graduated. My mom had died the previous year and I felt it was time to leave the neighborhood and see what the rest of the world looked like.

My childhood in Brooklyn was shaped by two profound realities. First, my mom, dad and older brother Larry, who graduated from Brooklyn College, lived in a 3

Delivered on May 30, 2017 at Brooklyn College, Brooklyn, NY.

1/2 room rent-controlled apartment. As with many families who don't have a lot of money, financial pressures caused friction and tension within our household. From those experiences I have never forgotten that there are millions of people throughout this country who struggle to put food on the table, pay the electric bill, try to save for their kids' education or for retirement—people who face painful and stress-filled decisions every single day.

The second reality that impacted my life was that my father left Poland at the age of 17 from a community which was not only very poor, but from a country where anti-semitism, pogroms and attacks on Jews were not uncommon. While my father emigrated to the United States, and escaped Hitler and the holocaust, many in his family did not. For them, racism, right-wing extremism and ultra-nationalism were not "political issues." They were issues of life and death—and they died.

From that experience, what was indelibly stamped on me was the understanding that we must never allow demagogues to divide us up by race, by religion, by national origin, by gender or sexual orientation. Black, white, Latino, Asian American, Native American, Christian, Jew, Muslim and every religion, straight or gay, male or female we must stand together. This country belongs to all of us.

As a United States senator from Vermont let me give you a very brief overview of some of the very serious crises we currently face—crises which do not often get the kind of discussion they deserve.

As a student at James Madison High School, many years ago, I recall my social-studies teacher talking about how there were small developing countries around the world that were oligarchic societies—places where the economic and political life of the nation were controlled by a handful of very wealthy families. It never occurred to me then that the United States of America, our great nation, could move in that direction. But that is precisely what is happening.

Today, the top 1/10 of 1% now owns almost as much wealth as the bottom 90%, 20 Americans now own as much wealth as the bottom half of America and one family—the Walton family—owns more wealth than the bottom 42 percent of our people. In the last 17 years, while the middle class continues to decline, we have seen a tenfold increase in the number of billionaires–going from 51 to 565. In America today, CEOs of major corporations now earn about 350 times more than the average worker makes. In terms of income, 52 percent of all new income goes to the top 1%. In other words, the very rich are becoming much richer.

At the same time as we have more income and wealth inequality than any other major nation, 43 million Americans live in poverty, we have the highest rate of childhood poverty of almost any major country in earth, half of older workers have nothing in the bank as they approach retirement and in some inner cities and rural communities youth unemployment is sky high.

Unbelievably, in many parts of this country today, as a result of hopelessness and despair, life expectancy is actually declining as a frightening number of people experience drug addiction, alcoholism and suicide. And, because of poverty, racism and a broken criminal justice system, we have more people in jail than any other country—disproportionately black, Latino and Native American.

Directly related to the oligarchic economy that we currently have is an oligarchic and corrupt political system which is undermining American democracy. As a result of the disastrous Citizens United Supreme Court decision, corporations and billionaires are able to spend unlimited sums of money on elections. The result is that today a handful of billionaire families are spending hundreds of millions a year to make sure that candidates who represent the rich and the powerful get elected.

And we are seeing the results of how oligarchy functions right now in Congress where the Republican leadership wants to throw 23 million people off of health insurance, cut Medicaid by over $800 billion, defund Planned Parenthood, cut food stamps and other nutrition programs by over $200 billion, cut Head Start and after school programs, make drastic cuts in Pell grants and other programs that help make college more affordable.

And, unbelievably, at exactly the same time, they want to provide the top one percent with $3 trillion in tax cuts. The very rich get much richer and they get huge tax cuts. The middle class shrinks and the poor struggle, and they will find it harder to get health care, housing, nutrition, education or clean water.

In response to these very serious problems it seems to me that we have two choices. First we can throw up our hands in despair. We can moan and groan. We can withdraw from the public reality that we face. We can loudly proclaim that we can't beat the system.

That is one response. It is an understandable response but it is not an acceptable response.

It is not an acceptable response because the reality that we face today impacts not only our lives, but the lives of our children, the lives of our grandchildren and, with regard to climate change, the very future of this planet. The truth is that the only rational choice we have, the only real response we can make, is to stand up and fight back—reclaim American democracy and create a government that works for all of us, and not just the 1 percent.

Print Citations

CMS: Sanders, Bernie. "Remarks to the Brooklyn College Class of 2017." Speech presented at the Brooklyn College Class of 2017 Commencement, Brooklyn, NY, May, 2017. In *The Reference Shelf: Representative American Speeches 2016-2017*, edited by Betsy Maury, 38-41. Ipswich, MA: H.W. Wilson, 2017.

MLA: Sanders, Bernie. "Remarks to the Brooklyn College Class of 2017." Brooklyn College Class of 2017 Commencement. Brooklyn, NY. May, 2017. Presentation. *The Reference Shelf: Representative American Speeches 2016-2017*. Ed. Betsy Maury. Ipswich: H.W. Wilson, 2017. 38-41. Print.

APA: Sanders, B. (2017). Remarks to the Brooklyn College class of 2017. [Presentation]. *Speech presented at the Brooklyn College class of 2017 commencement.* Brooklyn, NY. In Betsy Maury (Ed.), *The reference shelf: Representative American speeches 2016-2017* (pp. 38-41). Ipswich, MA: H.W. Wilson. (Original work published 2017)

Be Brave. Take the Leap. Do It. Dare It. Courage.

By Anna Quindlen

Author and journalist Anna Quindlen, known for her Pulitzer Prize-winning New York Times *series and celebrated novels, speaks to the 2017 graduating class of Washington University in St. Louis, Missouri. Quindlen, who is the author of eight novels and several autobiographical and other nonfiction books and is a former writer for* Newsweek, *speaks to students about courage, bravery, and self-confidence needed to attempt to follow one's own path and to challenge stereotypes and popular concepts towards the goal of forming a unique and fulfilling identity and career.*

Thank you, Chancellor Wrighton, and thank you so much for the profound honor of addressing the Washington University community on this very special day.

Commencement speeches are very difficult to craft, even in a year when the country doesn't seem to be going through a nervous breakdown. After all, no one is here to hear me. Everyone is here for the sake of just a few words; the name of someone they love, or their own name. It's almost the only thing I remember from my own commencement, even though the legendary anthropologist Margaret Mead was the commencement speaker. I don't even remember the weather, although you probably won't forget yours. I remember these three words: "Anna Marie Quindlen," and the look on my father's face.

But it's particularly hard to craft a message for people like you. Because you're receiving a degree today from Washington University, I know this about all of you: You are what my grandmother used to call "The smart ones." The children of the 99th percentile, the men and women of the top decile, accustomed to high test scores and high hopes. You are the people who make the checklists, who come up with plans, who are invested always in the right answer.

I know this, because I am one of you. And this is what I've learned, often with great difficulty: The checklist should be honored mostly in the breach. The plans are a tiny box that, followed slavishly, will smother you, and the right answer is sometimes the wrong answer.

What are the public names you recall sitting there of those people who did exactly what was considered the right thing, who followed the template, who met expectations? You cannot come up with one of them, because the people we know, the

Delivered on May 19, 2017 at Washington University, St. Louis, MO.

people we admire, the people whose names we carve into the cornices of buildings and see on the cover of books are deviants in the best sense of that term.

Jane Austen threw out the plan for a well-read regency-era woman. Frank Lloyd Wright threw out the plan for a young architect of his time. Bill Gates, Oprah Winfrey, Enrico Fermi, Lin-Manuel Miranda, Martin Luther King, Marie Curie, Pablo Picasso, Toni Morrison, they all threw out the plan. The right answer was safe; the wrong answer, the one no one else came up with or followed or believed in, was transformational.

Ah, you say to yourself sitting there, "I cannot expect to be Jane Austen or Frank Lloyd Wright," but what you can embrace is a life that feels like it belongs to you, not one made up of tiny fragments of the expectations of a society that, frankly, in most of its expectations, is not worthy of you. And that requires courage, not compliance; passion in lieu of simply plans.

Smart is good. Smart and hardworking is really good. Smart, hardworking and fearless, that's the hat trick. You possess an invaluable credential that will soon be ratified here, but are you strong and smart enough to become who you might be were you not afraid? That's the problem, isn't it?

We slavishly seek what is correct because we are afraid. Caution is nothing but fear dressed up as common sense. Coloring books have come back into vogue for adults because there's nothing quite so soothing as coloring inside the lines.

"The Road Less Traveled," popular poem, unpopular life choice. The well-trod road is so much safer. But I tell you absolutely that the most terrifying choices I made in my life and the ones that other people saw as most foolhardy are the ones that brought greatest rewards. Because of some strange little voice inside, I zigged where I was expected to zag. I traded more good jobs than most people had ever had for new roles I thought were even scarier and chancier and potentially more rewarding. I took the ultimate flying leap in life and had three children in five years while my career was at its very peak.

Five years in, I left the op-ed page of the *New York Times* to become a full-time novelist. The publisher told me that I was the first person to willingly give up a *Times* column. Someone wrote that my decision showed that women are afraid of success. But I'm not afraid of success. I'm afraid of living a life that seems more like a resume than an adventure story, that doesn't feel as though it belongs to me, a life full of dreams deferred until they evaporate entirely with the call of custom.

None of you want to have that sort of life, so you can't let fear rule you. For your own sake and for the sake of this great nation, fear is what has poisoned our culture, our community and our character. The very worst things in this country are done out of fear. Homophobia, sexism, racism, religious bigotry, xenophobia, the embrace of demagogues, they all arise out of fear of that which is unknown or different.

Our political leaders don't actually lead when they are afraid of being thrown out of office. Our corporations resist real innovation because they're afraid of taking a chance.

In my former business, the news business, which I was proud and continue to be proud to call home, fear is the greatest of enemies. Without fear or favor, the business has to provide readers, listeners and viewers with searching stories, even if those are stories the powerful do not want you to hear or believe and do not want us to publish or disseminate, even if they are stories that offend and rage and distress the very readers we are bound to inform.

What is the point of free speech if we are always afraid to speak freely or if we embrace an echo chamber?

If we embrace an echo chamber in which liberals talk only to other liberals and conservatives only to other conservatives, and moderates feel as though no one is talking to them, as an opinion columnist nothing was more important to me before I wrote on any issue than to listen to those people who were in opposition to my position.

You cannot marshal a cogent argument without knowing the counterpoint. Yet, too often we fall silent, becoming our own censors out of fear. If we fail to allow the unpopular or even the unacceptable to be heard because of some sense of plain vanilla civility, it's not civility at all. It is a denigration of the human capacity for thought, the suggestion that we are incapable of disagreement, argument or intellectual combat. It is the denial of everything this university stands for.

We parents sitting out there have known fear on your behalf. Make no mistake. We grew up with a simple equation. Our children would do better than we had. In my father's Irish Catholic household, it was a simple equation. Ditch digger to cop to lawyer to judge in four generations. My mother's Italian immigrant parents barely spoke English. Their granddaughter is a novelist. That's the American story.

Many of my generation fear that doing better is not in the cards for you. We feel chagrined that you won't inherit the SUV, the McMansion, the corner office, that you won't do better than we did, but you are going to define what doing better means and do it better than we did. Because if you are people who see race and ethnicity, sexual orientation and gender identity as attributes not stereotypes, you will have done better than us.

If those of you who are male recognize in every way that those of us who are female are capable, equal and human and live that in the way you behave every day, you will have done better than us.

And on a more personal level, if you as a group ditch what has somehow become the 80-hour work week and return us to a sane investment in our personal and professional lives, you will have done better than us.

Those of us of my generation have worked hard to pass on a better world, but we sometimes made a grave mistake in thinking that doing better was mathematical when it's actually spiritual. Perhaps my favorite quote and the one I evoke most often is from the great writer Henry James. "Three things in human life are important: The first is to be kind; the second is to be kind; and the third is to be kind."

If you follow those words in public service and private life, you will have done better, because we have today a world with too much of the kindness leached out of it, that is too often mean-spirited, that seems to have lost track of the most valuable verse from the New Testament, the one about loving your neighbor. Perhaps that's because we've forgotten how to be kind to ourselves.

The right answer about how we should be, how we should behave is today so often a punitive one. We should be thinner, richer, slicker, surer, we should be tougher, harder. That's all nonsense. I can assure you that when I look back over my life, "thin" and "rich" will be two of the last things I really care about.

Loving kindness, as Buddhism calls it, that's what matters. That's what lasts. That, and giving up on the right answer. In my line of work, the honorable creative failure is infinitely more important and more useful than the careful, little, connect-the-dots paragraph. You have to have the courage to frighten yourself with what you attempt, whether it is a start-up or a family, a novel or a marriage.

You're lucky people, all of you. Most Americans will never get the kind of education you've earned here. In a culture in which knowledge seems to be moving at the speed of sound, the one thing that's never obsolete is a world-class university education.

In a recent interview, the CEO of Logitech said he loves hiring English majors. And I don't just mention that because I was an English major. Critical thinking is a skill that never goes out of style, but being the lucky ones confers great responsibility and even a moral obligation. It is to model a particular kind of life, a life of audacity. America is greatest when it is audacious.

Never forget that this is a nation built on non-compliance, begun with righteous resistance against the despotism of the privileged class. It is called the American Revolution, not the American Compromise. It is audacious to come here from another country without language or means and add to the fabric of this polyglot place.

It is audacious to send your child off to college when no one in your family has ever been before.

It is audacious to work to overturn laws and customs that for centuries have held fellow citizens as less than.

It is audacious to invent and it is audacious to dare and it is audacious to care and to live that caring conspicuously. Playing it safe is a slog. Taking a chance is getting on a skateboard. When you come up with a checklist—job, check; spouse, check; home, check—don't forget to ask yourself, "Are these the things I really want or is each of them what I assume I ought to want?" The difference between those two is the difference between a life and an existence.

T. S. Eliot, "Only those who risk going too far can possibly find out how far they can go." George Eliot, or as it's now safe to call her, Mary Anne Evans , "It is never too late to be what you might have been." It is never too early, either.

The status quo, business as usual, the way things have always been done, even, if you will, the right answer has failed us in nearly every area of life. Fear of setting a foot wrong, of criticism and judgment and even failure is unworthy of people like you.

The voice you should sometimes heed is the one that tells you you can't, you shouldn't, it's too much, it's too chancy. Don't heed the fear. The fear a young English woman in a parsonage more than 200 years ago refused to acknowledge when she wrote *Pride and Prejudice*. The fear a neophyte architect refused to let steer his vision as he created uncommon buildings.

When I send a gift to a newborn, I always include the message, "Welcome to the world." Today I offer you a variation: "Welcome to my world." It's a world of achievers, planners, list makers, but it is greatest when it is the world that says, "Be brave. Take the leap. Do it. Dare it. Courage."

Congratulations.

Print Citations

CMS: Quindlen, Anna. "Be Brave. Take the Leap. Do It. Dare It. Courage." Speech presented at the Washington University Class of 2017 Commencement, St. Louis, MO, May, 2017. In *The Reference Shelf: Representative American Speeches 2016-2017*, edited by Betsy Maury, 42-46. Ipswich, MA: H.W. Wilson, 2017.

MLA: Quindlen, Anna. "Be Brave. Take the Leap. Do It. Dare It. Courage." Washington University Class of 2017 Commencement. St. Louis, MO. May, 2017. Presentation. *The Reference Shelf: Representative American Speeches 2016-2017.* Ed. Betsy Maury. Ipswich: H.W. Wilson, 2017. 42-46. Print.

APA: Quindlen, A. (2017). Be brave. Take the leap. Do it. Dare it. Courage. [Presentation]. *Speech presented at the Washington University Class of 2017 Commencement.* St. Louis, MO. In Betsy Maury (Ed.), *The reference shelf: Representative American speeches 2016-2017* (pp. 42-46). Ipswich, MA: H.W. Wilson. (Original work published 2017)

2
Making America Great

President Barack Obama speaks to supporters during his farewell speech at McCormick Place on January 10, 2017 in Chicago, Illinois. Obama addressed the nation in what is expected to be his last trip outside Washington as president.

Farewell Speech

By Barack Obama

Barack Obama, 44th President of the United States, delivers his farewell address in Chicago, Illinois. Obama, who was a graduate of Harvard University Law School and an expert in constitutional law, served in the US Senate representing Illinois before winning a historic landslide election in 2008 to become the nation's first African-American president. During his two presidential terms, Obama attempted a major overhaul of the nation's health insurance system and struggled against a divided Congress and numerous Republican filibusters. In his farewell address, Obama speaks about the nature of the American experiment and the need to continue working to ensure that the unalienable rights of the American creed are preserved for future generations. Obama argues further that the history of the nation has been defined by the march of forward progress and expresses his hopes that future generations will adhere to this same goal.

It's good to be home. My fellow Americans, Michelle and I have been so touched by all the well-wishes we've received over the past few weeks. But tonight it's my turn to say thanks. Whether we've seen eye-to-eye or rarely agreed at all, my conversations with you, the American people—in living rooms and schools; at farms and on factory floors; at diners and on distant outposts—are what have kept me honest, kept me inspired, and kept me going. Every day, I learned from you. You made me a better president, and you made me a better man.

I first came to Chicago when I was in my early 20s, still trying to figure out who I was; still searching for a purpose to my life. It was in neighborhoods not far from here where I began working with church groups in the shadows of closed steel mills. It was on these streets where I witnessed the power of faith, and the quiet dignity of working people in the face of struggle and loss. This is where I learned that change only happens when ordinary people get involved, get engaged, and come together to demand it.

After eight years as your president, I still believe that. And it's not just my belief. It's the beating heart of our American idea—our bold experiment in self-government.

It's the conviction that we are all created equal, endowed by our creator with certain unalienable rights, among them life, liberty, and the pursuit of happiness.

It's the insistence that these rights, while self-evident, have never been self-executing; that we, the people, through the instrument of our democracy, can form a more perfect union.

Delivered on January 10, 2017 at McCormick Place, Chicago, IL.

This is the great gift our Founders gave us. The freedom to chase our individual dreams through our sweat, toil, and imagination—and the imperative to strive together as well, to achieve a greater good.

For 240 years, our nation's call to citizenship has given work and purpose to each new generation. It's what led patriots to choose republic over tyranny, pioneers to trek west, slaves to brave that makeshift railroad to freedom. It's what pulled immigrants and refugees across oceans and the Rio Grande, pushed women to reach for the ballot, powered workers to organize. It's why GIs gave their lives at Omaha Beach and Iwo Jima; Iraq and Afghanistan—and why men and women from Selma to Stonewall were prepared to give theirs as well.

So that's what we mean when we say America is exceptional. Not that our nation has been flawless from the start, but that we have shown the capacity to change, and make life better for those who follow.

Yes, our progress has been uneven. The work of democracy has always been hard, contentious and sometimes bloody. For every two steps forward, it often feels we take one step back. But the long sweep of America has been defined by forward motion, a constant widening of our founding creed to embrace all, and not just some.

If I had told you eight years ago that America would reverse a great recession, reboot our auto industry, and unleash the longest stretch of job creation in our history...if I had told you that we would open up a new chapter with the Cuban people, shut down Iran's nuclear weapons program without firing a shot, and take out the mastermind of 9/11...if I had told you that we would win marriage equality, and secure the right to health insurance for another 20 million of our fellow citizens—you might have said our sights were set a little too high.

But that's what we did. That's what you did. You were the change. You answered people's hopes, and because of you, by almost every measure, America is a better, stronger place than it was when we started.

In 10 days, the world will witness a hallmark of our democracy: the peaceful transfer of power from one freely elected president to the next. I committed to President-elect Trump that my administration would ensure the smoothest possible transition, just as President Bush did for me. Because it's up to all of us to make sure our government can help us meet the many challenges we still face.

We have what we need to do so. After all, we remain the wealthiest, most powerful, and most respected nation on Earth. Our youth and drive, our diversity and openness, our boundless capacity for risk and reinvention mean that the future should be ours.

But that potential will be realized only if our democracy works. Only if our politics reflects the decency of our people. Only if all of us, regardless of our party affiliation or particular interest, help restore the sense of common purpose that we so badly need right now.

That's what I want to focus on tonight—the state of our democracy.

Understand, democracy does not require uniformity. Our founders quarreled and compromised, and expected us to do the same. But they knew that democracy does require a basic sense of solidarity—the idea that for all our outward differences, we are all in this together; that we rise or fall as one.

There have been moments throughout our history that threatened to rupture that solidarity. The beginning of this century has been one of those times. A shrinking world, growing inequality; demographic change and the specter of terrorism—these forces haven't just tested our security and prosperity, but our democracy as well. And how we meet these challenges to our democracy will determine our ability to educate our kids, and create good jobs, and protect our homeland.

In other words, it will determine our future.

Our democracy won't work without a sense that everyone has economic opportunity. Today, the economy is growing again; wages, incomes, home values, and retirement accounts are rising again; poverty is falling again. The wealthy are paying a fairer share of taxes even as the stock market shatters records. The unemployment rate is near a 10-year low. The uninsured rate has never, ever been lower. Healthcare costs are rising at the slowest rate in 50 years. And if anyone can put together a plan that is demonstrably better than the improvements we've made to our healthcare system—that covers as many people at less cost—I will publicly support it.

That, after all, is why we serve—to make people's lives better, not worse.

But for all the real progress we've made, we know it's not enough. Our economy doesn't work as well or grow as fast when a few prosper at the expense of a growing middle class. But stark inequality is also corrosive to our democratic principles. While the top 1% has amassed a bigger share of wealth and income, too many families, in inner cities and rural counties, have been left behind—the laid-off factory worker; the waitress and healthcare worker who struggle to pay the bills—convinced that the game is fixed against them, that their government only serves the interests of the powerful—a recipe for more cynicism and polarization in our politics.

There are no quick fixes to this long-term trend. I agree that our trade should be fair and not just free. But the next wave of economic dislocation won't come from overseas. It will come from the relentless pace of automation that makes many good, middle-class jobs obsolete.

And so we must forge a new social compact—to guarantee all our kids the education they need; to give workers the power to unionize for better wages; to update the social safety net to reflect the way we live now and make more reforms to the tax code so corporations and individuals who reap the most from the new economy don't avoid their obligations to the country that's made their success possible. We can argue about how to best achieve these goals. But we can't be complacent about the goals themselves. For if we don't create opportunity for all people, the disaffection and division that has stalled our progress will only sharpen in years to come.

There's a second threat to our democracy—one as old as our nation itself. After my election, there was talk of a post-racial America. Such a vision, however well-intended, was never realistic. For race remains a potent and often divisive force in our society. I've lived long enough to know that race relations are better than they were 10, or 20, or 30 years ago—you can see it not just in statistics, but in the attitudes of young Americans across the political spectrum.

But we're not where we need to be. All of us have more work to do. After all, if every economic issue is framed as a struggle between a hard-working white middle class and undeserving minorities, then workers of all shades will be left fighting for scraps while the wealthy withdraw further into their private enclaves. If we decline to invest in the children of immigrants, just because they don't look like us, we diminish the prospects of our own children—because those brown kids will represent a larger share of America's workforce. And our economy doesn't have to be a zero-sum game. Last year, incomes rose for all races, all age groups, for men and for women.

Going forward, we must uphold laws against discrimination—in hiring, in housing, in education and the criminal justice system. That's what our Constitution and highest ideals require. But laws alone won't be enough. Hearts must change. If our democracy is to work in this increasingly diverse nation, each one of us must try to heed the advice of one of the great characters in American fiction, Atticus Finch, who said, "You never really understand a person until you consider things from his point of view...until you climb into his skin and walk around in it."

For blacks and other minorities, it means tying our own struggles for justice to the challenges that a lot of people in this country face—the refugee, the immigrant, the rural poor, the transgender American, and also the middle-aged white man who from the outside may seem like he's got all the advantages, but who's seen his world upended by economic, cultural, and technological change.

For white Americans, it means acknowledging that the effects of slavery and Jim Crow didn't suddenly vanish in the '60s; that when minority groups voice discontent, they're not just engaging in reverse racism or practicing political correctness; that when they wage peaceful protest, they're not demanding special treatment, but the equal treatment our Founders promised.

For native-born Americans, it means reminding ourselves that the stereotypes about immigrants today were said, almost word for word, about the Irish, Italians, and Poles. America wasn't weakened by the presence of these newcomers; they embraced this nation's creed, and it was strengthened.

So regardless of the station we occupy; we have to try harder; to start with the premise that each of our fellow citizens loves this country just as much as we do; that they value hard work and family like we do; that their children are just as curious and hopeful and worthy of love as our own.

None of this is easy. For too many of us, it's become safer to retreat into our own bubbles, whether in our neighborhoods or college campuses or places of worship or our social media feeds, surrounded by people who look like us and share the same political outlook and never challenge our assumptions. The rise of naked partisanship, increasing economic and regional stratification, the splintering of our media into a channel for every taste—all this makes this great sorting seem natural, even inevitable. And increasingly, we become so secure in our bubbles that we accept only information, whether true or not, that fits our opinions, instead of basing our opinions on the evidence that's out there.

This trend represents a third threat to our democracy. Politics is a battle of ideas; in the course of a healthy debate, we'll prioritize different goals, and the different means of reaching them. But without some common baseline of facts; without a willingness to admit new information, and concede that your opponent is making a fair point, and that science and reason matter, we'll keep talking past each other, making common ground and compromise impossible.

Isn't that part of what makes politics so dispiriting? How can elected officials rage about deficits when we propose to spend money on preschool for kids, but not when we're cutting taxes for corporations? How do we excuse ethical lapses in our own party, but pounce when the other party does the same thing? It's not just dishonest, this selective sorting of the facts; it's self-defeating. Because as my mother used to tell me, reality has a way of catching up with you.

Take the challenge of climate change. In just eight years, we've halved our dependence on foreign oil, doubled our renewable energy, and led the world to an agreement that has the promise to save this planet. But without bolder action, our children won't have time to debate the existence of climate change; they'll be busy dealing with its effects: environmental disasters, economic disruptions, and waves of climate refugees seeking sanctuary.

Now, we can and should argue about the best approach to the problem. But to simply deny the problem not only betrays future generations; it betrays the essential spirit of innovation and practical problem-solving that guided our Founders.

It's that spirit, born of the Enlightenment, that made us an economic powerhouse—the spirit that took flight at Kitty Hawk and Cape Canaveral; the spirit that that cures disease and put a computer in every pocket.

It's that spirit—a faith in reason, and enterprise, and the primacy of right over might, that allowed us to resist the lure of fascism and tyranny during the Great Depression, and build a post-World War II order with other democracies, an order based not just on military power or national affiliations but on principles—the rule of law, human rights, freedoms of religion, speech, assembly, and an independent press.

That order is now being challenged—first by violent fanatics who claim to speak for Islam; more recently by autocrats in foreign capitals who see free markets, open democracies, and civil society itself as a threat to their power. The peril each poses to our democracy is more far-reaching than a car bomb or a missile. It represents the fear of change; the fear of people who look or speak or pray differently; a contempt for the rule of law that holds leaders accountable; an intolerance of dissent and free thought; a belief that the sword or the gun or the bomb or propaganda machine is the ultimate arbiter of what's true and what's right.

Because of the extraordinary courage of our men and women in uniform, and the intelligence officers, law enforcement, and diplomats who support them, no foreign terrorist organization has successfully planned and executed an attack on our homeland these past eight years; and although Boston and Orlando remind us of how dangerous radicalization can be, our law enforcement agencies are more effective and vigilant than ever. We've taken out tens of thousands of terrorists—including

Osama bin Laden. The global coalition we're leading against ISIL has taken out their leaders, and taken away about half their territory. ISIL will be destroyed, and no one who threatens America will ever be safe. To all who serve, it has been the honor of my lifetime to be your Commander-in-Chief.

But protecting our way of life requires more than our military. Democracy can buckle when we give in to fear. So just as we, as citizens, must remain vigilant against external aggression, we must guard against a weakening of the values that make us who we are. That's why, for the past eight years, I've worked to put the fight against terrorism on a firm legal footing. That's why we've ended torture, worked to close Gitmo, and reform our laws governing surveillance to protect privacy and civil liberties. That's why I reject discrimination against Muslim Americans. That's why we cannot withdraw from global fights—to expand democracy, and human rights, women's rights, and LGBT rights—no matter how imperfect our efforts, no matter how expedient ignoring such values may seem. For the fight against extremism and intolerance and sectarianism are of a piece with the fight against authoritarianism and nationalist aggression. If the scope of freedom and respect for the rule of law shrinks around the world, the likelihood of war within and between nations increases, and our own freedoms will eventually be threatened.

So let's be vigilant, but not afraid. ISIL will try to kill innocent people. But they cannot defeat America unless we betray our Constitution and our principles in the fight. Rivals like Russia or China cannot match our influence around the world—unless we give up what we stand for, and turn ourselves into just another big country that bullies smaller neighbors.

Which brings me to my final point—our democracy is threatened whenever we take it for granted. All of us, regardless of party, should throw ourselves into the task of rebuilding our democratic institutions. When voting rates are some of the lowest among advanced democracies, we should make it easier, not harder, to vote. When trust in our institutions is low, we should reduce the corrosive influence of money in our politics, and insist on the principles of transparency and ethics in public service. When Congress is dysfunctional, we should draw our districts to encourage politicians to cater to common sense and not rigid extremes.

And all of this depends on our participation; on each of us accepting the responsibility of citizenship, regardless of which way the pendulum of power swings.

Our Constitution is a remarkable, beautiful gift. But it's really just a piece of parchment. It has no power on its own. We, the people, give it power—with our participation, and the choices we make. Whether or not we stand up for our freedoms. Whether or not we respect and enforce the rule of law. America is no fragile thing. But the gains of our long journey to freedom are not assured.

In his own farewell address, George Washington wrote that self-government is the underpinning of our safety, prosperity, and liberty, but "from different causes and from different quarters much pains will be taken...to weaken in your minds the conviction of this truth;" that we should preserve it with "jealous anxiety;" that we should reject "the first dawning of every attempt to alienate any portion of our country from the rest or to enfeeble the sacred ties" that make us one.

We weaken those ties when we allow our political dialogue to become so corrosive that people of good character are turned off from public service; so coarse with rancor that Americans with whom we disagree are not just misguided, but somehow malevolent. We weaken those ties when we define some of us as more American than others; when we write off the whole system as inevitably corrupt, and blame the leaders we elect without examining our own role in electing them.

It falls to each of us to be those anxious, jealous guardians of our democracy; to embrace the joyous task we've been given to continually try to improve this great nation of ours. Because for all our outward differences, we all share the same proud title: Citizen.

Ultimately, that's what our democracy demands. It needs you. Not just when there's an election, not just when your own narrow interest is at stake, but over the full span of a lifetime. If you're tired of arguing with strangers on the Internet, try to talk with one in real life. If something needs fixing, lace up your shoes and do some organizing. If you're disappointed by your elected officials, grab a clipboard, get some signatures, and run for office yourself. Show up. Dive in. Persevere. Sometimes you'll win. Sometimes you'll lose. Presuming a reservoir of goodness in others can be a risk, and there will be times when the process disappoints you. But for those of us fortunate enough to have been a part of this work, to see it up close, let me tell you, it can energize and inspire. And more often than not, your faith in America—and in Americans—will be confirmed.

Mine sure has been. Over the course of these eight years, I've seen the hopeful faces of young graduates and our newest military officers. I've mourned with grieving families searching for answers, and found grace in a Charleston church. I've seen our scientists help a paralyzed man regain his sense of touch, and our wounded warriors walk again. I've seen our doctors and volunteers rebuild after earthquakes and stop pandemics in their tracks. I've seen the youngest of children remind us of our obligations to care for refugees, to work in peace, and above all to look out for each other.

That faith I placed all those years ago, not far from here, in the power of ordinary Americans to bring about change—that faith has been rewarded in ways I couldn't possibly have imagined. I hope yours has, too. Some of you here tonight or watching at home were there with us in 2004, in 2008, in 2012—and maybe you still can't believe we pulled this whole thing off.

You're not the only ones. Michelle—for the past 25 years, you've been not only my wife and mother of my children, but my best friend. You took on a role you didn't ask for and made it your own with grace and grit and style and good humor. You made the White House a place that belongs to everybody. And a new generation sets its sights higher because it has you as a role model. You've made me proud. You've made the country proud.

Malia and Sasha, under the strangest of circumstances, you have become two amazing young women, smart and beautiful, but more importantly, kind and thoughtful and full of passion. You wore the burden of years in the spotlight so easily. Of all that I've done in my life, I'm most proud to be your dad.

To Joe Biden, the scrappy kid from Scranton who became Delaware's favorite son: You were the first choice I made as a nominee, and the best. Not just because you have been a great vice president, but because in the bargain, I gained a brother. We love you and Jill like family, and your friendship has been one of the great joys of our life.

To my remarkable staff: For eight years—and for some of you, a whole lot more— I've drawn from your energy, and tried to reflect back what you displayed every day: heart, and character, and idealism. I've watched you grow up, get married, have kids, and start incredible new journeys of your own. Even when times got tough and frustrating, you never let Washington get the better of you. The only thing that makes me prouder than all the good we've done is the thought of all the remarkable things you'll achieve from here.

And to all of you out there—every organizer who moved to an unfamiliar town and kind family who welcomed them in, every volunteer who knocked on doors, every young person who cast a ballot for the first time, every American who lived and breathed the hard work of change—you are the best supporters and organizers anyone could hope for, and I will forever be grateful. Because, yes, you changed the world.

That's why I leave this stage tonight even more optimistic about this country than I was when we started. Because I know our work has not only helped so many Americans; it has inspired so many Americans—especially so many young people out there—to believe you can make a difference; to hitch your wagon to something bigger than yourselves. This generation coming up—unselfish, altruistic, creative, patriotic—I've seen you in every corner of the country. You believe in a fair, just, inclusive America; you know that constant change has been America's hallmark, something not to fear but to embrace, and you are willing to carry this hard work of democracy forward. You'll soon outnumber any of us, and I believe as a result that the future is in good hands.

My fellow Americans, it has been the honor of my life to serve you. I won't stop; in fact, I will be right there with you, as a citizen, for all my days that remain. For now, whether you're young or young at heart, I do have one final ask of you as your president—the same thing I asked when you took a chance on me eight years ago.

I am asking you to believe. Not in my ability to bring about change—but in yours.

I am asking you to hold fast to that faith written into our founding documents; that idea whispered by slaves and abolitionists; that spirit sung by immigrants and homesteaders and those who marched for justice; that creed reaffirmed by those who planted flags from foreign battlefields to the surface of the moon; a creed at the core of every American whose story is not yet written:

Yes We Can.

Yes We Did.

Yes We Can.

Thank you. God bless you. And may God continue to bless the United States of America.

Print Citations

CMS: Obama, Barack. "Farewell Speech." Speech presented at McCormick Place, Chicago, IL, January, 2017. In *The Reference Shelf: Representative American Speeches 2016-2017*, edited by Betsy Maury, 49-57. Ipswich, MA: H.W. Wilson, 2017.

MLA: Obama, Barack. "Farewell Speech." McCormick Place. Chicago, IL. January, 2017. Presentation. *The Reference Shelf: Representative American Speeches 2016-2017*. Ed. Betsy Maury. Ipswich: H.W. Wilson, 2017. 49-57. Print.

APA: Obama, B. (2017). Farewell speech. [Presentation]. *Speech presented at McCormick Place*. Chicago, IL. In Betsy Maury (Ed.), *The reference shelf: Representative American speeches 2016-2017* (pp. 49-57). Ipswich, MA: H.W. Wilson. (Original work published 2017)

Inaugural Address

By Donald Trump

US President Donald Trump delivers an inaugural address after winning an electoral victory to become the nation's 45th president. After gaining fame as a reality television personality and real estate mogul known for the chain of hotels sharing his name, Trump won the 2016 election despite losing the popular vote. In his address, echoing messages from his campaign trail, Trump alleges that a conspiracy of liberal politicians had taken power away from the people and that foreign agents and immigrants threatened the welfare of the American people. Trump promises that a new era of protectionism and an "America first" agenda would bring about a new and more prosperous era for the nation.

Chief Justice Roberts, President Carter, President Clinton, President Bush, President Obama, fellow Americans, and people of the world: thank you.

We, the citizens of America, are now joined in a great national effort to rebuild our country and to restore its promise for all of our people.

Together, we will determine the course of America and the world for years to come.

We will face challenges. We will confront hardships. But we will get the job done.

Every four years, we gather on these steps to carry out the orderly and peaceful transfer of power, and we are grateful to President Obama and First Lady Michelle Obama for their gracious aid throughout this transition. They have been magnificent.

Today's ceremony, however, has very special meaning. Because today we are not merely transferring power from one Administration to another, or from one party to another—but we are transferring power from Washington, D.C. and giving it back to you, the American People.

For too long, a small group in our nation's Capital has reaped the rewards of government while the people have borne the cost.

Washington flourished—but the people did not share in its wealth.

Politicians prospered—but the jobs left, and the factories closed.

The establishment protected itself, but not the citizens of our country.

Their victories have not been your victories; their triumphs have not been your triumphs; and while they celebrated in our nation's Capital, there was little to celebrate for struggling families all across our land.

Delivered on January 20, 2017 at the US Capitol, Washington, DC.

That all changes—starting right here, and right now, because this moment is your moment: it belongs to you.

It belongs to everyone gathered here today and everyone watching all across America.

This is your day. This is your celebration.

And this, the United States of America, is your country.

What truly matters is not which party controls our government, but whether our government is controlled by the people.

January 20th 2017, will be remembered as the day the people became the rulers of this nation again.

The forgotten men and women of our country will be forgotten no longer.

Everyone is listening to you now.

You came by the tens of millions to become part of a historic movement the likes of which the world has never seen before.

At the center of this movement is a crucial conviction: that a nation exists to serve its citizens.

Americans want great schools for their children, safe neighborhoods for their families, and good jobs for themselves.

These are the just and reasonable demands of a righteous public.

But for too many of our citizens, a different reality exists: Mothers and children trapped in poverty in our inner cities; rusted-out factories scattered like tombstones across the landscape of our nation; an education system, flush with cash, but which leaves our young and beautiful students deprived of knowledge; and the crime and gangs and drugs that have stolen too many lives and robbed our country of so much unrealized potential.

This American carnage stops right here and stops right now.

We are one nation—and their pain is our pain. Their dreams are our dreams; and their success will be our success. We share one heart, one home, and one glorious destiny.

The oath of office I take today is an oath of allegiance to all Americans.

For many decades, we've enriched foreign industry at the expense of American industry;

Subsidized the armies of other countries while allowing for the very sad depletion of our military;

We've defended other nation's borders while refusing to defend our own;

And spent trillions of dollars overseas while America's infrastructure has fallen into disrepair and decay.

We've made other countries rich while the wealth, strength, and confidence of our country has disappeared over the horizon.

One by one, the factories shuttered and left our shores, with not even a thought about the millions upon millions of American workers left behind.

The wealth of our middle class has been ripped from their homes and then redistributed across the entire world.

But that is the past. And now we are looking only to the future.

We assembled here today are issuing a new decree to be heard in every city, in every foreign capital, and in every hall of power.

From this day forward, a new vision will govern our land.

From this moment on, it's going to be America First.

Every decision on trade, on taxes, on immigration, on foreign affairs, will be made to benefit American workers and American families.

We must protect our borders from the ravages of other countries making our products, stealing our companies, and destroying our jobs. Protection will lead to great prosperity and strength.

I will fight for you with every breath in my body—and I will never, ever let you down.

America will start winning again, winning like never before.

We will bring back our jobs. We will bring back our borders. We will bring back our wealth. And we will bring back our dreams.

We will build new roads, and highways, and bridges, and airports, and tunnels, and railways all across our wonderful nation.

We will get our people off of welfare and back to work—rebuilding our country with American hands and American labor.

We will follow two simple rules: Buy American and Hire American.

We will seek friendship and goodwill with the nations of the world—but we do so with the understanding that it is the right of all nations to put their own interests first.

We do not seek to impose our way of life on anyone, but rather to let it shine as an example for everyone to follow.

We will reinforce old alliances and form new ones—and unite the civilized world against Radical Islamic Terrorism, which we will eradicate completely from the face of the Earth.

At the bedrock of our politics will be a total allegiance to the United States of America, and through our loyalty to our country, we will rediscover our loyalty to each other.

When you open your heart to patriotism, there is no room for prejudice.

The Bible tells us, "how good and pleasant it is when God's people live together in unity."

We must speak our minds openly, debate our disagreements honestly, but always pursue solidarity.

When America is united, America is totally unstoppable.

There should be no fear—we are protected, and we will always be protected.

We will be protected by the great men and women of our military and law enforcement and, most importantly, we are protected by God.

Finally, we must think big and dream even bigger.

In America, we understand that a nation is only living as long as it is striving.

We will no longer accept politicians who are all talk and no action—constantly complaining but never doing anything about it.

The time for empty talk is over.

Now arrives the hour of action.

Do not let anyone tell you it cannot be done. No challenge can match the heart and fight and spirit of America.

We will not fail. Our country will thrive and prosper again.

We stand at the birth of a new millennium, ready to unlock the mysteries of space, to free the Earth from the miseries of disease, and to harness the energies, industries and technologies of tomorrow.

A new national pride will stir our souls, lift our sights, and heal our divisions.

It is time to remember that old wisdom our soldiers will never forget: that whether we are black or brown or white, we all bleed the same red blood of patriots, we all enjoy the same glorious freedoms, and we all salute the same great American Flag.

And whether a child is born in the urban sprawl of Detroit or the windswept plains of Nebraska, they look up at the same night sky, they fill their heart with the same dreams, and they are infused with the breath of life by the same almighty Creator.

So to all Americans, in every city near and far, small and large, from mountain to mountain, and from ocean to ocean, hear these words:

You will never be ignored again.

Your voice, your hopes, and your dreams, will define our American destiny. And your courage and goodness and love will forever guide us along the way.

Together, We Will Make America Strong Again.

We Will Make America Wealthy Again.

We Will Make America Proud Again.

We Will Make America Safe Again.

And, Yes, Together, We Will Make America Great Again. Thank you, God Bless You, And God Bless America.

Print Citations

CMS: Trump, Donald. "Inaugural Address." Speech presented at the US Capitol, Washington, DC, January, 2017. In *The Reference Shelf: Representative American Speeches 2016-2017*, edited by Betsy Maury, 58-61. Ipswich, MA: H.W. Wilson, 2017.

MLA: Trump, Donald. "Inaugural Address." US Capitol. Washington, DC. January, 2017. Presentation. *The Reference Shelf: Representative American Speeches 2016-2017*. Ed. Betsy Maury. Ipswich: H.W. Wilson, 2017. 58-61. Print.

APA: Trump, D. (2017). Inaugural address. [Presentation]. *Speech presented at the US Capitol*. Washington, DC. In Betsy Maury (Ed.), *The reference shelf: Representative American speeches 2016-2017* (pp. 58-61). Ipswich, MA: H.W. Wilson. (Original work published 2017)

Remarks to US Department of State Employees

By Rex W. Tillerson

Secretary of State Rex Tillerson, who formerly served as CEO of the oil company Exx-onMobil delivers a speech upon taking the office of secretary of state after Trump's historic election. In his speech, Tillerson attempts to explain to gathered employees of the state department how Trump's "America first" campaign slogan will translate into State Department policy. Tillerson, who was approved to head the department by a narrow 11-10 margin, argues controversially that, in restructuring the department to adhere to the administration's agenda, it is important to separate the nation's values, like freedom and human dignity, from the nation's international policies.

SECRETARY TILLERSON: Good morning. (Applause.) Thank you. Thank you.

Are we on? Can you all hear me back there in the back? Can you hear me now? (Laughter.) Can you hear me now?

AUDIENCE: Yes.

SECRETARY TILLERSON: All right. I told them I have to walk around. My wife has always said if you tied my hands down to my side, I would be a complete mute. (Laughter.) So I'm not great at podiums. I do know how to read a speech, but I thought today we'd just have a chat.

So I've been here about three months now, we've been working alongside one another, and so I thought it'd be worthwhile to just share a few of my perspectives with you on where I think we are and some things that are coming that I know are of interest to you.

But before I do that, I would be remiss if I did not thank all of those who have stepped into acting roles during these past three months to help me, and starting with acting Deputy Secretary Tom Shannon, who's just been stellar. (Applause.) But I also want to acknowledge the large number of people who are—stepped into under secretary, assistant secretary roles, director roles, and a number of chief of missions around the world as well. Your willingness to step up and not just fill that role, but to take responsibility for the role and to lead the organization through some pretty challenging first 90 days—it's not like we haven't had some things to work on. And so I want to express my appreciation to all of you for helping me and helping my team as we came on board. And I've just been really gratified at the work that everyone's undertaken in that regard.

Delivered on May 3, 2017 at Dean Acheson Auditorium, Washington, DC.

So I thought we'd talk about a couple of things. I want to share my perspective as to how does this administration's policies of "America first" fit into our foreign policy and foreign affairs. And so I want to touch on that. And then I'll take a quick walk around the world. Most of you have some familiarity of what's going on around the world, but I thought just regionally I'd hit each one of them very quickly, to share with you my perspective on kind of where I feel we are, and then in some areas where we've not yet had time to devote the attention to we would like, and I don't want that to be in any way considered that we don't think those are important. It's kind of a—what's the hottest fire that we've got to deal with?

So I want to talk about that a little bit, and then spend some time at the end talking about where we're going in the future of the department, USAID, and, as you know, we just kicked off this listening exercise.

So let's talk first about my view of how you translate "America first" into our foreign policy. And I think I approach it really that it's America first for national security and economic prosperity, and that doesn't mean it comes at the expense of others. Our partnerships and our alliances are critical to our success in both of those areas. But as we have progressed over the last 20 years—and some of you could tie it back to the post-Cold War era as the world has changed, some of you can tie it back to the evolution of China since the post-Nixon era and China's rise as an economic power, and now as a growing military power—that as we participated in those changes, we were promoting relations, we were promoting economic activity, we were promoting trade with a lot of these emerging economies, and we just kind of lost track of how we were doing. And as a result, things got a little bit out of balance. And I think that's—as you hear the President talk about it, that's what he really speaks about, is: Look, things have gotten out of balance, and these are really important relationships to us and they're really important alliances, but we've got to bring them back into balance.

So whether it's our asking of NATO members to really meet their obligations, even though those were notional obligations, we understand—and aspirational obligation, we think it's important that those become concrete. And when we deal with our trading partners—that things have gotten a little out of bounds here, they've gotten a little off balance—we've got to bring that back into balance because it's not serving the interests of the American people well.

So it doesn't have to come at the expense of others, but it does have to come at an engagement with others. And so as we're building our policies around those notions, that's what we want to support. But at the end of it, it is strengthening our national security and promoting economic prosperity for the American people, and we do that, again, with a lot of partners.

Now, I think it's important to also remember that guiding all of our foreign policy actions are our fundamental values: our values around freedom, human dignity, the way people are treated. Those are our values. Those are not our policies; they're values. And the reason it's important, I think, to keep that well understood is policies can change. They do change. They should change. Policies change to adapt to the—our values never change. They're constant throughout all of this.

And so I think the real challenge many of us have as we think about constructing our policies and carrying out our policies is: How do we represent our values? And in some circumstances, if you condition our national security efforts on someone adopting our values, we probably can't achieve our national security goals or our national security interests. If we condition too heavily that others must adopt this value that we've come to over a long history of our own, it really creates obstacles to our ability to advance our national security interests, our economic interests. It doesn't mean that we leave those values on the sidelines. It doesn't mean that we don't advocate for and aspire to freedom, human dignity, and the treatment of people the world over. We do. And we will always have that on our shoulder everywhere we go.

But I think it is—I think it's really important that all of us understand the difference between policy and values, and in some circumstances, we should and do condition our policy engagements on people adopting certain actions as to how they treat people. They should. We should demand that. But that doesn't mean that's the case in every situation. And so we really have to understand, in each country or each region of the world that we're dealing with, what are our national security interests, what are our economic prosperity interests, and then as we can advocate and advance our values, we should—but the policies can do this; the values never change.

And so I would ask you to just—to the extent you could think about that a little bit, I think it's useful, because I know this is probably, for me, it's one of the most difficult areas as I've thought about how to formulate policy to advance all of these things simultaneously. It's a real challenge. And I hear from government leaders all over the world: You just can't demand that of us, we can't move that quickly, we can't adapt that quickly, okay? So it's how do we advance our national security and economic interests on this hand, our values are constant over here.

So I give you that as kind of an overarching view of how I think about the President's approach of "America first." We must secure the nation. We must protect our people. We must protect our borders. We must protect our ability to be that voice of our values now and forevermore. And we can only do that with economic prosperity. So it's foreign policy projected with a strong ability to enforce the protection of our freedoms with a strong military. And all of you that have been at this a long time understand the value of speaking with a posture of strength—not a threatening posture, but a posture of strength. People know we can back it up.

So with that in mind, let me just quickly walk around the world and give you my assessment of where we are in some of the early stages of policy that's underway and some that's yet to be developed.

So as all of you clearly understand, when we came in to the State Department, the administration came in, was sworn in, immediately confronted with a serious situation in North Korea. Now, the prior administration, as all of you know, President Obama told President Trump this was going to be your greatest threat that you're going to have to manage, and he was right.

So it was—it's right on the doorstep. And so it got immediate attention. It was the first policy area that we began to develop in terms of what is our overarching strategic approach and how do we want to execute against that. In evaluating that, what was important to us and to me to understand was, first, where are our allies? And so engaging with our allies and ensuring that our allies and we see the situation the same—our allies in South Korea, our allies in Japan.

And then, secondly, it was to engage with the other regional powers as to how do they see it. And so it was useful and helpful to have the Chinese and now the Russians articulate clearly that their policy is unchanged; they—their policy is a denuclearized Korean Peninsula. And of course we did our part many years ago. We took all the nuclear weapons out of South Korea. So now we have a shared objective, and that's very useful, from which you then build out your policy approaches and your strategies.

So many people are saying, well, gee, this is just the same thing we've tried over and over—we're going to put pressure on the regime in Pyongyang, they're not going to do anything, and then in the end we'll all cave. Well, the difference, I think, in our approach this time is we're going to test this assumption, and when the—when folks came in to review the situation with me, the assumption was that China has limited influence on the regime in Pyongyang, or they have a limited willingness to assert their influence. And so I told the President we've got to test that, and we're going to test it by leaning hard into them, and this is a good place to start our engagement with China.

And so that's what we've been doing, is leaning hard into China to test their willingness to use their influence, their engagement with the regime in North Korea. All of it backed up by very strong resolve on our part to have a denuclearized peninsula with a commitment to our security alliances on the peninsula and in the region to our important allies Japan and South Korea.

So it's a pressure campaign that has a knob on it. I'd say we're at about dial setting 5 or 6 right now, with a strong call of countries all over the world to fully implement the UN Security Council resolutions regarding sanctions, because no one has ever fully implemented those. So we're going to lean into people to fully implement them. We've told them we're watching what you're doing. When we see you not implementing, we see companies or we see individuals that are violating these sanctions, we're going to contact you and we're going to ask you to take care of it. If you can't take care of it or you simply don't want to take care of it for your own internal political reasons, we will. We'll sanction them through third-country sanctions.

So we are being very open and transparent about our intentions, and we're asking our partners around the world to please take actions on your own. We want you to control how that happens. We're not trying to control it for you, but we have an expectation of what you will do. So we're putting that pressure on. We are preparing additional sanctions, if it turns out North Korea's actions warrant additional sanctions. We're hopeful that the regime in North Korea will think about this and come to a conclusion that there's another way to the future. We know they have— they're—they aspire to nuclear weapons because it's the regime's belief it's the only way they can secure their future.

We are clear—we've been clear to them this is not about regime change, this is not about regime collapse, this is not about an accelerated reunification of the peninsula, this is not about us looking for an excuse to come north of the 38th Parallel. So we're trying to be very, very clear and resolute in our message to them that your future security and economic prosperity can only be achieved through your following your commitments to denuclearize.

So this is where we are. We're at—I would say we're at about the 20 to 25 percent stage of this strategy. Thus far, our assessment is it is going like we had hoped for in terms of the response we're getting from others, but we've got a lot of work left to do to keep that pressure on. And so that's what the folks that are in the bureaus and out in the missions are doing to help us right now, is to continue this steady, resolute message and continue to talk out here to the North Koreans, but not here, yet, about what our intentions are and what we want. We are ready and prepared to engage in talks when conditions are right. But as you've heard me say, we are not going to negotiate our way to the negotiating table. That is what Pyongyang has done for the last 20 years, is cause us to have to negotiate to get them to sit down. We'll sit down when they're ready to sit down under the right terms. So that's North Korea.

And then if I pivoted over to China, because it really took us directly to our China foreign policy, we really had to assess China's situation, as I said, from the Nixon era up to where we find things today, and we saw a bit of an inflection point with the Sochi—with the Beijing Olympics. Those were enormously successful for China. They kind of put China on the map, and China really began to feel its oats about that time, and rightfully. They have achieved a lot. They moved 500 million Chinese people out of poverty into middle class status. They've still got a billion more they need to move.

So China has its own challenges, and we want to work with them and be mindful of what they're dealing with in the context of our relationship. And our relationship has to be one of understanding that we have security interests throughout northeast Asia and security interests throughout the Pacific, and we need to work with them on how those are addressed. So that gets to the island building in the South China Sea, the militarization of those islands, and obviously, we have huge trading issues to talk with them about.

So we are using the entree of the visit in Mar-a-Lago, which was heavy on some issues with North Korea but also heavy on a broader range of issues. And what we've asked the Chinese to do is we're—we want to take a fresh look at where's this relationship going to be 50 years from now, because I think we have an opportunity to define that. And so I know there have been a lot of dialogue areas that have been underway for the last several years with China. We have asked China to narrow the dialogue areas and elevate the participants to the decision-making level.

So we outlined four major dialogue areas with China, and we've asked them to bring people who report directly to the decision-maker, which is President Xi. So for the first time, we are seeking and we—so far it appears we will get people at the politburo level and at much higher levels of the government within China to participate in these dialogues so we can reframe what we want the relationship to be and begin to deal with some of the problems and issues that have just been sitting out there kind of stuck in neutral for a while. So it is a—it's a much narrower—as we make progress, those things will result in working groups where we can get after solving these things.

So we're going to have the first meeting of the Diplomatic and Security Dialogue, which is chaired by myself and Secretary Mattis, with our counterparts here in Washington in June, and we've put it up as a kind of top priority. The second one is economic and trade, which is chaired by Treasury Secretary Mnuchin and Commerce Secretary Ross, and it's well underway also.

So that's kind of the new approach we're taking with China, is elevate, let's kind of revisit this relationship, and what is it going to be over the next half century. I think it's a tremendous opportunity we have to define that, and there seems to be a great interest on the part of the Chinese leadership to do that as well. They feel we're at a point of inflection also. So that's China.

Obviously, throughout Asia we've got a lot of work do with ASEAN nations and re-solidifying our leadership with ASEAN on a number of security issues but also trade issues and the South China Sea, strengthen relations with Australia and New Zealand—really important partners with us on a number of counterterrorism fronts. And so throughout the region those engagements are underway. And the President has committed to make the trip to Vietnam and to the Philippines for those meetings this fall, and I think that's going to be very important that he is going, and we'll be going in advance, obviously, to prepare for all of that.

So if we walk around to the next hot spot that we worked on, pretty quickly it was the Middle East around the campaign to defeat ISIS and instability that that's created in, obviously, Syria, Iraq, the issues in Afghanistan. And as those of you who work that region well know, you can just kind of draw the concentric circles out all the way into North Africa, parts of Africa, all of the Middle East, parts of Central Asia, and this is really a D-ISIS and a counterterrorism effort, is what it really boils down to. And so how do we develop policies and bring regional players together to address these threats of ISIS and counterterrorism?

And we hosted I think what was a very successful coalition to defeat ISIS ministerial here at the State Department. I think there is a real renewed sense of energy and commitment to win this war against ISIS. We will; we are defeating ISIS in their caliphate in Syria and Iraq, but we know that ISIS exists more broadly than that. And so, as we said in that coalition effort, we've got to move beyond the battlefield, we've got to move into the cyberspace, we've got to move into the social communications space, and get inside of the messaging that allows them to recruit people around the world to their terrorism efforts.

So there is a big effort underway with players in the region, most notably the Kingdom of Saudi Arabia, and working with other partners to get inside of this conversation that's going on within the Muslim community around what this is doing to the way the Muslim faith is understood by others in the world. And I would say it's a very open conversation we're having and a renewed commitment on the part of leaders in the Muslim world that want to take this on. So we're going to be leveraging on that as well.

So as you're seeing this play out in the Middle East, still a lot of hard work to do to get coalition partners together around ceasefires and peace processes in Syria. How do we advance our interest in Afghanistan to a legitimate peace process is what we're pursuing in Afghanistan, and then keeping this terrorism network confined as it wants to spread itself through North Africa and Central Africa. So a lot of work ahead of us, and many of you are directly engaged in it already; many more of you are going to become engaged in it, I think you can expect.

The next kind of area of priority is our re-engagement with Russia. Obviously, they are part of the engagement in Syria, but we have other issues with Russia, as you all well know, in Europe, and the situation in Ukraine. As I know many of you heard from my trip to Moscow, characterized to President Putin that the relationship between our two nations was the lowest it's been since the Cold War. He did not disagree. He shrugged his shoulders and nodded in agreement. And I said it's spiraling down, it's getting worse. And my comment to him was you—we cannot have, the two greatest nuclear powers in the world cannot have this kind of relationship. We have to change it.

And so we have a number of efforts underway to first stabilize the relationship. And Deputy Secretary—acting Deputy Secretary Shannon is leading a working group effort to see if we can address some of the things that are just irritating the relationship, that make it hard for us to talk to one another even in civil tones. So we're working hard on that and we're hoping to begin to solve some of that, while Foreign Minister Lavrov and I, under the direction of President Putin and now President Trump, coming out of the call yesterday are going to continue to see if we can work together on the first big area of cooperation, which would be Syria, and can we achieve a ceasefire that will hold long enough for us to get a peace process underway.

I don't want to say we're off to a great start on this, because it's very early stages. I don't know where it will go. So I've got a bilateral with Foreign Minister Lavrov in Alaska next week on the margins of the Arctic Council. Both our presidents have charged us to take this further and see where we can go with it. So obviously, close coordination with the Department of Defense, with our intelligence agencies, and importantly our allies in the region, because we want them to always know what we're doing, because we're going to need their support as well.

So a lot of work ahead of us on the Russia engagement—work some small things, can we work one big thing together. If we can find space for something we feel we can begin to rebuild some level of trust, because today there is almost no trust between us. Can we build some level of trust? We've got a long list of things to work on from our arms agreements and issues we have with our nuclear arms agreements, to obviously, getting to Ukraine, Crimea, and other places where Russia is not being particularly helpful today.

So that's what we're hoping, is that we can begin to build a way in which we can learn how to work with one another. I don't know whether we can or not. We'll— we're going to find out.

So quickly to other parts of the world that are really important to us as well—the continent of Africa is so important from the standpoint that first, from a national security view, we cannot let Africa become the next breeding ground for a re-emergence of a caliphate for ISIS. We also cannot allow the terrorist networks that weave their way through Africa to continue unabated. You can connect the dots between countries throughout the central part of Africa and northern part of Africa where the terrorist networks are connected. We've got to get into the middle of that and disrupt that to save those countries.

But Africa is also a continent of enormous opportunity, and needs and will get and will continue to receive our attention to support stabilizing governments as they are emerging and continuing to develop their own institutional capacity, but also looking at Africa for potential economic and trading opportunities. It's a huge, I think, potential sitting out there, waiting for us to capture it, and then, obviously, a big focus of our health initiatives, because Africa still struggles with huge health challenges. And those are important to us and they're going to continue to get our attention.

So we're going to—we're working—today we have some things we're working in North Africa relative to its relationship to the Middle East challenges and our ISIS challenges. We've got to step back and take a more comprehensive look at our approach to the entire continent, and that's out in front of us as well.

And then lastly, I want to go to the Western Hemisphere. And in the Western Hemisphere, obviously, our neighbors are vitally important to us, Canada and Mexico. It's not as rocky as it looks sometimes, and I think, in fact, the relationships are quite good. Both of our neighbors understand we have to refresh some of the agreements that have governed our relationship, particularly in the areas of trade, and both countries are ready to engage in a good-faith effort with us as well.

In particular, we're investing a lot of effort into Mexico because of the transmigration issues and organized crime. And so we have an initiative underway where the senior members of the Mexican Government will be coming up here on May the 18th to participate in an interagency process with us to see if we can get at transnational organized crime and begin to break these organized crime units up. Not only are they a threat to us and to Mexico's stability and the scourge of drugs that just flow into this country, they also are part of the integrated terrorist financing networks as well. So this is vital to us for a number of reasons and we look forward to making some progress there.

South of Mexico, we've got some initiatives underway to work with the Latin American countries, which are where a lot of the people are trying to leave to come up to the U.S., to continue economic development, security investments in Latin America, and working with the Department of Homeland Security. We're actually hosting an event in Miami to bring those leaders up so we can talk with them about how we get better organized to address these issues and how we can bring more private capital into investment opportunities in Central and Latin America.

Southern cone, we have a lot of opportunity and some challenges down there. What we want to do is step back and develop a Western Hemisphere strategy that thinks about South America in its entirety and its relationship to Central America, but Cuba and the Caribbean as well. There are terrorist financing issues. There are terrorist networks that are beginning to emerge in parts of South America that have our attention. There are governance issues in certain countries—certainly all of you are following the situation in Venezuela; a real tragedy, but we're hopeful that working with others, including interventions by others in Europe, that we may be able to gain some traction in Venezuela. So we have a number of things in front of us yet to develop clear policies on how we want to go forward.

So my view is that we want to look at these regions almost in their entirety first, because everything is interconnected. We can take a country and develop something, but if we don't have the perspective regionally, we're probably not going to be as effective. So we're trying to start out here, and then we'll bring it down to a country-by-country level so we can execute. So that's just to give you a little perspective on how we're approaching these things in policy planning, and then we try to get a big-picture view and then we bring the bureau people in, the experts in, and help us start developing, now, how do you execute something like this? How do you implement it?

So for those of you that have participated in these early efforts, thank you. I feel quite good about the one—the pieces that have been completed and are in execution, I feel good about those. I can tell you the White House feels good about it. The National Security Council really values the work that we provide in the interagency process. And I would share with you I hear that from them all the time, that the stuff that comes over from the State Department, we've done our homework. It's a complete piece of work, it's useful, we can use it, and that's not always the case from all of the other agencies. So thank you for the efforts you're putting into that in that regard.

So let me turn now quickly to the last thing I wanted to talk about, which is the future and where we're going. And I alluded to this a little bit when I was commenting about the post-Cold War era. And during the Cold War—and I've had this conversation with some of you in this room before in our interactions—in many respects the Cold War was a lot easier. Things were pretty clear, the Soviet Union had a lot of things contained, and I had a conversation with Secretary-General Guterres at the UN. He described it as during the Cold War, we froze history. History just stopped in its tracks because so many of the dynamics that existed for centuries were contained. They were contained with heavy authoritarianism. And when the Cold War ended and the Soviet Union broke up, we took all of that off and history regained its march. And the world got a whole lot more complicated. And I think that's what we see. It has become much more complicated in terms of old conflicts have renewed themselves because they're not contained now. So that's the world as it is and that's the world we have to engage with.

And so I'm going to—I'm saying this as a preface to as we get into thinking about how we should deliver on mission is to be thinking about how the way we have been delivering was in many ways shaped and as a residual of the Cold War era. And in many respects, we've not yet transitioned ourselves to this new reality either. And

I don't say that just about the State Department, I say that about institutions globally. In fact, this is the—this—I had this same conversation with Secretary Guterres about the United Nations, that there are many institutions—and you can see when we have our conversations with NATO, another example, but there are many institutions around the world that were created during a different era. And so they were set up to deal with certain conditions and their processes and their organizations were set up, and as things have changed, we've not really fully adapted those. It's not that we've not recognized, but we've not fully adapted how we deliver on mission.

So one of the things, as we get into this opportunity to look at how we get our work done, is to think about the world as it is today and to leave behind—we've been—well, we do it this way because we've been doing it this way for the last 30 years or 40 years or 50 years, because all of that was created in a different environment. And so I think—I guess what I'm inviting all of you to do is to approach this effort that we're going to undertake with no constraints to your thinking—with none.

One of the great honors for me serving in this department, the Department of State, and all of you know, the Department of State, first cabinet created and chartered under the Constitution. Secretary of State, first cabinet position chartered and created under the Constitution. So we are part of a living history and we're going to get to carve our little piece of it, our increment, in that clock of time. We're going to carve our piece into that history.

And I think the question is how we will do that and how effectively we will do that. And history is moving around us as we just spoke. And how do we adapt to that? And so I want to ask all of you to be very free in your thinking. So the process going forward, as you know we've just kicked off this listening exercise and I really encourage all of you to please go online and participate in the survey online. This is vital to how we understand where we want to go and I think we have about 300 individuals that we've selected to sit down face-to-face and do some interviews so we have a more fulsome understanding. We want to collect all of these—all this input and your thoughts and ideas, both here and at USAID, and that is going to guide how we approach both our organizational structure, but more importantly, our work process design: How do we actually deliver on mission? That's the real key. How do you deliver on mission?

And really, the way I have found these things to be the most successful is I understand how to deliver on mission first, I understand how the work processes work, and then I'll put the boxes around it to make all that work. Most people like to start with the boxes and then try to design it. I'm—I do it the other way around. How do we get the work done? We'll then put the organization structure in place to support that. So we need a lot of creative thinking. We need to hear from you. This is going to inform how this turns out. I want to emphasize to you we have no preconceived notions on the outcome. I didn't come with a solution in a box when I showed up. I came with a commitment to look at it and see if we can't improve it.

And I know change like this is really stressful for a lot of people. There's nothing easy about it, and I don't want to diminish in any way the challenges I know this presents for individuals, it presents to families, it presents to organizations. I'm very well aware of all of that. All I can offer you on the other side of that equation is an opportunity to shape the future way in which we will deliver on mission, and I can almost promise you—because I have never been through one of these exercises where it wasn't true—that I can promise you that when this is all done, you're going to have a much more satisfying, fulfilling career, because you're going to feel better about what you're doing because of the impact of what you are doing. You will know exactly how what you do every day contributes to our delivery on mission, and that is when I find people are most satisfied with their professional careers. And you're going to have clear line of sight about what do you want for yourself in the future.

So this is a—it's a big undertaking. This is a big department, between this and USAID, and we are including all of our missions, all of our embassies, all of our consular offices, because we all are part of how we deliver on mission. So we want to look at it in its entirety as to how we do that. So I appreciate your participating openly in this listening exercise, but importantly, I want to condition you to be ready to participate in the next phase, because that's when it'll become more challenging. But we're all on this boat, on this voyage—I'm not going to call it a cruise; it's not— may not be that much fun. (Laughter.) But we're on all this ship, on this voyage together. And so we're going to get on the ship and we're going to take this voyage, and when we get there, we're all going to get off the ship at wherever we arrive. But we're all going to get on and we're going to get off together. We don't intend to leave anybody out.

So I appreciate your participation. I hope you will approach this with a level of excitement as to what it may hold for this State Department first and then for you as an individual and what it means for you. So we're asking all of you to do that.

Let me lastly say that I do appreciate all of the work that you do. Believe it or not, I do read all these memos that come to me from—all the way from missions to the various bureaus. I appreciate those of you that get them on one page, because I'm not a fast reader. But they're extraordinarily helpful to me, and so keep sending me insights as to what you're doing, how you're doing it, and in particular the perspective on how we got to where we are. It is very valuable to me.

I had the opportunity to address a group of young people yesterday—about 700 middle school, high school people—that were here participating in the model UN conference. We were hosting it here at the State Department. One of the—there's a few fun things you get to do in this job, and talking to young people is one of them. So I had a Q&A time, and a young lady—I think she was in middle school—asked a question. She said, "What inspires you as Secretary of State when you come to work every day?" And I told her it's quite easy. I said the men and women of the State Department inspire me, my colleagues—their professionalism, their commitment, their patriotism. And I said, then our partners over at the Department of Defense, the men and women in uniform, because it's really the State Department and the Defense Department that deliver our national security. I'm inspired by you, and I thank you for that, and I'm honored to serve alongside of you.

We'll be talking again. Thank you. (Applause.)

Print Citations

CMS: Tillerson, Rex W. "Remarks to US Department of State Employees." Speech presented at the Dean Acheson Auditorium, Washington, DC, May, 2017. In *The Reference Shelf: Representative American Speeches 2016-2017*, edited by Betsy Maury, 62-73. Ipswich, MA: H.W. Wilson, 2017.

MLA: Tillerson, Rex W. "Remarks to US Department of State Employees." Dean Acheson Auditorium. Washington, DC. May, 2017. Presentation. *The Reference Shelf: Representative American Speeches 2016-2017*. Ed. Betsy Maury. Ipswich: H.W. Wilson, 2017. 62-73. Print.

APA: Tillerson, R.W. (2017). Remarks to US Department of State employees. [Presentation]. *Speech presented at the Dean Acheson Auditorium*. Washington, DC. In Betsy Maury (Ed.), *The reference shelf: Representative American speeches 2016-2017* (pp. 62-73). Ipswich, MA: H.W. Wilson. (Original work published 2017)

Address to the People of Poland

By Donald Trump

US President Donald Trump, visiting the nation of Poland to attend a meeting on the Three Seas Initiative, delivers a speech encouraging cooperating between Poland, the United States, and other nations to defend "Western" society from Islamic terrorism and other forms of extremism. The speech highlights cultural and historic connections between the United States and Poland and reinforces shared values calling the US and nations of Europe a "community of nations". Trump's appearance in Poland was controversial given that Poland's ruling "Law and Justice" party, which gained power in 2015, has been widely criticized for authoritarian policies, including passing laws that prohibit liberal political parties and eliminated press outlets critical of the current government. Trump was also criticized for suggesting that the United States and Poland were part of a "Western" society, which, as numerous analysts pointed out is a reference to the concept of white, Christian dominated societies, and not a reference to a geographic or political collection of nations.

MRS. TRUMP: Hello, Poland! Thank you very much. My husband and I have enjoyed visiting your beautiful country. I want to thank President and Mrs. Duda for the warm welcome and their generous hospitality. I had the opportunity to visit the Copernicus Science Centre today, and found it not only informative but thoughtful, its mission, which is to inspire people to observe, experiment, ask questions, and seek answers.

I can think of no better purpose for such a wonderful science center. Thank you to all who were involved in giving us the tour, especially the children who made it such a wonderful experience.

As many of you know, a main focus of my husband's presidency is safety and security of the American people. I think all of us can agree people should be able to live their lives without fear, no matter what country they live in. That is my wish for all of us around the world. (Applause.)

Thank you again for this wonderful welcome to your very special country. Your kindness and gracious hospitality will not be forgotten. (Applause.)

And now it is my honor to introduce to you my husband, the President of the United States, Donald J. Trump. (Applause.)

PRESIDENT TRUMP: Thank you very much. That's so nice. The United States has many great diplomats, but there is truly no better ambassador for our country

---

Delivered on July 6, 2017 at Krasinski Square, Warsaw, Poland.

than our beautiful First Lady, Melania. Thank you, Melania. That was very nice. (Applause.)

We've come to your nation to deliver a very important message: America loves Poland, and America loves the Polish people. (Applause.) Thank you.

The Poles have not only greatly enriched this region, but Polish-Americans have also greatly enriched the United States, and I was truly proud to have their support in the 2016 election. (Applause.)

It is a profound honor to stand in this city, by this monument to the Warsaw Uprising, and to address the Polish nation that so many generations have dreamed of: a Poland that is safe, strong, and free. (Applause.)

President Duda and your wonderful First Lady, Agata, have welcomed us with the tremendous warmth and kindness for which Poland is known around the world. Thank you. (Applause.) My sincere—and I mean sincerely thank both of them. And to Prime Minister Syzdlo, a very special thanks also. (Applause.)

We are also pleased that former President Lech Walesa, so famous for leading the Solidarity Movement, has joined us today, also. (Applause.) Thank you. Thank you. Thank you.

On behalf of all Americans, let me also thank the entire Polish people for the generosity you have shown in welcoming our soldiers to your country. These soldiers are not only brave defenders of freedom, but also symbols of America's commitment to your security and your place in a strong and democratic Europe.

We are proudly joined on stage by American, Polish, British, and Romanian soldiers. Thank you. (Applause.) Thank you. Great job.

President Duda and I have just come from an incredibly successful meeting with the leaders participating in the Three Seas Initiative. To the citizens of this great region, America is eager to expand our partnership with you. We welcome stronger ties of trade and commerce as you grow your economies. And we are committed to securing your access to alternate sources of energy, so Poland and its neighbors are never again held hostage to a single supplier of energy. (Applause.)

Mr. President, I congratulate you, along with the President of Croatia, on your leadership of this historic Three Seas Initiative. Thank you. (Applause.)

This is my first visit to Central Europe as President, and I am thrilled that it could be right here at this magnificent, beautiful piece of land. It is beautiful. (Applause.) Poland is the geographic heart of Europe, but more importantly, in the Polish people, we see the soul of Europe. Your nation is great because your spirit is great and your spirit is strong. (Applause.)

For two centuries, Poland suffered constant and brutal attacks. But while Poland could be invaded and occupied, and its borders even erased from the map, it could never be erased from history or from your hearts. In those dark days, you have lost your land but you never lost your pride. (Applause.)

So it is with true admiration that I can say today, that from the farms and villages of your countryside to the cathedrals and squares of your great cities, Poland lives, Poland prospers, and Poland prevails. (Applause.)

Despite every effort to transform you, oppress you, or destroy you, you endured and overcame. You are the proud nation of Copernicus—think of that—(applause)—Chopin, Saint John Paul II. Poland is a land of great heroes. (Applause.) And you are a people who know the true value of what you defend.

The triumph of the Polish spirit over centuries of hardship gives us all hope for a future in which good conquers evil, and peace achieves victory over war.

For Americans, Poland has been a symbol of hope since the beginning of our nation. Polish heroes and American patriots fought side by side in our War of Independence and in many wars that followed. Our soldiers still serve together today in Afghanistan and Iraq, combatting the enemies of all civilization.

For America's part, we have never given up on freedom and independence as the right and destiny of the Polish people, and we never, ever will. (Applause.)

Our two countries share a special bond forged by unique histories and national characters. It's a fellowship that exists only among people who have fought and bled and died for freedom. (Applause.)

The signs of this friendship stand in our nation's capital. Just steps from the White House, we've raised statues of men with names like Pułaski and Kościuszko. (Applause.) The same is true in Warsaw, where street signs carry the name of George Washington, and a monument stands to one of the world's greatest heroes, Ronald Reagan. (Applause.)

And so I am here today not just to visit an old ally, but to hold it up as an example for others who seek freedom and who wish to summon the courage and the will to defend our civilization. (Applause.) The story of Poland is the story of a people who have never lost hope, who have never been broken, and who have never, ever forgotten who they are. (Applause)

AUDIENCE: Donald Trump! Donald Trump! Donald Trump!

PRESIDENT TRUMP: Thank you. Thank you so much. Thank you. Thank you so much. Such a great honor. This is a nation more than one thousand years old. Your borders were erased for more than a century and only restored just one century ago.

In 1920, in the Miracle of Vistula, Poland stopped the Soviet army bent on European conquest. (Applause.) Then, 19 years later in 1939, you were invaded yet again, this time by Nazi Germany from the west and the Soviet Union from the east. That's trouble. That's tough.

Under a double occupation the Polish people endured evils beyond description: the Katyn forest massacre, the occupations, the Holocaust, the Warsaw Ghetto and the Warsaw Ghetto Uprising, the destruction of this beautiful capital city, and the deaths of nearly one in five Polish people. A vibrant Jewish population—the largest in Europe—was reduced to almost nothing after the Nazis systematically murdered millions of Poland's Jewish citizens, along with countless others, during that brutal occupation.

In the summer of 1944, the Nazi and Soviet armies were preparing for a terrible and bloody battle right here in Warsaw. Amid that hell on earth, the citizens of

Poland rose up to defend their homeland. I am deeply honored to be joined on stage today by veterans and heroes of the Warsaw Uprising. (Applause.)

AUDIENCE: (Chanting.)

PRESIDENT TRUMP: What great spirit. We salute your noble sacrifice and we pledge to always remember your fight for Poland and for freedom. Thank you. Thank you. (Applause.)

This monument reminds us that more than 150,000 Poles died during that desperate struggle to overthrow oppression.

From the other side of the river, the Soviet armed forces stopped and waited. They watched as the Nazis ruthlessly destroyed the city, viciously murdering men, women, and children. They tried to destroy this nation forever by shattering its will to survive.

But there is a courage and a strength deep in the Polish character that no one could destroy. The Polish martyr, Bishop Michael Kozal, said it well: "More horrifying than a defeat of arms is a collapse of the human spirit."

Through four decades of communist rule, Poland and the other captive nations of Europe endured a brutal campaign to demolish freedom, your faith, your laws, your history, your identity—indeed the very essence of your culture and your humanity. Yet, through it all, you never lost that spirit. (Applause.) Your oppressors tried to break you, but Poland could not be broken. (Applause.)

And when the day came on June 2nd, 1979, and one million Poles gathered around Victory Square for their very first mass with their Polish Pope, that day, every communist in Warsaw must have known that their oppressive system would soon come crashing down. (Applause.) They must have known it at the exact moment during Pope John Paul II's sermon when a million Polish men, women, and children suddenly raised their voices in a single prayer. A million Polish people did not ask for wealth. They did not ask for privilege. Instead, one million Poles sang three simple words: "We Want God." (Applause.)

In those words, the Polish people recalled the promise of a better future. They found new courage to face down their oppressors, and they found the words to declare that Poland would be Poland once again.

As I stand here today before this incredible crowd, this faithful nation, we can still hear those voices that echo through history. Their message is as true today as ever. The people of Poland, the people of America, and the people of Europe still cry out "We want God." (Applause.)

Together, with Pope John Paul II, the Poles reasserted their identity as a nation devoted to God. And with that powerful declaration of who you are, you came to understand what to do and how to live. You stood in solidarity against oppression, against a lawless secret police, against a cruel and wicked system that impoverished your cities and your souls. And you won. Poland prevailed. Poland will always prevail. (Applause.)

AUDIENCE: Donald Trump! Donald Trump! Donald Trump!

PRESIDENT TRUMP: Thank you. You were supported in that victory over communism by a strong alliance of free nations in the West that defied tyranny. Now, among the most committed members of the NATO Alliance, Poland has resumed its place as a leading nation of a Europe that is strong, whole, and free.

A strong Poland is a blessing to the nations of Europe, and they know that. A strong Europe is a blessing to the West and to the world. (Applause.) One hundred years after the entry of American forces into World War I, the transatlantic bond between the United States and Europe is as strong as ever and maybe, in many ways, even stronger.

This continent no longer confronts the specter of communism. But today we're in the West, and we have to say there are dire threats to our security and to our way of life. You see what's happening out there. They are threats. We will confront them. We will win. But they are threats. (Applause.)

AUDIENCE: Donald Trump! Donald Trump! Donald Trump!

PRESIDENT TRUMP: We are confronted by another oppressive ideology—one that seeks to export terrorism and extremism all around the globe. America and Europe have suffered one terror attack after another. We're going to get it to stop. (Applause.)
During a historic gathering in Saudi Arabia, I called on the leaders of more than 50 Muslim nations to join together to drive out this menace which threatens all of humanity. We must stand united against these shared enemies to strip them of their territory and their funding, and their networks, and any form of ideological support that they may have. While we will always welcome new citizens who share our values and love our people, our borders will always be closed to terrorism and extremism of any kind. (Applause.)

AUDIENCE: Donald Trump! Donald Trump! Donald Trump!

PRESIDENT TRUMP: We are fighting hard against radical Islamic terrorism, and we will prevail. We cannot accept those who reject our values and who use hatred to justify violence against the innocent.

Today, the West is also confronted by the powers that seek to test our will, undermine our confidence, and challenge our interests. To meet new forms of aggression, including propaganda, financial crimes, and cyberwarfare, we must adapt our alliance to compete effectively in new ways and on all new battlefields.

We urge Russia to cease its destabilizing activities in Ukraine and elsewhere, and its support for hostile regimes—including Syria and Iran—and to instead join the community of responsible nations in our fight against common enemies and in defense of civilization itself. (Applause.)

Finally, on both sides of the Atlantic, our citizens are confronted by yet another danger—one firmly within our control. This danger is invisible to some but familiar to the Poles: the steady creep of government bureaucracy that drains the vitality and wealth of the people. The West became great not because of paperwork and regulations but because people were allowed to chase their dreams and pursue their destinies.

Americans, Poles, and the nations of Europe value individual freedom and sovereignty. We must work together to confront forces, whether they come from inside or out, from the South or the East, that threaten over time to undermine these values and to erase the bonds of culture, faith and tradition that make us who we are. (Applause.) If left unchecked, these forces will undermine our courage, sap our spirit, and weaken our will to defend ourselves and our societies.

But just as our adversaries and enemies of the past learned here in Poland, we know that these forces, too, are doomed to fail if we want them to fail. And we do, indeed, want them to fail. (Applause.) They are doomed not only because our alliance is strong, our countries are resilient, and our power is unmatched. Through all of that, you have to say everything is true. Our adversaries, however, are doomed because we will never forget who we are. And if we don't forget who we are, we just can't be beaten. Americans will never forget. The nations of Europe will never forget. We are the fastest and the greatest community. There is nothing like our community of nations. The world has never known anything like our community of nations.

We write symphonies. We pursue innovation. We celebrate our ancient heroes, embrace our timeless traditions and customs, and always seek to explore and discover brand-new frontiers.

We reward brilliance. We strive for excellence, and cherish inspiring works of art that honor God. We treasure the rule of law and protect the right to free speech and free expression. (Applause.)

We empower women as pillars of our society and of our success. We put faith and family, not government and bureaucracy, at the center of our lives. And we debate everything. We challenge everything. We seek to know everything so that we can better know ourselves. (Applause.)

And above all, we value the dignity of every human life, protect the rights of every person, and share the hope of every soul to live in freedom. That is who we are. Those are the priceless ties that bind us together as nations, as allies, and as a civilization.

What we have, what we inherited from our—and you know this better than anybody, and you see it today with this incredible group of people—what we've inherited from our ancestors has never existed to this extent before. And if we fail to preserve it, it will never, ever exist again. So we cannot fail.

This great community of nations has something else in common: In every one of them, it is the people, not the powerful, who have always formed the foundation of freedom and the cornerstone of our defense. The people have been that foundation here in Poland—as they were right here in Warsaw—and they were the foundation from the very, very beginning in America.

Our citizens did not win freedom together, did not survive horrors together, did not face down evil together, only to lose our freedom to a lack of pride and confidence in our values. We did not and we will not. We will never back down. (Applause.)

AUDIENCE: Donald Trump! Donald Trump! Donald Trump!

PRESIDENT TRUMP: As long as we know our history, we will know how to build our future. Americans know that a strong alliance of free, sovereign and independent nations is the best defense for our freedoms and for our interests. That is why my administration has demanded that all members of NATO finally meet their full and fair financial obligation.

As a result of this insistence, billions of dollars more have begun to pour into NATO. In fact, people are shocked. But billions and billions of dollars more are coming in from countries that, in my opinion, would not have been paying so quickly.

To those who would criticize our tough stance, I would point out that the United States has demonstrated not merely with words but with its actions that we stand firmly behind Article 5, the mutual defense commitment. (Applause.)

Words are easy, but actions are what matters. And for its own protection—and you know this, everybody knows this, everybody has to know this—Europe must do more. Europe must demonstrate that it believes in its future by investing its money to secure that future.

That is why we applaud Poland for its decision to move forward this week on acquiring from the United States the battle-tested Patriot air and missile defense system—the best anywhere in the world. (Applause.) That is also why we salute the Polish people for being one of the NATO countries that has actually achieved the benchmark for investment in our common defense. Thank you. Thank you, Poland. I must tell you, the example you set is truly magnificent, and we applaud Poland. Thank you. (Applause.)

We have to remember that our defense is not just a commitment of money, it is a commitment of will. Because as the Polish experience reminds us, the defense of the West ultimately rests not only on means but also on the will of its people to prevail and be successful and get what you have to have. The fundamental question of our time is whether the West has the will to survive. Do we have the confidence in our values to defend them at any cost? Do we have enough respect for our citizens to protect our borders? Do we have the desire and the courage to preserve our civilization in the face of those who would subvert and destroy it? (Applause.)

We can have the largest economies and the most lethal weapons anywhere on Earth, but if we do not have strong families and strong values, then we will be weak and we will not survive. (Applause.) If anyone forgets the critical importance of these things, let them come to one country that never has. Let them come to

Poland. (Applause.) And let them come here, to Warsaw, and learn the story of the Warsaw Uprising.

When they do, they should learn about Jerusalem Avenue. In August of 1944, Jerusalem Avenue was one of the main roads running east and west through this city, just as it is today.

Control of that road was crucially important to both sides in the battle for Warsaw. The German military wanted it as their most direct route to move troops and to form a very strong front. And for the Polish Home Army, the ability to pass north and south across that street was critical to keep the center of the city, and the Uprising itself, from being split apart and destroyed.

Every night, the Poles put up sandbags amid machine gun fire—and it was horrendous fire—to protect a narrow passage across Jerusalem Avenue. Every day, the enemy forces knocked them down again and again and again. Then the Poles dug a trench. Finally, they built a barricade. And the brave Polish fighters began to flow across Jerusalem Avenue. That narrow passageway, just a few feet wide, was the fragile link that kept the Uprising alive.

Between its walls, a constant stream of citizens and freedom fighters made their perilous, just perilous, sprints. They ran across that street, they ran through that street, they ran under that street—all to defend this city. "The far side was several yards away," recalled one young Polish woman named Greta. That mortality and that life was so important to her. In fact, she said, "The mortally dangerous sector of the street was soaked in the blood. It was the blood of messengers, liaison girls, and couriers."

Nazi snipers shot at anybody who crossed. Anybody who crossed, they were being shot at. Their soldiers burned every building on the street, and they used the Poles as human shields for their tanks in their effort to capture Jerusalem Avenue. The enemy never ceased its relentless assault on that small outpost of civilization. And the Poles never ceased its defense.

The Jerusalem Avenue passage required constant protection, repair, and reinforcement, but the will of its defenders did not waver, even in the face of death. And to the last days of the Uprising, the fragile crossing never, ever failed. It was never, ever forgotten. It was kept open by the Polish people.

The memories of those who perished in the Warsaw Uprising cry out across the decades, and few are clearer than the memories of those who died to build and defend the Jerusalem Avenue crossing. Those heroes remind us that the West was saved with the blood of patriots; that each generation must rise up and play their part in its defense—(applause)—and that every foot of ground, and every last inch of civilization, is worth defending with your life.

Our own fight for the West does not begin on the battlefield—it begins with our minds, our wills, and our souls. Today, the ties that unite our civilization are no less vital, and demand no less defense, than that bare shred of land on which the hope of Poland once totally rested. Our freedom, our civilization, and our survival depend on these bonds of history, culture, and memory.

And today as ever, Poland is in our heart, and its people are in that fight. (Applause.) Just as Poland could not be broken, I declare today for the world to hear that the West will never, ever be broken. Our values will prevail. Our people will thrive. And our civilization will triumph. (Applause.)

AUDIENCE: Donald Trump! Donald Trump! Donald Trump!

PRESIDENT TRUMP: Thank you. So, together, let us all fight like the Poles—for family, for freedom, for country, and for God.

Thank you. God Bless You. God bless the Polish people. God bless our allies. And God bless the United States of America.

Thank you. God bless you. Thank you very much. (Applause.)

Print Citations

CMS: Trump, Donald. "Address to the People of Poland." Speech presented at Krasinski Square, Warsaw, Poland, July, 2017. In *The Reference Shelf: Representative American Speeches 2016-2017*, edited by Betsy Maury, 74-82. Ipswich, MA: H.W. Wilson, 2017.

MLA: Trump, Donald. "Address to the People of Poland." Krasinski Square. Warsaw, Poland. July, 2017. Presentation. *The Reference Shelf: Representative American Speeches 2016-2017*. Ed. Betsy Maury. Ipswich: H.W. Wilson, 2017. 74-82. Print.

APA: Trump, D. (2017). Address to the people of Poland. [Presentation]. *Speech presented at Krasinski Square*. Warsaw, Poland. In Betsy Maury (Ed.), *The reference shelf: Representative American speeches 2016-2017* (pp. 74-82). Ipswich, MA: H.W. Wilson. (Original work published 2017)

Press Briefing on US Immigration Policy

By Sarah Sanders and Stephen Miller

White House press secretary Sarah Sanders and senior policy adviser Stephen Miller deliver speech on immigration policy on August 2, 2017. Sanders and Miller explain a new "points" system for issuing green cards based on qualities such as language ability, education, and financial stability and repeat frequent Trump administration claims, widely refuted by economists, that immigration policy has reduced wages and employment opportunities for American workers. Miller, former press secretary for Congresswoman Michele Bachmann and Congressmen John Shadegg, was one of the primary authors of the Trump administration's aborted attempts to initiate a "Muslim ban" barring immigration from several Muslim-majority countries.

MS. SANDERS: Good afternoon, everyone.

Before we get started, I'd like to hand it over to Stephen Miller, senior advisor to the President, to speak with you about the RAISE Act that the President endorsed this morning. And I know you guys will have lot of fun.

Take it away, Stephen.

MR. MILLER: Thank you. Great to be here today to talk with you about the President's new proposal for immigration reform. I'll just walk through the basics of it and then we'll take some questions and hopefully be able to answer all of them.

So this is the largest proposed reform to our immigration policy in half a century. The most important question when it comes to the U.S. immigration system is who gets a green card. A green card is the golden ticket of U.S. immigration.

Every year we issue a million green cards to foreign nationals from all the countries of the world, but we do so without regard to whether that applicant has demonstrated the skill that can add to the U.S. economy, whether they can pay their own way or be reliant on welfare, or whether they'll displace or take a job from an American worker.

And as a result of this policy, in place now for many years, we've seen significant reductions in wages for blue collar workers, massive displacement of African American and Hispanic workers, as well as the displacement of immigrant workers from previous years who oftentimes compete directly against new arrivals who are being paid even less.

So it's a policy that's actually exacerbated wealth inequality in the country in a pretty significant way. So you've seen over time, as a result of this historic flow of

Delivered on August 2, 2017 at the White House, Washington, DC.

unskilled immigration, a shift in wealth from the working class to wealthier corporations and businesses. And it's been very unfair for American workers, but especially for immigrant workers, African American workers, and Hispanic workers, and blue collar workers in general across the country.

At the same time, it has cost taxpayers enormously because roughly half of immigrant head of households in the United States receive some type of welfare benefit—which I know is a fact that many people might consider astonishing, but it's not surprising when you have an immigration system that doesn't look at questions like skill level or self-sufficiency.

And so this proposal has several major historic changes. First, it eliminates so-called chain migration. So right now, what does chain migration mean? It means that if you come into the United States on a green card—and just so we're all clear, a green card gives the recipient lifetime work authorization, the ability to bring in their family members. It gives them a fast track to U.S. citizenship and, with that, all the benefits that come with being an American citizen.

And so the individuals right now who are receiving green cards, they can bring in, say, an elderly relative who could immediately go on to public assistance if they become unable to support themselves financially. And then that person can bring in a relative who can bring in a relative who can bring in a relative, and that's why they call it chain migration. And over years, that has massively de-skilled the migrant flow into America and produced all of those effects I'm talking about.

So we're proposing to limit family-based migration to spouses and minor children. Additionally, we're establishing a new entry system that's points-based. Australia has a points-based system, Canada has a points-based system. And what will this system look at? It will look at: Does the applicant speak English? Can they support themselves and their families financially? Do they have a skill that will add to the U.S. economy? Are they being paid a high wage?

The last part is very important because it will help prevent displacement of U.S. workers. So if a company—let's say they're offering three times the median wage, that person will get more points on their application than if they're being offered two times the median wage or one time the median wage. So all of a sudden, you're putting upward pressure on wages instead of downward pressure, and you're making it very hard to use immigrant labor to substitute for American workers because by prioritizing higher paid workers, you basically end the practice, more or less, of being able to seek out permanent residents to come in at lower pay.

And so that's a major historic change to U.S. immigration policy. The effect of this, switching to a skills-based system and ending unfettered chain migration, would be, over time, you would cut net migration in half, which polling shows is supported overwhelmingly by the American people in very large numbers.

And I'll just conclude by saying this is what President Trump campaigned on. He talked about it throughout the campaign, throughout the transition, and since coming into office.

This is a major promise to the American people to push for merit-based immigration reform that protects U.S. workers, protects U.S. taxpayers, and protects the

U.S. economy, and that prioritizes the needs of our own citizens, our own residents, and our own workers. It's pro-American immigration reform that the American people want, that the American people deserve, and that puts the needs of the working class ahead of the investor class.

So with that, I would gladly take a few questions.

Q: Thank you, Stephen. You talk about the President's agenda and wanting to implement it. But obviously if this doesn't become law, it won't be implemented, and there's already resistance in Congress, specifically from Republicans, even the day that you're rolling out this plan. How do you plan to overcome that? Where are the compromise points for the President and this White House?

MR. MILLER: It's been my experience in the legislative process that there's two kinds of proposals. There's proposals that can only succeed in the dark of night and proposals that can only succeed in the light of day. This is the latter of those two.

The more that we as a country have a national conversation about what kind of immigration system we want and to whom we want to give green cards to, the more unstoppable the momentum for something like this becomes.

Q: So there's room for change?

MR. MILLER: Public support is so immense on this—if you just look at the polling data in many key battleground states across the country—that over time you're going to see massive public push for this kind of legislation. Because immigration affects every aspect of our lives. It affects our schools, our hospitals, our working conditions, our labor market, our tax base, our communities, and it's a deeply personal issue for Americans.

And so you're going to see massive public support for this. And ultimately, members of Congress will have a choice to make. They can either vote with the interests of U.S. citizens and U.S. workers, or they can vote against their interests, and whatever happens as a result of that, I think would be somewhat predictable.

Let me go to John and then we'll move back.

Q: How do you wedge this into an already jam-packed legislative calendar?

MR. MILLER: Well, ultimately we're going to have to have conversations with Senate leadership and House leadership about the steps forward. But this is an issue that we campaigned on, the American people voted for by electing Donald J. Trump as their President, and that is of enormous importance to the American economy. Because again, we're protecting blue-collar workers and we're bringing in workers who can add to the economy.

And so I really think this is a really historic moment that happened today. Again, the biggest proposed change that would take place in 50 years. At a time in which you have automation that is replacing a lot of jobs in the United States, you have American workers without high school diplomas who have very low participation rates in the labor force, and then you're bringing in workers to compete directly against the workers who are either losing their jobs to automation or who can't find work because there's not enough jobs for workers in our own country without education.

And so particularly—I mean, go to an American city that has labor force problems, wherever that may be—say, Detroit. How is it fair or right or proper that if, say, you open up a new business in Detroit, that the unemployed workers of Detroit are going to have to compete against an endless flow of unskilled workers for the exact same jobs, reducing pay for those positions, and reducing their chance of getting those jobs while, at the same time, ultra-high-skilled workers are in the back of the line to get into the country? It makes no sense. The numbers are too large, and the numbers of low-skilled workers in particular is a major detriment to U.S. workers.

So I think the more we have this conversation publicly and ask America who ought to get a green card in this country, the more momentum there's going to be, the more support there's going to be. And our message to folks in Congress is, if you are serious about immigration reform, then ask yourselves, what's in the best interest of Americans and American workers, and ultimately this has to be a part of that.

All right, let's go to Glenn.

Q: Two quick questions. First of all, let's have some statistics. There have been a lot of studies out there that don't show a correlation between low-skilled immigration and the loss of jobs for native workers. Cite for me, if you could, one or two studies with specific numbers that prove the correlation between those two things—because your entire policy is based on that.

And secondly, I have sources that told me, about a month ago, that you guys have sort of elbowed infrastructure out of the way to get immigration on the legislative queue. Tell me why this is more important than infrastructure.

MR. MILLER: Look, the latter statement isn't true.

I think the most recent study I would point to is the study from George Borjas that he just did about the Mariel boatlift. And he went back and reexamined and opened up the old data, and talked about how it actually did reduce wages for workers who were living there at the time.

And Borjas has, of course, done enormous amounts of research on this, as has Peter Kirsanow on the U.S. Civil Rights Commission, as has Steve Camarota at the Center for Immigration Studies, and so on and so—

Q: How about the National Academies of Sciences, Engineering, and Medicine?

MR. MILLER: Right. And their recent study said that as much as $300 billion a year may be lost as a result of our current immigration system in terms of folks drawing more public benefits than they're paying in.

But let's also use common sense here, folks. At the end of the day, why do special interests want to bring in more low-skilled workers? And why historically—

Q: Stephen, I'm not asking for common sense. I'm asking for specific statistical data.

MR. MILLER: Well, I think it's very clear, Glenn, that you're not asking for common sense, but if I could just answer your question.

Q: No, no, not common sense. Common sense is fungible. Statistics are not.
MR. MILLER: I named the studies, Glenn.

Q: Let me just finish the question. Tell me the specific—

MR. MILLER: Glenn, Glenn, Glenn—I named the studies. I named the studies.

Q: I asked you for a statistic. Can you tell me how many—

MR. MILLER: Glenn, maybe we'll make a carve-out in the bill that says the *New York Times* can hire all the low-skilled, less-paid workers they want from other countries, and see how you feel then about low-wage substitution. This is a reality that's happening in our country.

Q: (Inaudible.)

MR. MILLER: Maybe it's time we had compassion, Glenn, for American workers. President Trump has met with American workers who have been replaced by foreign workers.

Q: Oh, I understand. I'm not questioning any of that. I'm asking for—

MR. MILLER: And ask them—ask them how this has affected their lives.

Q: I'm not asking them. I'm asking you for a number.

MR. MILLER: Look at—I just told you.

Q: Give me the number of low-skilled jobs that Americans might otherwise have—

MR. MILLER: If you look at—first of all, if you look at the premise, Glenn, of bringing in low-skilled labor, it's based on the idea that there's a labor shortage for lower-skilled jobs. There isn't. The number of people living in the United States in the working ages who aren't working today is at a record high.

One in four Americans—or almost one in four Americans between the ages of 25 and 54 aren't even employed. For African American workers, their labor force participation rate who don't have a high school diploma—I guess, African American males without a high school diploma has plummeted some 40 percentage points since the mass wave of unskilled migration began.

The reality is that, if you just use common sense—and, yes, I will use common sense—the reason why some companies want to bring in more unskilled labor is because they know that it drives down wages and reduces labor costs.

Our question as a government is, to whom is our duty? Our duty is to U.S. citizens and U.S. workers to promote rising wages for them. If low-skilled immigration was an unalloyed good for the economy, then why have we been growing at 1.5 percent for the last 17 years at a time of unprecedented new low-wage arrivals? The facts speak for themselves. At some point, we're accountable to reality.

On the other hand, like I said, you have ultra-high-skilled workers who are at the back of the line, which makes no sense in the year 2017.

Neil, let me go to you.

Q: You brought up the African American male stats. Are you now targeting the black unemployment rate that is traditionally and historically higher than the average American? Is that what you're looking at with this—

MR. MILLER: There's no doubt at all—and then I'll go to Neil—but there's no doubt that it's very, very sad and very unfair that immigration policy, both legal and illegal, over the last several decades has had a deleterious impact on African American employment in general, and certainly African American males that has been quite tragic. And we, as a country, have to have a conversation about that.

Neil.

Q: Thanks very much. So one of the arguments made against this bill is that large-scale immigration will increase the total number of jobs. Senator Graham, for example, said he wants more immigration to bring in more restaurant jobs, more resort jobs, bed cleaning jobs, and such like. Is it better for this country to have more jobs or higher wages and higher productivity for Americans?

MR. MILLER: Well, I think at the end of the day, President Trump has been clear that he is a pro-high-wage President. He ran as a pro-high-wage candidate, and that's what this policy will accomplish.

At the same time, to the point about economic growth, we're constantly told that unskilled immigration boosts the economy. But again, if you look at the last 17 years, we just know from reality that's not true. And if you look at wages, you can see the effects there. If you look at the labor force, you can see the effects there.

And so again, we're ending unskilled chain migration, but we're also making sure that the great inventors of the world, the great scientists of the world, that people who have the next great piece of technology can come into the United States and compete in a competitive application process—a points-based system that makes sense in the year 2017.

All right, let me go to you.

Q: Two questions. One, you did personalize it with the *New York Times*, so normally this wouldn't be a question, but will the Trump organization stop bringing in foreign workers on visa programs to set an example for other businesses in the interim before this bill becomes law?

MR. MILLER: Well, as you know, the only way to have immigration policy work is it has to be national; it has to be uniform. You can't have different rules and different procedures for different companies.

This bill, of course, doesn't deal with guest workers and temporary non-immigrant visas, which is, I think, what you're asking about, and that's a separate thing. But the President was clear, if you go back and look at his debate on this during the primary, where he said, as a businessman, my responsibility is to operate my business according to the laws of the United States as they exist. He said, as President, my responsibility is to pass laws that make sure we have an immigration system that prioritizes American workers. He said that throughout the campaign, and he said it as a candidate, and he said it now.

But just as a technical matter, you're talking about a different aspect of the immigration system. Today, we're talking about the green card system, but it's a good question.

Let me move on. Over there.

Q: My second question was—

MR. MILLER: Hold on a second.

Q: Thank you, Stephen. Just to take the question in another direction, *USA Today* and others have shown that over the last seven years, there's been a negative flow of immigration across the southern border. And of course, unemployment is at, perhaps, a 10-year low right now. So will there be enough workers in the southwest states if this policy were to go into effect?

MR. MILLER: Well, yeah. So I think we're talking about different things, and I appreciate the question. Net migration overall has been at a record pace. You're talking, I think, just about some questions about net migration illegally across the southern border.

Q: Correct.

MR. MILLER: We're talking today about green card policy. Every year, we issue a million more green cards and it just keeps adding on every year after year after year. And so the supply of foreign labor is at a record high. I think the foreign-born population right now is 45 million and I think there's 25 million foreign workers in the United States.

All right. Right there.

Q: Thank you, Stephen. Two questions for you. First, does the Trump administration plan to defend the DACA program that Texas and eight other states bring a lawsuit challenging the court?

MR. MILLER: Well, we are not going to make an announcement on that today because there is ongoing litigation, and DOJ and DHS are reviewing that. But I will say that whatever we do is going to prioritize the interests of American citizens and workers.

Q: Stephen, Zoe Daniel from Australian Broadcasting. You've talked about the Australian policy. Can you speak more specifically about what the administration likes and also how that extends into things like family sponsorship? You mentioned bringing in elderly relatives, for example, who might not be productive. Yet in Australia, adult children can sponsor their parents to immigrate. So which elements of the policy are you choosing that you might liken to Australia's?

MR. MILLER: Right. So we looked at the Australian system, the Canadian system. We took things we liked. We added things that made sense for America and where we are as a country right now.

One of the things I think is the most compelling about the Australian system is the efforts to make sure that immigrants are financially self-sufficient and make sure they're able to pay for their own healthcare and things of that nature. And that's certainly one of the things we took from that, and obviously the points-based system that Canada has has a lot to recommend it. And we actually—we took that and we added things that are all new to it and that were released today, and made sure that we have a highly competitive application process.

Look, there's 7 billion people in the world, and so the question of who gets that golden ticket needs to be a discerning process that makes sense. Again, in an environment in which you have this huge pool of unemployed labor in the United States, and you're spending massive amounts of money putting our own workers on welfare, doesn't it make sense economically to say, let's get our own workers, immigrant and U.S.-born, off of welfare, into the labor market, earning a living wage, able to pay into taxes, instead of bringing in lower-wage substitutes while at the same time ensuring that the inventors, the innovators, and the scientists are able to come into our country and add to our economy and our GDP, but not as substitutes for Americans?

NBC.

Q: Thank you so much. Can you respond to some of the critics within your own party who say what we really should be focused on is comprehensive immigration reform in order to really tackle the problem in a serious way? And secondly, what do you say to those who say this just separates families and it's effectively cutting an effective (inaudible)?

MR. MILLER: Well, actually, legislation for folks who are already here, they are able—who have pending family-based sponsorships—they're actually grandfathered in. So it's a new system moving forward. Point one.

And point two is that, beyond the immediate family members that are covered in the bill—i.e., your minor children and your spouses—your other relatives can come in; they just have to come in through the points-based system.

And then your first part of your question?

Q: My question about comprehensive immigration reform. Some Republicans are saying that you should be focused on comprehensive immigration reform instead of a sliver of the problem in order to really address the growing—problem of immigration. Why not tackle it from that stance?

MR. MILLER: Let me ask a hypothetical, and I mean it in all sincerity. Let's say that we had introduced a 2000-page comprehensive immigration reform bill. Would we be having this conversation today about Green Card policy? I suspect we wouldn't be. I think it's time that we forced the conversation onto this core issue. I know the President feels that it's enormously advantageous to have a conversation about this core aspect of immigration reform because it does receive so little discussion, and yet it's so enormously important.

Q: Follow-up on that Stephen?

MR. MILLER: Hold on. Let's go to you.

Q: Thank you, Stephen. You mentioned lawmakers have a choice to make. Is President Trump going to make this a campaign issue next year?

MR. MILLER: Well, we're making it an issue, period, starting—well, he started in the campaign when he was running, but as far as a real push for change, that begins in earnest aggressively starting today. And I do think—I just work on the policy side—but I do think that voters across the country are going to demand these kinds of changes because, again, of the effects it has on their lives and their communities.

And this is overwhelmingly popular. And I challenge any news organization here: Do a poll. Ask these questions: Do you think we should favor applicants to our country who speaks English? Yes or no? Do you think that we should make sure that workers who come into our country don't displace existing American workers? Do you think people who come into our country should receive welfare or be financially self-sufficient? Do you think we should prioritize people based on skill? Do you think that we should reduce overall net migration? Do you think we should have unlimited family chain migration?

If you ask any of these questions—look at the polls. Look at the results you'll get in your own news organizations, and they'll be very clear.

Q: Two for you. First, following up on Noah's question, the President has talked a lot about immigration reform—this has been held up in the past. He has the power today to take personal action on this by changing the way his Trump properties, Mar-a-Lago and others, bring in unskilled foreign workers, displacing, as you talked about, large numbers of Americans who are looking for work in these states. So is the President planning on taking that action?

And secondly, does this signal that the White House does not believe that any sort of comprehensive action on immigration is possible with this Congress; that immigration needs to be tackled in a piecemeal fashion going forward?

MR. MILLER: Well, again, just as a technical matter, you're talking about non-immigrant and guest worker visas, and this legislation deals with Green Cards, i.e., permanent immigration. So they're two totally separate categories.

But I'll just refer everyone here today back to the President's comments during the primary when this was raised in a debate, and he said: My job as a businessman is to follow the laws of the United States. And my job as President is to create an immigration system that works for American workers.

And that's one of the reasons why I think Americans so deeply admire President Trump is because they see every day he's not working for himself. He has said over and over again: I've been very successful. I've had a great life. Now I'm here to work for the American people.

But for any immigration system to be functional and to work, it has to be uniform across the board. One standard for everyone.

Q: Can you say how close the President is to getting a nominee for DHS? And can you add—if this legislation is not moving by the end of the year, how much is it possible for you to do through executive action, if any?

MR. MILLER: Well, I certainly think that on the administrative action front, you can tighten up and continue to tighten up enforcement on visas rules and standards. And I think that's certainly something that we'd been looking at doing. But we'd like to create a permanent change to our immigration system that will endure through time, that will still be in place many decades from now. And that's what this legislation would accomplish.

And I would just, again, encourage everyone to understand the depth of this change. What President Trump has done today is one of the most important legislative moves that we've seen on this issue in many, many years. The President of the United States said, I'm taking a stand today for American workers and the American economy, and we're putting American families first on immigration. We're saying our compassion, first and foremost, is for struggling American families, and our focus is on the national interest.

That is a major event, and all of your news organizations should take a hard look at the polls on these questions and see where folks are. And you'll see that this is an issue that's supported by Democrats, independents, and Republicans across the board.

One last question and then I'll hand it back to Sarah.

Q: (Inaudible) any polls?

MR. MILLER: Maybe more than one. Maybe two. I hear a lot of energy—I'm getting a lot of energy from upfront here.

Q: If this is so huge and major—you make it sound so enormously important—why did the senators who were with the President today call it modest and incremental? Is it modest and incremental? And aside from that, you seem to be suggesting this is immigration reform. Does this come even close to stemming illegal immigration for the President?

MR. MILLER: So, of course, the answer is that it's the divide between how Americans think about immigration and how Washington thinks about immigration. So to everyday Americans, this is the most rational, modest, commonsense, basic thing you can do. Of course, you shouldn't have foreign workers—

Q: So it's modest and incremental?

MR. MILLER: Of course, you shouldn't have foreign workers displacing American workers. In Washington, this represents a sea change from decades of practice. So it just depends what lens you're looking at it through.

Q: An incremental sea change? (Laughter.)

MR. MILLER: It just depends what lens you're looking at it through. I guarantee you, go to, say, like an ed board for a couple of your papers, and see what they think about it. They'll see it as a sea change. Talk to an everyday guy in the street and he'll say this is the most commonsense thing—or she'll say this is the most commonsense thing that I've seen in my entire life. And it's right down, straight, the center of American politics and American political views.

So I'll take one last question. Who has—so I'll do for the last question, right here.

Q: Thank you. I appreciate it. And thank you very much for coming out here and talking to us on camera. But I'd like to ask you if you've recently spoken with your old boss and what you make of the rift between President Trump and the Attorney General. You worked for Jeff Sessions for many years.

MR. MILLER: I think Sarah has already spoken about that at length, and that's not why I'm here today. But I think, if I remember what she said correctly, I'll say it again: The President has confidence in all of his Cabinet and expects them to perform their duties honorably and fully and on behalf of the American people.

But since the last question is not on the subject at hand, I will take one actual last question on the subject at hand.

Yes.

Q: What you're proposing, or what the President is proposing here does not sound like it's in keeping with American tradition when it comes to immigration. The Statue of Liberty says, "Give me your tired, your poor, your huddled masses yearning to breathe free." It doesn't say anything about speaking English or being able to be a computer programmer.

Aren't you trying to change what it means to be an immigrant coming into this country if you're telling them you have to speak English? Can't people learn how to speak English when they get here?

MR. MILLER: Well, first of all, right now it's a requirement that to be naturalized you have to speak English. So the notion that speaking English wouldn't be a part of our immigration system would be actually very ahistorical.

Secondly, I don't want to get off into a whole thing about history here, but the Statue of Liberty is a symbol of liberty and lighting the world. It's a symbol of American liberty lighting the world. The poem that you're referring to, that was added later, is not actually a part of the original Statue of Liberty.

But more fundamentally, the history—

Q: You're saying that that does not represent what the country—

MR. MILLER: I'm saying that the notion—

Q: —has always thought of as immigration coming into this country?

MR. MILLER: I'm saying the notion—

Q: Stephen, I'm sorry, but that sounds like some—

MR. MILLER: Jim, let me ask you a question.

Q: That sounds like some National Park revisionism. (Laughter.)

MR. MILLER: No. What I'm asking you is—

Q: The Statue of Liberty has always been a beacon of hope to the world for people to send their people to this country—

MR. MILLER: Jim—Jim, do you believe—

Q:—and they're not always going to speak English, Stephen. They're not always going to be highly skilled. They're not always going to be somebody who can go to work
at Silicon Valley right away.

MR. MILLER: Jim, I appreciate your speech. So let's talk about this.

Q: It was a modest and incremental speech.

MR. MILLER: Jim, let's talk about this. In 1970, when we let in 300,000 people a
year, was that violating or not violating the Statue of Liberty law of the land? In the
1990s, when it was half-a-million a year, was it violating or not violating the Statue
of Liberty law of the land?

Q: Was it violating the Statue of Liberty and the—

MR. MILLER: No, tell me what years—tell me what years—

Q: (Inaudible) call for a deportation force?

MR. MILLER: Tell me what years meet Jim Acosta's definition of the Statue of Liberty poem law of the land. So you're saying a million a year is the Statue of Liberty
number? 900,000 violates it? 800,000 violates it?

Q: You're sort of bringing a "press one for English" philosophy here to immigration,
and that's never been what the United States has been about, Stephen. I mean,
that's just the case—

MR. MILLER: But your statement is also shockingly ahistorical in another respect,
too—which is, if you look at the history of immigration, it's actually ebbed and
flowed. You've had periods of very large waves, followed by periods of less immigration and more immigration. And during the—

Q: We're in a low period of immigration right now. The President wants to build
a wall and you want to bring about a sweeping change to the immigration system.

MR. MILLER: Surely, Jim, you don't actually think that a wall affects Green Card
policy. You couldn't possibly believe that, or do you? Actually, the notion that you
actually think immigration is at a historic lull—the foreign-born population in the
United States today—

Q: The President was just with the new Chief of Staff on Monday talking about
how border crossings were way down.

MR. MILLER: I want to be serious, Jim. Do you really at CNN not know the difference between Green Card policy and illegal immigration? You really don't know
the—

Q: Sir, my father was a Cuban immigrant. He came to this country in 1962 right
before the Cuban Missile Crisis and obtained a Green Card.

Yes, people who immigrate to this country can eventually—people who immigrate to this country not through Ellis Island, as your family may have, but in other ways, do obtain a Green Card at some point. They do it through a lot of hard work. And, yes, they may learn English as a second language later on in life. But this whole notion of "well, they have to learn English before they get to the United States," are we just going to bring in people from Great Britain and Australia?

MR. MILLER: Jim, it's actually—I have to honestly say I am shocked at your statement that you think that only people from Great Britain and Australia would know English. It's actually—it reveals your cosmopolitan bias to a shocking degree that in your mind—

Q: Sir, it's not a cosmopolitan—

MR. MILLER: No, this is an amazing moment. This an amazing moment. That you think only people from Great Britain or Australia would speak English is so insulting to millions of hardworking immigrants who do speak English from all over the world.

Q: My father came to this country not speaking any English.

MR. MILLER: Jim, have you honestly never met an immigrant from another country who speaks English outside of Great Britain and Australia? Is that your personal experience?

Q: Of course, there are people who come into this country from other parts of the world.

MR. MILLER: But that's not what you said, and it shows your cosmopolitan bias. And I just want to say—

Q: It just sounds like you're trying to engineer the racial and ethnic flow of people into this country through this policy.

MR. MILLER: Jim, that is one of the most outrageous, insulting, ignorant, and foolish things you've ever said, and for you that's still a really—the notion that you think that this is a racist bill is so wrong and so insulting.

Q: I didn't say it was a racist bill.

MR. MILLER: Jim, the reality is, is that the foreign-born population into our country has quadrupled since 1970. That's a fact. It's been mostly driven by Green Card policy. Now, this bill allows for immediate nuclear family members to come into the country, much as they would today, and it adds an additional points-based system. The people who have been hurt the most—

Q: You're saying that people have to be English speaking when they're naturalized. What is this English-speaking component that you've inserted into this? I don't understand.

MR. MILLER: The people who have been hurt the most by the policy you're advocating are—

Q: What policy am I advocating?

MR. MILLER: Apparently, just unfettered, uncontrolled migration. The people who have been hurt the most by the policy—

Q: (Inaudible) is for open borders. That's the same tired thing that—

MR. MILLER: The people who have been hurt the most by the policy you're advocating are immigrant workers and minority workers and African American workers and Hispanic workers.

Q: Are you targeting the African American community? Now you brought it up again—you said you wanted to have a conversation and not target. Is it going to be a targeted effort? You keep using the African American community. Are you going to target? I'm not trying to be funny, but you keep saying this.

MR. MILLER: Right, I know. What you're saying is 100 percent correct.

Q: Thank you.

MR. MILLER: We want to help unemployed African Americans in this country and unemployed workers of all backgrounds get jobs. And insinuations like Jim made trying to ascribe nefarious motives to a compassion immigration measure designed to help newcomers and current arrivals alike is wrong. And this is a positive, optimist proposal that says 10 years, 20 years, 30 years from now—

Q: Sir, I didn't call you ignorant. You called me ignorant on national television. Honestly, I think that's just inappropriate.

MR. MILLER:—we want to have an immigration system that takes care of the people who are coming here and the people who are already living here by having standards, by having a real clear requirement that you should be able to support yourself financially, by making sure that employers can pay a living wage. That's the right policy for our country, and it's the President's commitment to taking care of American workers.

I apologize, Jim, if things got heated. But you did make some pretty rough insinuations.

Q: I don't know what you mean by rough insinuations. I don't know what that means.

MR: MILLER: So, thank you. Thank you. And I'll hand it over to Sarah.

I think that went exactly as planned. I think that was what Sarah was hoping would happen. (Laughter.)

Q: I think she'd like to reclaim her time.

MR. MILLER: I think that was exactly what we were hoping to have happened. Thank you.

MS. SANDERS: Thank you, Stephen. Well, the transition back should be pretty fun and simple. Thank you. That was exciting.

Throughout this week we've been talking about the American Dream and all that it signifies for people of all ages and nationalities. This morning, Counselor to the President Kellyanne Conway and Advisor to the President Ivanka Trump hosted a listening session with military spouses on the unique challenges they face in finding and maintaining employment to support their families.

And yesterday, we hosted over 100 small businesses for a discussion on how they help to keep the American Dream alive for millions of workers around the country.

As I mentioned last week, I want to take time to recognize people from around the country that write in and ask the President questions. And today I wanted to read you a special letter to the President from someone who embodies the enterprising and ambitious spirit of America.

Frank from Falls Church, Virginia wrote: "Dear Mr. President, it would be my honor to mow the White House lawn for some weekend for you. Even though I'm only 10, I'd like to show the nation what young people like me are ready for. I admire your business background and have started my own business.

I have been mowing my neighbors' lawns for some time. (Please see the attached flier). Here's a list of what I have and you are free to pick whatever you want: power mower, push mower, and weed whacker. I can bring extra fuel for the power mower and charged batteries for the weed whacker." And he'll do that with no charge.

"Sincerely,

Frank"

Frank, I'm happy to report back to you that I just spoke with the President and he wanted me to be sure and tell you that you're doing a great job and keep working hard. He also asked me—we found out when we called—to let you know that we would be reading this letter to wish you a Happy Birthday. I think Frank went from

10 to 11 in the time that we received and were able to respond to this letter. And he also wanted me to invite you to spend a morning here at the White House with the groundskeeper. The groundskeeper—we've talked to them, and they would love to show you how the U.S. Park Service maintains the 18 acres of the White House complex. And he'd love to give you the opportunity to cut the grass in the Rose Garden.

It's our responsibility to keep the American Dream alive for kids like Frank, immigrants who are already here, and those who dream of immigrating here in the future.

And with that, I'll take your questions.

Justin.

Q: Does the President believe that white applicants to college are the victims of discrimination?

MS. SANDERS: I'm sorry?

Q: Does the President believe that white applicants to college are the victims of discrimination?

MS. SANDERS: I'm not aware of that opinion at all. I certainly haven't had that conversation or have any reason to—

Q: So can you explain why the Justice Department's Civil Rights Division is devoting its limited time and resources to—

MS. SANDERS: Quite an accusatory question, but I'd be happy to respond. The *New York Times* article is based entirely on uncorroborated inferences from a leaked internal personnel posting in violation of Department of Justice policy. And while the White House does not confirm or deny the existence of potential investigations, the Department of Justice will always review credible allegations of discrimination on the basis of any race. And I don't have anything further on that.

Q: Sarah, thank you. Why did the President say that he received a phone call from the leader of the Boy Scouts and the President of Mexico when he did not? Did he lie?

MS. SANDERS: No. On Mexico, he was referencing the conversation that they had had at the G20 Summit, where they specifically talked about the issues that he referenced.

In terms of the Boy Scouts, multiple members of the Boy Scout leadership, following his speech there that day, congratulated him, praised him, and offered quite—I'm looking for the word—quite powerful compliments following his speech. And those were what those references were about.

Q: But the President specifically said that he received a phone call from the President of Mexico and the leader of the—

MS. SANDERS: They were actually—they were direct conversations, not actual phone calls.

Q: So he lied? He didn't receive that phone call?

MS. SANDERS: I wouldn't say it was a lie. That's a pretty bold accusation.

Q: How would you—

MS. SANDERS: The conversations took place. They just simply didn't take place over a phone call; that he had them in person.
   John.

Q: Sarah, if I could ask a couple of questions about Russia. Dmitry Medvedev, the Prime Minister, has weighed in on the President's signing of the sanctions, saying that this proves that the Trump administration is "utterly powerless" and ends hopes for better ties. What's the White House response?

MS. SANDERS: Look, this morning, the President signed the Countering America's Adversaries Through Sanctions Act. The President favors tough measures to punish and deter the bad behavior of the rogue regimes in Iran and North Korea. And he also sent a clear signal that we won't tolerate interference in our democratic process by Russia.
   The bill was improved, but Congress has encroached on the power of the presidency, and he signed it in the interest of national unity. We've been very clear that we support tough sanctions on all three of those countries. We continue to do so. And that has certainly not changed, and I think that was reflected in the statements today.

Q: One point on one of the finer aspects of the bill and the findings—it stated that Russia did, in fact, try to interfere in the U.S. election. In the President's statement—on the signing statement, he did not quibble with that. Is that an indication that he does accept the finding that Russia interfered in our election?

MS. SANDERS: The President has already said that himself directly at the press conference in Poland.

Q: He's also said that other actors may have been involved.

MS. SANDERS: May have been involved as well. But he doesn't dispute the fact that Russia was, and he said that in Poland at the press conference that I believe you were present for.

Q: One more. You said on Monday that, when you had something to say about the Russian action on the 755 diplomats, you would say something about it. Do you have anything to say about it today?

MS. SANDERS: No, I don't. But when I do, I'll let you know.
     Kristen.

Q: Sarah, thanks. Did President Trump speak with Russia's President, Vladimir Putin, prior to signing the bill or at all today?

MS. SANDERS: No.

Q: That's definitive? That's confirmed? Let me just ask you something about North Korea. General McCaffrey said that, "I think at some point we are clearly going to take dramatic action short of war against North Korea." Can you respond to that? Do you think that's an accurate characterization? Can you tell us where the administration's thinking is right now when it comes to taking some type of military action against North Korea to stop its provocations?

MS. SANDERS: As I've said many times before, we're not going to broadcast our actions, and we're keeping all options on the table.
     Jordan.

Q: Thank you. I'll ask you the question I was going to ask Stephen. The President said in an *Economist* interview in May—he was asked whether he supports cutting the number of immigrants who can come here legally. He said, no. This bill today that he supports would cut the number of green cards issued by half. So when did the President have a change of heart on this issue?

MS. SANDERS: I'd have to see the specific reference. But I know that the President has talked pretty frequently about merit-based immigration reform, not just on the campaign trail, but he's been talking about this for years. And I can't comment on a story I haven't seen specifically.

Q: I mean, merit-based wouldn't necessarily lead to the reduction of total green cards. So does he have a separate opinion about the number of green cards that—

MS. SANDERS: I think Stephen spoke pretty extensively on that, and I don't have anything to add beyond that.
     Jon.

Q: Thanks a lot, Sarah. The President, in signing this sanctions bill today, issued a signing statement. And in that signing statement, he said that the bill is significantly flawed. He said that there are provisions in this bill that are clearly unconstitutional. Why would he sign this bill if he felt so strongly that this bill inhibits his ability to act as the Commander-in-Chief and to carry out his duties as President?

MS. SANDERS: I think I spoke on this already, but primarily because the President favors tough measures to punish and deter the bad behavior of the rogue regimes in Iran and North Korea, and he also sent a clear signal that we won't tolerate interference in our democratic process by Russia. I also said that he signed it in the interest of national unity and, again, in support of—there's no question that there isn't support for the principles of the bill; it's maybe just some of the process pieces.
Steve.

Q: I'm sorry—does he also send a signal in signing this particular legislation that, if another bill comes before his desk that he also finds significantly flawed and clearly unconstitutional, that he'd sign that legislation as well?

MS. SANDERS: I'm not going to speak about a hypothetical bill that we don't know and doesn't exist and whether or not the President is going to sign it.
    Steve.

Q: Sarah, can you clear up some confusion? There were almost simultaneously two signing statements that went out. They had slightly different language. Did you intend to send both out, or was that a mistake?

MS. SANDERS: It was actually one signing statement and one press statement, so that's the difference. One is more of a legal document that goes with the executive secretary, and the other one is a press document. So that's the difference.

Q: I wanted to bring up some unfinished business. When you were named Press Secretary, because there was so much focus on the other announcement, that you only had a chance to talk about the job in one question. So I wanted to give you a chance to answer two questions that all of your predecessors faced. The first one is, what is your overall approach to the job, especially in terms of balancing whether you're serving the President or serving the public? And secondly, do you see any circumstances where it's appropriate to lie from the podium?

MS. SANDERS: I'll take the second one first. Absolutely not. I don't think it's appropriate to lie from the podium or any other place.
    On the first question, I think that the balance—my job is to communicate the President's agenda, the President's message, and answer your questions on that as best that I can, as honestly as I can, and as transparent as I can possibly be at any given moment.

Francesca.

Q: Thank you, Sarah. Following up on the question about the position, what exactly is Sean Spicer's role in this administration at this point? And how much longer do you expect him to stay on staff? And then something on the signing statement.

MS. SANDERS: As he said, I believe that was, gosh, a week or so ago. The days all kind of run together now. But he was going to stay on in a transition process through August, and nothing has changed.

Q: So nothing changed because of Anthony Scaramucci leaving?

MS. SANDERS: No, nothing has changed at this point.

Q: Okay, and then on the signing statement, one of the things that it said was that it would drive China, Russia, and North Korea much closer together—these sanctions. Can you elaborate on that? Because yesterday you suggested that China was both an ally and a partner.

MS. SANDERS: I don't have anything to comment beyond the signing statement itself.
Alexis.

Q: Sarah, can I just follow up? Two questions. On DHS, should we expect that more into September, when Congress comes back, a nomination? Or is that possible soon? And the second question is, lots of lawmakers, Republicans on the Hill, and the business community have been concerned that the President won't stay focused on tax reform, that this is something they really want him to talk about. And you just introduced immigration. You've got healthcare still hanging. Is the President going to focus on all of those issues in the weeks ahead, going into September? Or does he really want to showcase just one or two things?

MS. SANDERS: As we've said many times before, we can walk and chew gum at the same time, and we can work on a multitude of issues at the same time.
In terms of the DHS appointment, I don't have any personnel announcements at this time.
John Gizzi.

Q: Yeah, thank you, Sarah. This morning, New Orleans Mayor Mitch Landrieu, president of the U.S. Conference of Mayors, took a shot at Tom Homan, the head of the Immigration and Customs Enforcement. On June the 28th, right from that podium, Mr. Homan said, and I quote, "Most law enforcement officials in cities work with us but many don't in the largest cities. And that's where criminal aliens and criminal gangs flourish." Mayor Landrieu this morning said he's wrong about that; that kind of rhetoric is not helpful. And he added that police officers keep the streets safe irrespective of immigration status, and do so all the time. Your response to Mayor Landrieu and his charge against someone who is mentioned frequently to be the next Secretary of Homeland Security?

MS. SANDERS: Look, I think Tom has served our country well. He's been active in law enforcement. And I would certainly trust his opinion very—a lot of confidence in him and his ability, having been in a multitude of different positions within law enforcement and been able to see it in a lot of different places, not just one location, like the mayor. So I would certainly defer to Tom on this issue.

Q: So then you would—you trust him more than you would Mayor Landrieu on that issue?

MS. SANDERS: I think that's pretty safe to say, John.
     Jim.

Q: Yes. Jeff Flake, in a *Politico* magazine article, said the President was—he suggested the President was a carnival barker and had eroded conservatism. Is the President still thinking of helping to fund the $10 million challenge against Senator Flake? And does he have any response to Senator Flake's comments?

MS. SANDERS: I'm not sure about any potential funding of a campaign. But I think that Senator Flake would serve his constituents much better if he was less focused on writing a book and attacking the President, and passing legislation.
     Alex.

Q: Two American soldiers were killed today in Afghanistan. That's nine on the year. Does the President know about this? And does he feel any sense of urgency to implement a new plan in the conflict there?

MS. SANDERS: I can't comment on that at this time, but I'll certainly keep you posted.
     Trey.

Q: Thanks, Sarah. Did President Trump feel pressured into sign the Russia sanctions bill?

MS. SANDERS: No. As I've said, the President supports putting pressure on these three countries in particular, and so he supports the principle of it and wanted to take action in that course.
     Steve.

Q: I just wanted to follow up. You were asked yesterday by Jared Rizzi whether the

President would weigh in on this question of cost-sharing payments. Can you put this to bed? Will the administration continue making these cost-sharing payments or not?

MS. SANDERS: The CSR payments are bailing out at this point—a failed law that the President wants to repeal and replace. Since last year's campaign, the President has been clear that Obamacare is a failed law. He's working with his staff and his Cabinet to consider the issues raised by the CSR payments. And without Congress fulfilling its promise to American voters in repealing and replacing Obamacare, insurers will continue to flee this failing system. We need real reform that actually lowers cost and provides more choice for Americans. And we'll keep you posted when we have a final announcement on that.

Thanks so much, guys.

Print Citations

CMS: Sanders, Sarah, and Stephen Miller. "Press Briefing on US Immigration Policy." Briefing presented at the White House, Washington, DC, August, 2017. In *The Reference Shelf: Representative American Speeches 2016-2017*, edited by Betsy Maury, 83-105. Ipswich, MA: H.W. Wilson, 2017.

MLA: Sanders, Sarah, and Stephen Miller. "Press Briefing on US Immigration Policy." The White House. Washington, DC. August, 2017. Presentation. *The Reference Shelf: Representative American Speeches 2016-2017*. Ed. Betsy Maury. Ipswich: H.W. Wilson, 2017. 83-105. Print.

APA: Sanders, S., & S. Miller. (2017). Press briefing on US immigration policy. [Presentation]. *Briefing presented at the White House*. Washington, DC. In Betsy Maury (Ed.), *The reference shelf: Representative American speeches 2016-2017* (pp. 83-105). Ipswich, MA: H.W. Wilson. (Original work published 2017)

3
The Year in Review

Photo by Chris Kleponis-Pool/Getty Images

President Donald Trump makes a statement on the violence this past weekend in Charlottesville, Virginia at the White House on August 14, 2017 in Washington, DC.

Remarks at the United Nations Advocating for Action against the Assad Regime

By Nikki Haley

Nikki Haley, former governor of South Carolina and United States ambassador to the United Nations, delivers a speech to the United Nations on April 8, 2017, on the state of Syria. Haley claims that the administration will make the ousting of Syrian president Bashar al-Assad a priority in an effort to combat Islamic extremism and stabilize Syria and the surrounding region. Haley's speech was a major departure from Haley's previous statements on Syria and occurred after the United States launched an air attack on Syria in response to reports that Syrian military used chemical weapons to attack a town allegedly occupied by antigovernment forces.

It was interesting to hear of the talk from my Russian colleague about the independent investigations and the importance of them, because this entire Security Council decided on what the Joint Investigative Mechanism would be and decided what it would do, and it was actually voted on unanimously. And the joint mechanism came back and said that the Syrian government committed chemical weapons acts against their own people three different times. But somehow now we don't like what the Joint Investigative Mechanism does.

Having said that, I will say in the life of the United Nations, there are times when we are compelled to do more than just talk. There are times we are compelled to take collective action. This Security Council thinks of itself as a defender of peace, security, and human rights. We will not deserve that description if we do not rise to action today.

Yesterday morning, we awoke to pictures, to children foaming at the mouth, suffering convulsions, being carried in the arms of desperate parents. We saw rows of lifeless bodies. Some still in diapers. Some with the visible scars of a chemical weapons attack.

Look at those pictures. We cannot close our eyes to those pictures. We cannot close our minds of the responsibility to act. We don't yet know everything about yesterday's attack. But there are many things we do know.

We know that yesterday's attack bears all the hallmarks of the Assad regime's use of chemical weapons. We know that Assad has used these weapons against the Syrian people before. That was confirmed by this Council's own independent team of

Delivered on April 5, 2017 at the United Nations, New York, NY.

investigators. We know that yesterday's attack was a new low, even for the barbaric Assad regime.

Evidence reported from the scene indicates that Assad is now using even more lethal chemical agents than he did before. The gas that fell out of the sky yesterday was more deadly, leaving men, women, the elderly, and children, gasping for their very last breath.

And as first responders, doctors, and nurses rushed to help the victims, a second round of bombs rained down. They died in the same slow, horrendous manner as the civilians they were trying to save.

We all also know this: Just a few weeks ago, this Council attempted to hold Assad accountable for suffocating his own people to death with toxic chemicals. Russia stood in the way of this accountability. They made an unconscionable choice. They chose to close their eyes to the barbarity. They defied the conscience of the world. Russia cannot escape responsibility for this. In fact, if Russia had been fulfilling its responsibility, there would not even be any chemical weapons left for the Syrian regime to use.

There is one more thing we know: We know that if nothing is done, these attacks will continue.

Assad has no incentive to stop using chemical weapons as long as Russia continues to protect his regime from consequences. I implore my colleagues to take a hard look at their words in this Council. We regularly repeat tired talking points in support of a peace process that is regularly undermined by the Assad regime.

Time and time again, Russia uses the same false narrative to deflect attention from their allies in Damascus. Time and time again, without any factual basis, Russia attempts to place blame on others.

There is an obvious truth here that must be spoken. The truth is that Assad, Russia, and Iran have no interest in peace.

The illegitimate Syrian government, led by a man with no conscience, has committed untold atrocities against his people for more than six years. Assad has made it clear that he doesn't want to take part in a meaningful political process. Iran has reinforced Assad's military, and Russia has shielded Assad from UN sanctions.

If Russia has the influence in Syria that it claims to have, we need to see them use it. We need to see them put an end to these horrific acts. How many more children have to die before Russia cares?

The United States sees yesterday's attack as a disgrace at the highest level, an assurance that humanity means nothing to the Syrian government.

The question members of this Council must ask themselves is this: If we are not able to enforce resolutions preventing the use of chemical weapons, what does that say for our chances of ending the broader conflict in Syria? What does that say of our ability to bring relief to the Syrian people? If we are not able to enforce resolutions preventing the use of chemical weapons, what does that say about our effectiveness in this institution?

If we are not prepared to act, then this Council will keep meeting, month after month, to express outrage at the continuing use of chemical weapons, and it will not end. We will see more conflict in Syria. We will see more pictures that we can never un-see.

I began my remarks by saying that in the life of the United Nations, there are times when we are compelled to take collective action. I will now add this: When the United Nations consistently fails in its duty to act collectively, there are times in the life of states that we are compelled to take our own action.

For the sake of the victims, I hope the rest of the Council is finally willing to do the same. The world needs to see the use of chemical weapons and the fact that they will not be tolerated.

Thank you.

Print Citations

CMS: Haley, Nikki. "Remarks at the United Nations Advocating for Acting against the Assad Regime." Speech presented at the United Nations, New York, NY, April, 2017. In *The Reference Shelf: Representative American Speeches 2016-2017*, edited by Betsy Maury, 109-111. Ipswich, MA: H.W. Wilson, 2017.

MLA: Haley, Nikki. "Remarks at the United Nations Advocating for Acting against the Assad Regime." United Nations. New York, NY. April, 2017. Presentation. *The Reference Shelf: Representative American Speeches 2016-2017*. Ed. Betsy Maury. Ipswich: H.W. Wilson, 2017. 109-111. Print.

APA: Haley, N. (2017). Remarks at United Nations advocating for acting against the Assad regime. [Presentation]. *Speech presented at the United Nations*. New York, NY. In Betsy Maury (Ed.), *The reference shelf: Representative American speeches 2016-2017* (pp. 109-111). Ipswich, MA: H.W. Wilson. (Original work published 2017)

Racism Is Evil

By Donald Trump

Criticized for failing to explicitly condemn racism and white nationalism after a white nationalist protestor drove a vehicle through a group of antiracism protestors in Charlottesville, Virginia, killing one woman and injuring 19 others, US President Donald Trump delivers a second statement on the Charlottesville incident. In the speech, Trump explicitly calls racism "evil" and condemns the KKK, neo-Nazis, and white supremacists. After critics complained that Trump's statements were delivered too late, Trump issued a third, impromptu statement in which he again maintained that there had been fault on both sides and criticized the movement to remove Confederate monuments from public land.

I'm in Washington today to meet with my economic team about trade policy and major tax cuts and reform. We are renegotiating trade deals and making them good for the American worker, and it's about time. The economy is now strong. The stock market continues to hit record highs, unemployment is at a 16-year low, and businesses are more optimistic than ever before. Companies are moving back to the United States and bringing many thousands of jobs with them. We have already created over one million jobs since I took office.

We will be discussing economic issues in greater detail later this afternoon, but based on the events that took place over the weekend in Charlottesville, Virginia, I would like to provide the nation with an update on the ongoing federal response to the horrific attack and violence that was witnessed by everyone. I just met with FBI director Christopher Wray and Attorney General Jeff Sessions. The Department of Justice has opened a civil-rights investigation into the deadly car attack that killed one innocent American and wounded 20 others. To anyone who acted criminally in this weekend's racist violence, you will be held accountable. Justice will be delivered.

As I said on Saturday, we condemn in the strongest possible terms this egregious display of bigotry, hatred, and violence. It has no place in America. And as I have said many times before, no matter the color of our skin, we all live under the same laws; we all salute the same great flag; and we are all made by the same almighty God. We must love each other, show affection for each other, and unite together in condemnation of hatred, bigotry, and violence. We must discover the bonds of love and loyalty that bring us together as Americans. Racism is evil, and those who cause violence in its name are criminals and thugs, including the KKK, neo-Nazis, white

Delivered on August 14, 2017 at the White House, Washington, DC.

supremacists, and other hate groups that are repugnant to everything we hold dear as Americans. We are a nation founded on the truth that all of us are created equal. We are equal in the eyes of our creator, we are equal under the law, and we are equal under our constitution. Those who spread violence in the name of bigotry strike at the very core of America.

Two days ago, a young American woman, Heather Heyer, was tragically killed. Her death fills us with grief and we send her family our thoughts, our prayers, and our love. We also mourn the two Virginia state troopers who died in service to their community, their commonwealth, and their country. Troopers H. Jay Cullen and Berke Bates exemplify the very best of America, and our hearts go out to their families, their friends, and every member of American law enforcement. These three fallen Americans embody the goodness and decency of our nation. In times such as these, America has always shown its true character, responding to hate with love, division with unity, and violence with an unwavering resolve for justice. As a candidate, I promised to restore law and order to our country, and our federal law-enforcement agencies are following through on that pledge. We will spare no resource in fighting so that every American child can grow up free from violence and fear. We will defend and protect the sacred rights of all Americans, and we will work together so that every citizen in this blessed land is free to follow their dreams in their hearts and to express the love and joy in their souls.

Thank you. God bless you, and God bless America.

Print Citations

CMS: Trump, Donald. "Racism Is Evil." Speech presented at the White House, Washington, DC, August, 2017. In *The Reference Shelf: Representative American Speeches 2016-2017*, edited by Betsy Maury, 112-113. Ipswich, MA: H.W. Wilson, 2017.

MLA: Trump, Donald. "Racism Is Evil." The White House. Washington, DC. August, 2017. Presentation. *The Reference Shelf: Representative American Speeches 2016-2017*. Ed. Betsy Maury. Ipswich: H.W. Wilson, 2017. 112-113. Print.

APA: Trump, D. (2017). Racism is evil. [Presentation]. *Speech presented at the White House*. Washington, DC. In Betsy Maury (Ed.), *The reference shelf: Representative American speeches 2016-2017* (pp. 112-113). Ipswich, MA: H.W. Wilson. (Original work published 2017)

Returning to the Senate after Defeating the "Skinny" Health Care Bill Speech

By John McCain

Senator and former Presidential Candidate John McCain delivers a speech on his deci-sion to vote against a Republican plan to repeal the Affordable Care Act on July 25th. McCain, arguing against the process of pushing through legislation along strict party lines advocated for bipartisan cooperation and negotiation to create a compromised bill that would provide solutions to some of the problems facing the public. McCain also delivered a passionate plea to Congress to recognize that the body might achieve more working together than it had by remaining locked behind partisan lines. The Republi-can-led Senate attempted three votes to repeal Obamacare, each failing to achieve suffi-cient support from either moderate or hard conservatives within the Republican senate.

Mr. President, I've stood in this place many times and addressed as president many presiding officers. I have been so addressed when I have sat in that chair, as close as I will ever be to a presidency.

It is an honorific we're almost indifferent to, isn't it. In truth, presiding over the Senate can be a nuisance, a bit of a ceremonial bore, and it is usually relegated to the more junior members of the majority.

But as I stand here today—looking a little worse for wear I'm sure—I have a refreshed appreciation for the protocols and customs of this body, and for the other ninety-nine privileged souls who have been elected to this Senate.

I have been a member of the United States Senate for thirty years. I had another long, if not as long, career before I arrived here, another profession that was pro-foundly rewarding, and in which I had experiences and friendships that I revere. But make no mistake, my service here is the most important job I have had in my life. And I am so grateful to the people of Arizona for the privilege—for the honor— of serving here and the opportunities it gives me to play a small role in the history of the country I love.

I've known and admired men and women in the Senate who played much more than a small role in our history, true statesmen, giants of American politics. They came from both parties, and from various backgrounds. Their ambitions were fre-quently in conflict. They held different views on the issues of the day. And they often had very serious disagreements about how best to serve the national interest.

Delivered on July 25, 2017 at the US Senate, Washington, DC.

But they knew that however sharp and heartfelt their disputes, however keen their ambitions, they had an obligation to work collaboratively to ensure the Senate discharged its constitutional responsibilities effectively. Our responsibilities are important, vitally important, to the continued success of our Republic. And our arcane rules and customs are deliberately intended to require broad cooperation to function well at all. The most revered members of this institution accepted the necessity of compromise in order to make incremental progress on solving America's problems and to defend her from her adversaries.

That principled mindset, and the service of our predecessors who possessed it, come to mind when I hear the Senate referred to as the world's greatest deliberative body. I'm not sure we can claim that distinction with a straight face today.

I'm sure it wasn't always deserved in previous eras either. But I'm sure there have been times when it was, and I was privileged to witness some of those occasions.

Our deliberations today—not just our debates, but the exercise of all our responsibilities—authorizing government policies, appropriating the funds to implement them, exercising our advice and consent role—are often lively and interesting. They can be sincere and principled. But they are more partisan, more tribal more of the time than any other time I remember. Our deliberations can still be important and useful, but I think we'd all agree they haven't been overburdened by greatness lately. And right now they aren't producing much for the American people.

Both sides have let this happen. Let's leave the history of who shot first to the historians. I suspect they'll find we all conspired in our decline—either by deliberate actions or neglect. We've all played some role in it. Certainly I have. Sometimes, I've let my passion rule my reason. Sometimes, I made it harder to find common ground because of something harsh I said to a colleague. Sometimes, I wanted to win more for the sake of winning than to achieve a contested policy.

Incremental progress, compromises that each side criticize but also accept, just plain muddling through to chip away at problems and keep our enemies from doing their worst isn't glamorous or exciting. It doesn't feel like a political triumph. But it's usually the most we can expect from our system of government, operating in a country as diverse and quarrelsome and free as ours.

Considering the injustice and cruelties inflicted by autocratic governments, and how corruptible human nature can be, the problem solving our system does make possible, the fitful progress it produces, and the liberty and justice it preserves, is a magnificent achievement.

Our system doesn't depend on our nobility. It accounts for our imperfections, and gives an order to our individual strivings that has helped make ours the most powerful and prosperous society on earth. It is our responsibility to preserve that, even when it requires us to do something less satisfying than "winning." Even when we must give a little to get a little. Even when our efforts manage just three yards and a cloud of dust, while critics on both sides denounce us for timidity, for our failure to "triumph."

I hope we can again rely on humility, on our need to cooperate, on our dependence on each other to learn how to trust each other again and by so doing better serve the people who elected us. Stop listening to the bombastic loudmouths on the radio and television and the Internet. To hell with them. They don't want anything done for the public good. Our incapacity is their livelihood.

Let's trust each other. Let's return to regular order. We've been spinning our wheels on too many important issues because we keep trying to find a way to win without help from across the aisle. That's an approach that's been employed by both sides, mandating legislation from the top down, without any support from the other side, with all the parliamentary maneuvers that requires.

We're getting nothing done. All we've really done this year is confirm Neil Gorsuch to the Supreme Court. Our healthcare insurance system is a mess. We all know it, those who support Obamacare and those who oppose it. Something has to be done. We Republicans have looked for a way to end it and replace it with something else without paying a terrible political price. We haven't found it yet, and I'm not sure we will. All we've managed to do is make more popular a policy that wasn't very popular when we started trying to get rid of it.

I voted for the motion to proceed to allow debate to continue and amendments to be offered. I will not vote for the bill as it is today. It's a shell of a bill right now. We all know that. I have changes urged by my state's governor that will have to be included to earn my support for final passage of any bill. I know many of you will have to see the bill changed substantially for you to support it.

We've tried to do this by coming up with a proposal behind closed doors in consultation with the administration, then springing it on skeptical members, trying to convince them it's better than nothing, asking us to swallow our doubts and force it past a unified opposition. I don't think that is going to work in the end. And it probably shouldn't.

The Obama administration and congressional Democrats shouldn't have forced through Congress without any opposition support a social and economic change as massive as Obamacare. And we shouldn't do the same with ours.

Why don't we try the old way of legislating in the Senate, the way our rules and customs encourage us to act. If this process ends in failure, which seem likely, then let's return to regular order.

Let the Health, Education, Labor, and Pensions Committee under Chairman Alexander and Ranking Member Murray hold hearings, try to report a bill out of committee with contributions from both sides. Then bring it to the floor for amendment and debate, and see if we can pass something that will be imperfect, full of compromises, and not very pleasing to implacable partisans on either side, but that might provide workable solutions to problems Americans are struggling with today.

What have we to lose by trying to work together to find those solutions? We're not getting much done apart. I don't think any of us feels very proud of our incapacity. Merely preventing your political opponents from doing what they want isn't the most inspiring work. There's greater satisfaction in respecting our differences, but not letting them prevent agreements that don't require abandonment of core principles, agreements made in good faith that help improve lives and protect the American people.

The Senate is capable of that. We know that. We've seen it before. I've seen it happen many times. And the times when I was involved even in a modest way with working out a bipartisan response to a national problem or threat are the proudest moments of my career, and by far the most satisfying.

This place is important. The work we do is important. Our strange rules and seemingly eccentric practices that slow our proceedings and insist on our cooperation are important. Our founders envisioned the Senate as the more deliberative, careful body that operates at a greater distance than the other body from the public passions of the hour.

We are an important check on the powers of the Executive. Our consent is necessary for the President to appoint jurists and powerful government officials and in many respects to conduct foreign policy. Whether or not we are of the same party, we are not the President's subordinates. We are his equal!

As his responsibilities are onerous, many and powerful, so are ours. And we play a vital role in shaping and directing the judiciary, the military, and the cabinet, in planning and supporting foreign and domestic policies. Our success in meeting all these awesome constitutional obligations depends on cooperation among ourselves.

The success of the Senate is important to the continued success of America. This country – this big, boisterous, brawling, intemperate, restless, striving, daring, beautiful, bountiful, brave, good and magnificent country—needs us to help it thrive. That responsibility is more important than any of our personal interests or political affiliations.

"We are the servants of a great nation, "a nation conceived in liberty and dedicated to the proposition that all men are created equal." More people have lived free and prosperous lives here than in any other nation. We have acquired unprecedented wealth and power because of our governing principles, and because our government defended those principles.

America has made a greater contribution than any other nation to an international order that has liberated more people from tyranny and poverty than ever before in history. We have been the greatest example, the greatest supporter and the greatest defender of that order. We aren't afraid. We don't covet other people's land and wealth. We don't hide behind walls. We breach them. We are a blessing to humanity.

What greater cause could we hope to serve than helping keep America the strong, aspiring, inspirational beacon of liberty and defender of the dignity of all human beings and their right to freedom and equal justice? That is the cause that binds us and is so much more powerful and worthy than the small differences that divide us.

What a great honor and extraordinary opportunity it is to serve in this body.

It's a privilege to serve with all of you. I mean it. Many of you have reached out in the last few days with your concern and your prayers, and it means a lot to me. It really does. I've had so many people say such nice things about me recently that I think some of you must have me confused with someone else. I appreciate it though, every word, even if much of it isn't deserved.

I'll be here for a few days, I hope managing the floor debate on the defense authorization bill, which, I'm proud to say is again a product of bipartisan cooperation and trust among the members of the Senate Armed Services Committee.

After that, I'm going home for a while to treat my illness. I have every intention of returning here and giving many of you cause to regret all the nice things you said about me. And, I hope, to impress on you again that it is an honor to serve the American people in your company.

Thank you, fellow senators.

Print Citations

CMS: McCain, John. "Returning to the Senate after Defeating the 'Skinny' Health Care Bill Speech." Speech presented at the US Senate, Washington, DC, July, 2017. In *The Reference Shelf: Representative American Speeches 2016-2017*, edited by Betsy Maury, 114-118. Ipswich, MA: H.W. Wilson, 2017.

MLA: McCain, John. "Returning to the Senate after Defeating the 'Skinny' Health Care Bill Speech." US Senate. Washington, DC. July, 2017. Presentation. *The Reference Shelf: Representative American Speeches 2016-2017*. Ed. Betsy Maury. Ipswich: H.W. Wilson, 2017. 114-118. Print.

APA: McCain, J. (2017). Returning to the Senate after defeating the "skinny" health care bill speech. [Presentation]. *Speech presented at US Senate*. Washington, DC. In Betsy Maury (Ed.), *The reference shelf: Representative American speeches 2016-2017* (pp. 114-118). Ipswich, MA: H.W. Wilson. (Original work published 2017)

Working Together

By Chuck Schumer

Democratic Senator Chuck Schumer speaks on the Senate floor after the defeat of the second attempt to repeal and replace the Affordable Care Act. Schumer, echoing Republican Senator John McCain's comments on the bill, also called for a bipartisan effort, returning to regular order and convening a committee to debate and discuss the various aspects of the bill in an attempt to craft a functional revision, rather than an outright repeal. Schumer, a former US representative and senator for the State of New York since 1999 is the minority leader of the Senate since the 2016 election of Donald Trump.

Mr. President, first, let me say that it has been a long, long road for both sides. Each side had sincere convictions, and we are at this point.

I want to say three things. First, I suggest that we turn the page. It is time to turn the page.

I say to my dear friend the majority leader that we are not celebrating. We are relieved that millions and millions of people who would have been so drastically hurt by the three proposals put forward will, at least, retain their healthcare, be able to deal with preexisting conditions, deal with nursing homes and opioids that Medicaid has paid for.

We are relieved, not for ourselves, but for the American people. But as I have said over and over again, ObamaCare was hardly perfect. It did a lot of good things, but it needs improvement. I hope one part of turning that page is that we go back to regular order, work in the committees together to improve ObamaCare.

We have good leaders—the Senator from Tennessee, the Senator from Washington, the Senator from Utah, the Senator from Oregon. They have worked well together in the past and can work well together in the future.

There are suggestions we are interested in that come from Members on the other side of the aisle—the Senator from Maine and the Senator from Louisiana.

So let's turn the page and work together to improve our healthcare system, and let's turn the page in another way. All of us are so inspired by the speech and the life of the Senator from Arizona, and he asked us to go back to regular order, to bring back the Senate that some of us who have been here a while remember. Maybe this can be a moment where we start doing that.

Both sides will have to give. The blame hardly falls on one side or the other, but if we can take this moment—a solemn moment—and start working this body the

Delivered on July 27, 2017 in the US Senate, Washington, DC.

way it had always worked until the last decade or so, with both sides to blame for the deterioration, we will do a better job for our country, a better job for this body, a better job for ourselves.

Finally, I am glad that the leader asked us to move to NDAA. We need to do it. I can say that on this side of the aisle, we will move expeditiously. I know that the Senator from Rhode Island has worked with the Senator from Arizona on a list of amendments that can be agreed to, and we can finish this bill up rather quickly. As I mentioned to the majority leader, there are some other things we can do rather quickly, including moving a whole lot of nominations.

We can work together. Our country demands it. Every place in every corner of the country where we go, the No. 1 thing we are asked—and I know this because I have talked to my colleagues from the other side of the aisle—is: Can't you guys work together? Let's give it a shot. Let's give it a shot.

Print Citations

CMS: Schumer, Chuck. "Working Together." Speech presented at the US Senate, Washington, DC, July, 2017. In *The Reference Shelf: Representative American Speeches 2016-2017*, edited by Betsy Maury, 119-120. Ipswich, MA: H.W. Wilson, 2017.

MLA: Schumer, Chuck. "Working Together." US Senate. Washington, DC. July, 2017. Presentation. *The Reference Shelf: Representative American Speeches 2016-2017*. Ed. Betsy Maury. Ipswich: H.W. Wilson, 2017. 119-120. Print.

APA: Schumer, C. (2017). Working together. [Presentation]. *Speech presented at the US Senate*. Washington, DC. In Betsy Maury (Ed.), *The reference shelf: Representative American speeches 2016-2017* (pp. 119-120). Ipswich, MA: H.W. Wilson. (Original work published 2017)

Removing New Orleans' Confederate Monuments

By Mitch Landrieu

New Orleans Mayor Mitch Landrieu delivers an eloquent speech about the city's decision to remove Confederate monuments from city property. Landrieu speaks about slavery in the city's history, the nature of patriotism, and the importance of confronting history as it occurs, rather than hiding from it, as the nation struggles to cope with its violent past of abuse, dehumanization, and racial inequality. Landrieu, the first white mayor elected in New Orleans since 1978, formerly served as lieutenant governor. Landrieu's speech was widely covered in national news and became symbolic of the movement to remove Confederate monuments from public property.

Thank you for coming.

The soul of our beloved City is deeply rooted in a history that has evolved over thousands of years; rooted in a diverse people who have been here together every step of the way—for both good and for ill. It is a history that holds in its heart the stories of Native Americans—the Choctaw, Houma Nation, the Chitimacha. Of Hernando de Soto, Robert Cavelier, Sieur de La Salle, the Acadians, the Islenos, the enslaved people from Senegambia, Free People of Colorix, the Haitians, the Germans, both the empires of France and Spain. The Italians, the Irish, the Cubans, the south and central Americans, the Vietnamese and so many more.

You see - New Orleans is truly a city of many nations, a melting pot, a bubbling cauldron of many cultures. There is no other place quite like it in the world that so eloquently exemplifies the uniquely American motto: E Pluribus Unum—out of many we are one. But there are also other truths about our city that we must confront. New Orleans was America's largest slave market: a port where hundreds of thousands of souls were bought, sold and shipped up the Mississippi River to lives of forced labor of misery of rape, of torture. America was the place where nearly 4000 of our fellow citizens were lynched, 540 alone in Louisiana; where the courts enshrined "separate but equal"; where Freedom riders coming to New Orleans were beaten to a bloody pulp. So when people say to me that the monuments in question are history, well what I just described is real history as well, and it is the searing truth.

And it immediately begs the questions; why there are no slave ship monuments, no prominent markers on public land to remember the lynchings or the slave blocks;

Delivered on May 19, 2017 at Gallier Hall, New Orleans, LA.

nothing to remember this long chapter of our lives; the pain, the sacrifice, the shame...all of it happening on the soil of New Orleans. So for those self-appointed defenders of history and the monuments, they are eerily silent on what amounts to this historical malfeasance, a lie by omission. There is a difference between remembrance of history and reverence of it.

For America and New Orleans, it has been a long, winding road, marked by great tragedy and great triumph. But we cannot be afraid of our truth. As President George W. Bush said at the dedication ceremony for the National Museum of African American History & Culture, "A great nation does not hide its history. It faces its flaws and corrects them." So today I want to speak about why we chose to remove these four monuments to the Lost Cause of the Confederacy, but also how and why this process can move us towards healing and understanding of each other. So, let's start with the facts.

The historic record is clear, the Robert E. Lee, Jefferson Davis, and P.G.T. Beauregard statues were not erected just to honor these men, but as part of the movement which became known as the Cult of the Lost Cause. This "cult" had one goal—through monuments and through other means—to rewrite history to hide the truth, which is that the Confederacy was on the wrong side of humanity. First erected over 166 years after the founding of our city and 19 years after the end of the Civil War, the monuments that we took down were meant to rebrand the history of our city and the ideals of a defeated Confederacy. It is self-evident that these men did not fight for the United States of America, they fought against it. They may have been warriors, but in this cause they were not patriots. These statues are not just stone and metal. They are not just innocent remembrances of a benign history. These monuments purposefully celebrate a fictional, sanitized Confederacy; ignoring the death, ignoring the enslavement, and the terror that it actually stood for.

After the Civil War, these statues were a part of that terrorism as much as a burning cross on someone's lawn; they were erected purposefully to send a strong message to all who walked in their shadows about who was still in charge in this city. Should you have further doubt about the true goals of the Confederacy, in the very weeks before the war broke out, the Vice President of the Confederacy, Alexander Stephens, made it clear that the Confederate cause was about maintaining slavery and white supremacy. He said in his now famous "corner-stone speech" that the Confederacy's "cornerstone rests upon the great truth, that the negro is not equal to the white man; that slavery—subordination to the superior race—is his natural and normal condition. This, our new government, is the first, in the history of the world, based upon this great physical, philosophical, and moral truth."

Now, with these shocking words still ringing in your ears...I want to try to gently peel from your hands the grip on a false narrative of our history that I think weakens us. And make straight a wrong turn we made many years ago—we can more closely connect with integrity to the founding principles of our nation and forge a clearer and straighter path toward a better city and a more perfect union.

Last year, President Barack Obama echoed these sentiments about the need to contextualize and remember all our history. He recalled a piece of stone, a slave auction block engraved with a marker commemorating a single moment in 1830 when Andrew Jackson and Henry Clay stood and spoke from it. President Obama said, "Consider what this artifact tells us about history...on a stone where day after day for years, men and women...bound and bought and sold and bid like cattle on a stone worn down by the tragedy of over a thousand bare feet. For a long time the only thing we considered important, the singular thing we once chose to commemorate as history with a plaque were the unmemorable speeches of two powerful men."

A piece of stone—one stone. Both stories were history. One story told. One story forgotten or maybe even purposefully ignored. As clear as it is for me today...for a long time, even though I grew up in one of New Orleans' most diverse neighborhoods, even with my family's long proud history of fighting for civil rights...I must have passed by those monuments a million times without giving them a second thought. So I am not judging anybody, I am not judging people. We all take our own journey on race.

I just hope people listen like I did when my dear friend Wynton Marsalis helped me see the truth. He asked me to think about all the people who have left New Orleans because of our exclusionary attitudes. Another friend asked me to consider these four monuments from the perspective of an African American mother or father trying to explain to their fifth grade daughter who Robert E. Lee is and why he stands atop of our beautiful city. Can you do it? Can you look into that young girl's eyes and convince her that Robert E. Lee is there to encourage her? Do you think she will feel inspired and hopeful by that story? Do these monuments help her see a future with limitless potential? Have you ever thought that if her potential is limited, yours and mine are too? We all know the answer to these very simple questions. When you look into this child's eyes is the moment when the searing truth comes into focus for us. This is the moment when we know what is right and what we must do. We can't walk away from this truth.

And I knew that taking down the monuments was going to be tough, but you elected me to do the right thing, not the easy thing and this is what that looks like. So relocating these Confederate monuments is not about taking something away from someone else. This is not about politics, this is not about blame or retaliation. This is not a naive quest to solve all our problems at once.

This is however about showing the whole world that we as a city and as a people are able to acknowledge, understand, reconcile and most importantly, choose a better future for ourselves making straight what has been crooked and making right what was wrong. Otherwise, we will continue to pay a price with discord, with division and yes with violence.

To literally put the Confederacy on a pedestal in our most prominent places of honor is an inaccurate recitation of our full past. It is an affront to our present, and it is a bad prescription for our future. History cannot be changed. It cannot be moved like a statue. What is done is done. The Civil War is over, and the Confederacy lost and we are better for it. Surely we are far enough removed from this dark time to acknowledge that the cause of the Confederacy was wrong.

And in the second decade of the 21st century, asking African Americans—or anyone else—to drive by property that they own; occupied by reverential statues of men who fought to destroy the country and deny that person's humanity seems perverse and absurd. Centuries old wounds are still raw because they never healed right in the first place. Here is the essential truth. We are better together than we are apart.

Indivisibility is our essence. Isn't this the gift that the people of New Orleans have given to the world? We radiate beauty and grace in our food, in our music, in our architecture, in our joy of life, in our celebration of death; in everything that we do. We gave the world this funky thing called jazz, the most uniquely American art form that is developed across the ages from different cultures. Think about second lines, think about Mardi Gras, think about muffaletta, think about the Saints, gumbo, red beans and rice. By God, just think.

All we hold dear is created by throwing everything in the pot; creating, producing something better; everything a product of our historic diversity. We are proof that out of many we are one—and better for it! Out of many we are one - and we really do love it! And yet, we still seem to find so many excuses for not doing the right thing. Again, remember President Bush's words, "A great nation does not hide its history. It faces its flaws and corrects them."

We forget, we deny how much we really depend on each other, how much we need each other. We justify our silence and inaction by manufacturing noble causes that marinate in historical denial. We still find a way to say "wait"/not so fast, but like Dr. Martin Luther King Jr. said, "wait has almost always meant never." We can't wait any longer. We need to change. And we need to change now.

No more waiting. This is not just about statues, this is about our attitudes and behavior as well. If we take these statues down and don't change to become a more open and inclusive society this would have all been in vain. While some have driven by these monuments every day and either revered their beauty or failed to see them at all, many of our neighbors and fellow Americans see them very clearly. Many are painfully aware of the long shadows their presence casts; not only literally but figuratively. And they clearly receive the message that the Confederacy and the cult of the lost cause intended to deliver.

Earlier this week, as the cult of the lost cause statue of P.G.T. Beauregard came down, world renowned musician Terence Blanchard stood watch, his wife Robin and their two beautiful daughters at their side. Terence went to a high school on the edge of City Park named after one of America's greatest heroes and patriots, John F. Kennedy. But to get there he had to pass by this monument to a man who fought to deny him his humanity.

He said, "I've never looked at them as a source of pride...it's always made me feel as if they were put there by people who don't respect us. This is something I never thought I'd see in my lifetime. It's a sign that the world is changing." Yes, Terence, it is and it is long overdue. Now is the time to send a new message to the next generation of New Orleanians who can follow in Terence and Robin's remarkable footsteps.

A message about the future, about the next 300 years and beyond; let us not miss this opportunity New Orleans and let us help the rest of the country do the same. Because now is the time for choosing. Now is the time to actually make this the City we always should have been, had we gotten it right in the first place.

We should stop for a moment and ask ourselves - at this point in our history - after Katrina, after Rita, after Ike, after Gustav, after the national recession, after the BP oil catastrophe and after the tornado - if presented with the opportunity to build monuments that told our story or to curate these particular spaces…these monuments be what we want the world to see? Is this really our story?

We have not erased history; we are becoming part of the city's history by righting the wrong image these monuments represent and crafting a better, more complete future for all our children and for future generations. And unlike when these Confederate monuments were first erected as symbols of white supremacy, we now have a chance to create not only new symbols, but to do it together, as one people. In our blessed land we all come to the table of democracy as equals. We have to reaffirm our commitment to a future where each citizen is guaranteed the uniquely American gifts of life, liberty and the pursuit of happiness.

That is what really makes America great and today it is more important than ever to hold fast to these values and together say a self-evident truth that out of many we are one. That is why today we reclaim these spaces for the United States of America. Because we are one nation, not two; indivisible with liberty and justice for all…not some. We all are part of one nation, all pledging allegiance to one flag, the flag of the United States of America. And New Orleanians are in…all of the way. It is in this union and in this truth that real patriotism is rooted and flourishes. Instead of revering a 4-year brief historical aberration that was called the Confederacy we can celebrate all 300 years of our rich, diverse history as a place named New Orleans and set the tone for the next 300 years.

After decades of public debate, of anger, of anxiety, of anticipation, of humiliation and of frustration. After public hearings and approvals from three separate community led commissions. After two robust public hearings and a 6-1 vote by the duly elected New Orleans City Council. After review by 13 different federal and state judges. The full weight of the legislative, executive and judicial branches of government has been brought to bear and the monuments in accordance with the law have been removed. So now is the time to come together and heal and focus on our larger task. Not only building new symbols, but making this city a beautiful manifestation of what is possible and what we as a people can become.

Let us remember what the once exiled, imprisoned and now universally loved Nelson Mandela and what he said after the fall of apartheid. "If the pain has often been unbearable and the revelations shocking to all of us, it is because they indeed bring us the beginnings of a common understanding of what happened and a steady restoration of the nation's humanity." So before we part let us again state the truth clearly.

The Confederacy was on the wrong side of history and humanity. It sought to tear apart our nation and subjugate our fellow Americans to slavery. This is the history we should never forget and one that we should never again put on a pedestal to be revered. As a community, we must recognize the significance of removing New Orleans' Confederate monuments. It is our acknowledgment that now is the time to take stock of, and then move past, a painful part of our history.

Anything less would render generations of courageous struggle and soul-searching a truly lost cause. Anything less would fall short of the immortal words of our greatest President Abraham Lincoln, who with an open heart and clarity of purpose calls on us today to unite as one people when he said: "With malice toward none, with charity for all, with firmness in the right, as God gives us to see the right, let us strive on to finish the work we are in, to bind up the nation's wounds...to do all which may achieve and cherish—a just and lasting peace among ourselves and with all nations."

Thank you.

Print Citations

CMS: Landrieu, Mitch. "Removing New Orleans' Confederate Monuments." Speech presented at Gallier Hall, New Orleans, LA, May, 2017. In *The Reference Shelf: Representative American Speeches 2016-2017*, edited by Betsy Maury, 121-126. Ipswich, MA: H.W. Wilson, 2017.

MLA: Landrieu, Mitch. "Removing New Orleans' Confederate Monuments." Gallier Hall. New Orleans, LA. May, 2017. Presentation. *The Reference Shelf: Representative American Speeches 2016-2017*. Ed. Betsy Maury. Ipswich: H.W. Wilson, 2017. 121-126. Print.

APA: Landrieu, M. (2017). Removing New Orleans' confederate monuments. [Presentation]. *Speech presented at Gallier Hall*. New Orleans, LA. In Betsy Maury (Ed.), *The reference shelf: Representative American speeches 2016-2017* (pp. 121-126). Ipswich, MA: H.W. Wilson. (Original work published 2017)

How Facebook Is Fighting Back Against Russia's Election Interference

By Mark Zuckerberg

Facebook founder and famed entrepreneur Mark Zuckerberg speaks about Facebook company policy on "fake news" and announces new policies designed to combat the use of Facebook to distribute political propaganda and fake news. Zuckerberg unveiled plans for more stringent reviews of advertisements, transparency in political advertising, and partnerships with security and tech companies, as well as election commissions, to promote the democratic process and the distribution of legitimate news and information on political issues. Zuckerberg is one of the nation's most famous entrepreneurs and faced harsh criticism after it was revealed that fake user profiles on Facebook were used to distribute and spread information used to manipulate voters with misinformation during the 2016 election.

Today is my first day back in the office after taking parental leave. It was really special to be with Priscilla and August after she was born, and to get to spend some more time with Max.

While I was out on leave, I spent a lot of time with our teams on the question of Russian interference in the US elections. I made some decisions on the next steps we're taking, and I want to share those with you now.

First, let me say this. I care deeply about the democratic process and protecting its integrity. Facebook's mission is all about giving people a voice and bringing people closer together. Those are deeply democratic values and we're proud of them. I don't want anyone to use our tools to undermine democracy. That's not what we stand for.

The integrity of our elections is fundamental to democracy around the world. That's why we've built teams dedicated to working on election integrity and preventing governments from interfering in the elections of other nations. And as we've shared before, our teams have found and shut down thousands of fake accounts that could be attempting to influence elections in many countries, including recently in the French elections.

Now, I wish I could tell you we're going to be able to stop all interference, but that wouldn't be realistic. There will always be bad people in the world, and we can't prevent all governments from all interference. But we can make it harder. We can make it a lot harder. And that's what we're going to do.

So today I want to share the steps we're taking to protect election integrity and

---

Delivered on September 21, 2017 on Facebook Live.

make sure that Facebook is a force for good in democracy. While the amount of problematic content we've found so far remains relatively small, any attempted interference is a serious issue. Here are 9 things we'll be working on over the next few months:

1. We are actively working with the US government on its ongoing investigations into Russian interference. We have been investigating this for many months, and for a while we had found no evidence of fake accounts linked to Russia running ads. When we recently uncovered this activity, we provided that information to the special counsel. We also briefed Congress—and this morning I directed our team to provide the ads we've found to Congress as well. As a general rule, we are limited in what we can discuss publicly about law enforcement investigations, so we may not always be able to share our findings publicly. But we support Congress in deciding how to best use this information to inform the public, and we expect the government to publish its findings when their investigation is complete.

2. We will continue our investigation into what happened on Facebook in this election. We may find more, and if we do, we will continue to work with the government. We are looking into foreign actors, including additional Russian groups and other former Soviet states, as well as organizations like the campaigns, to further our understanding of how they used our tools. These investigations will take some time, but we will continue our thorough review.

3. Going forward—and perhaps the most important step we're taking—we're going to make political advertising more transparent. When someone buys political ads on TV or other media, they're required by law to disclose who paid for them. But you still don't know if you're seeing the same messages as everyone else. So we're going to bring Facebook to an even higher standard of transparency. Not only will you have to disclose which page paid for an ad, but we will also make it so you can visit an advertiser's page and see the ads they're currently running to any audience on Facebook. We will roll this out over the coming months, and we will work with others to create a new standard for transparency in online political ads.

4. We will strengthen our ad review process for political ads. To be clear, it has always been against our policies to use any of our tools in a way that breaks the law—and we already have many controls in place to prevent this. But we can do more. Most ads are bought programmatically through our apps and website without the advertiser ever speaking to anyone at Facebook. That's what happened here. But even without our employees involved in the sales, we can do better.

Now, I'm not going to sit here and tell you we're going to catch all bad content in our system. We don't check what people say before they say it, and frankly, I don't think our society shouldn't want us to. Freedom means you don't have to ask permission first, and that by default you can say what you want. If you break our community standards or the law, then you're going to face consequences afterwards. We won't catch everyone immediately, but we can make it harder to try to interfere.

5. We are increasing our investment in security and specifically election integrity. In the next year, we will more than double the team working on election integrity.

In total, we'll add more than 250 people across all our teams focused on security and safety for our community.

6. We will expand our partnerships with election commissions around the world. We already work with electoral commissions in many countries to help people register to vote and learn about the issues. We'll keep doing that, and now we're also going to establish a channel to inform election commissions of the online risks we've identified in their specific elections.

7. We will increase sharing of threat information with other tech and security companies. We already share information on bad actors on the internet through programs like ThreatExchange, and now we're exploring ways we can share more information about anyone attempting to interfere with elections. It is important that tech companies collaborate on this because it's almost certain that any actor trying to misuse Facebook will also be trying to abuse other internet platforms too.

8. We are working proactively to strengthen the democratic process. Beyond pushing back against threats, we will also create more services to protect our community while engaging in political discourse. For example, we're looking at adapting our anti-bullying systems to protect against political harassment as well, and we're scaling our ballot information tools to help more people understand the issues.

9. We have been working to ensure the integrity of the German elections this weekend, from taking actions against thousands of fake accounts, to partnering with public authorities like the Federal Office for Information Security, to sharing security practices with the candidates and parties. We're also examining the activity of accounts we've removed and have not yet found a similar type of effort in Germany. This is incredibly important and we have been focused on this for a while.

At the same time, it's important not to lose sight of the more straightforward and larger ways Facebook plays a role in elections—and these effects operate at much larger scales of 100x or 1000x bigger than what we're discussing here.

In 2016, people had billions of interactions and open discussions on Facebook that may never have happened offline. Candidates had direct channels to communicate with tens of millions of citizens. Campaigns spent tens of millions organizing and advertising online to get their messages out further. And we organized "get out the vote" efforts that helped as many as 2 million people register to vote who might not have voted otherwise. Many of these dynamics were new in this election, or at much larger scale than ever before in history, and at much larger scale than the interference we've found.

But we are in a new world. It is a new challenge for internet communities to deal with nation states attempting to subvert elections. But if that's what we must do, we are committed to rising to the occasion. Our sophistication in handling these threats is growing and improving quickly. We will continue working with the government to understand the full extent of Russian interference, and we will do our part not only to ensure the integrity of free and fair elections around the world, but also to give everyone a voice and to be a force for good in democracy everywhere.

Thanks for tuning in, and we'll keep you updated with more soon.

Print Citations

CMS: Zuckerberg, Mark. "How Facebook Is Fighting Back against Russia's Election Interference." Speech presented over Facebook Live, September, 2017. In *The Reference Shelf: Representative American Speeches 2016-2017*, edited by Betsy Maury, 127-130. Ipswich, MA: H.W. Wilson, 2017.

MLA: Zuckerberg, Mark. "How Facebook Is Fighting Back against Russia's Election Interference." Facebook Live. September, 2017. Presentation. *The Reference Shelf: Representative American Speeches 2016-2017*. Ed. Betsy Maury. Ipswich: H.W. Wilson, 2017. 127-130. Print.

APA: Zuckerberg, M. (2017). How Facebook is fighting back against Russia's election interference. [Presentation]. Facebook Live. In Betsy Maury (Ed.), *The reference shelf: Representative American speeches 2016-2017* (pp. 127-130). Ipswich, MA: H.W. Wilson. (Original work published 2017)

4
Resistance and Persistence
2017

Gloria Steinem attends the Women's March on Washington on January 21, 2017 in Washington, DC.

2016 Postelection Speech

By Elizabeth Warren

Senator Elizabeth Warren delivers a speech on November 10, 2016, two days after the election of Donald Trump. Warren sympathizes with Americans worried by Trump's victory and called upon the president to adhere to his promise to represent all Americans while in office. Warren also remarked that it would be the role of Democrats in the new era to combat racism and bigotry and pledged to work alongside the Trump administration so long as the administration worked for the welfare of the American people. Warren was elected senator of Massachusetts in 2013 and formerly served as a special adviser to the Obama administration. Warren is considered one of the Democratic Party's current leaders and has been an outspoken critic of income inequality.

We're now two days removed from an incredibly close and hard-fought election, and many people here in Washington and around the country are trying to make sense of what happened.

This wasn't a pretty election. In fact, it was ugly, and we should not sugarcoat the reason why. Donald Trump ran a campaign that started with racial attacks and then rode the escalator down. He encouraged a toxic stew of hatred and fear. He attacked millions of Americans. And he regularly made statements that undermined core values of our democracy.

And he won. He won—and now Latino and Muslim-American children are worried about what will happen to their families. LGBT couples are worried that their marriages could be dissolved by a Trump-Pence Supreme Court. Women are worried that their access to desperately needed health services will disappear. Millions of people in this country are worried, deeply worried. And they are right to be worried.

Today, as President-Elect, Donald Trump has an opportunity to chart a different course: to govern for all Americans and to respect our institutions. In his victory speech, he pledged that he would be "President for all" of the American people. And when he takes the oath of office as the leader of our democracy and the leader of all Americans, I sincerely hope that he will fulfill that pledge with respect and concern for every single human being in this country, no matter who they are, no matter where they come from, no matter what they believe, no matter whom they love.

And that marks Democrats' first job in this new era: We will stand up to bigotry. There is no compromise here. In all its forms, we will fight back against attacks on Latinos, African Americans, women, Muslims, immigrants, disabled Americans-on

Delivered on November 10, 2016 to the AFL-CIO Executive Council, Washington, DC.

anyone. Whether Donald Trump sits in a glass tower or sits in the White House, we will not give an inch on this, not now, not ever.

But there are many millions of people who did not vote for Donald Trump because of the bigotry and hate that fueled his campaign rallies. They voted for him despite the hate. They voted for him out of frustration and anger—and also out of hope that he would bring change.

If we have learned nothing else from the past two years of electioneering, we should hear the message loud and clear that the American people want Washington to change. It was clear in the Democratic Primaries. It was clear in the Republican Primaries. It was clear in the campaign and it was clear on Election Day. The final results may have divided us—but the entire electorate embraced deep, fundamental reform of our economic system and our political system.

Working families across this country are deeply frustrated about an economy and a government that doesn't work for them. Exit polling on Tuesday found that 72 percent of voters believe that, quote, "the American economy is rigged to advantage the rich and powerful." 72 percent of ALL voters—Democrats and Republicans. The polls were also made clear that the economy was the top issue on voters' minds. Americans are angry about a federal government that works for the rich and powerful and that leaves everyone else in the dirt.

Lobbyists and Washington insiders have spent years trying to convince themselves and each other that Americans don't actually believe this. Now that the returns are in and the people have spoken, they're already trying to wave their hands and dismiss these views as some sort of mass delusion. They are wrong—very wrong.

The truth is that people are right to be angry. Angry that wages have been stagnant for a generation, while basic costs like housing, health care, and child care have skyrocketed. Angry that our political system is awash in barely legalized campaign bribery. Angry that Washington eagerly protects tax breaks for billionaires while it refuses to raise the minimum wage, or help the millions of Americans struggling with student loans, or enforce the law when the millionaire CEOs who fund our political campaigns break it. Angry that Washington pushes big corporate interests in trade deals, but won't make the investments in infrastructure to create good jobs right here in America. Angry that Washington tilts the playing field for giant corporations—giving them special privileges, letting them amass enormous economic and political power.

Angry that while Washington dithers and spins and does the backstroke in an ocean of money, while the American Dream moves further and further out of reach for too many families. Angry that working people are in debt. Angry that seniors can't stretch a Social Security check to cover the basics.

President-Elect Trump spoke to these issues. Republican elites hated him for it. But he didn't care. He criticized Wall Street and big money's dominance in Washington—straight up. He supported a new Glass-Steagall. He spoke of the need to reform our trade deals so they aren't raw deals for the American people. He said he will not cut Social Security benefits. He talked about the need to address the rising cost of college and about helping working parents struggling with the high cost of child care. He spoke of the urgency of rebuilding our crumbling infrastructure and putting people back to work. He spoke to the very real sense of millions of Americans that their government and their economy has abandoned them. And he promised to rebuild our economy for working people.

The deep worry that people feel over an America that does not work for them is not liberal or conservative worry. It is not Democratic or Republican worry. It is the deep worry that led even Americans with very deep reservations about Donald Trump's temperament and fitness to vote for him anyway.

So let me be 100% clear about this. When President-Elect Trump wants to take on these issues, when his goal is to increase the economic security of middle class families, then count me in. I will put aside our differences and I will work with him to accomplish that goal. I offer to work as hard as I can and to pull as many people as I can into this effort. If Trump is ready to go on rebuilding economic security for millions of Americans, so am I and so are a lot of other people—Democrats and Republicans.

But let's also be clear about what rebuilding our economy does not mean.

It does not mean handing the keys to our economy over to Wall Street so they can run it for themselves. Americans want to hold the big banks accountable. That will not happen if we gut Dodd-Frank and fire the cops responsible for watching over those banks, like the Consumer Financial Protection Bureau. If Trump and the Republican Party try to turn loose the big banks and financial institutions so they can once again gamble with our economy and bring it all crashing down, then we will fight them every step of the way.

It does not mean crippling our economy and ripping working families apart by rounding up and deporting millions of our coworkers, our friends and neighbors, our mothers and fathers, our sons and daughters. And if Republicans choose that path, we will fight them every single step of the way.

Americans want reform to Obamacare—Democrats included. We must bring down the costs of health insurance and the cost of health care. But if the Republicans want to strip away health insurance from 20 million Americans, if they want to let cancer survivors get kicked to the curb, if they want to throw 24-year-olds off their parents' health insurance, then we will fight them every step of the way.

Americans want to close tax loopholes that benefit the very rich, and Donald Trump claimed to support closing the carried interest loophole and other loopholes. We need a fairer tax system, but if Republicans want to force through massive tax breaks that blow a hole in our deficit and tilt the playing field even further toward the wealthy and big corporations, then we will fight them every step of the way.

The American people—Democrats, Republicans, and Independents—have been clear about what economic policies they want Washington to pursue. Two-thirds of people support raising the federal minimum wage. Three-quarters of Americans want the federal government to increase its infrastructure investments. Over 70 percent of people believe students should have a chance at a debt-free education. Nearly three-quarters support expanding Social Security. These are the kinds of policies that will help level the playing field for working families and address the frustrations felt by millions of people across the country.

The American people sent one more message as well. Economic reform requires political reform. Why has the federal government worked so long only for those at the top? The answer is money—and they want this system changed. The American people are sick of politicians wallowing in the campaign contributions and dark money. They are revolted by influence peddling by wealthy people and giant corporations. When Bernie Sanders proved his independence by running a campaign based on small dollar contributions and when Donald Trump promised to spend his own money, both were sending an important message that they could not be bought. And once again, if Donald Trump is ready to make good on his promise to get corruption out of politics, to end dark money and pay-to-play, count me in. I will work as hard as I can and to pull as many people as I can to end the influence of big money and return democracy to the people.

Donald Trump won the Presidency under a Republican flag. But Mitch Mc-Connell, Paul Ryan and the Republicans in Congress—and their way of doing business—were rejected—rejected by their own primary voters, rejected during the campaign, and rejected in Tuesday's election. Regardless of political party, working families are disgusted by a Washington that works for the rich and powerful and leaves everyone else behind.

The American people have called out loudly for economic and political reform. For years, too many Republicans and too many Democrats have refused to hear their demands.

The majority of Americans voted against Donald Trump. Democrats picked up seats in both the House and the Senate. And yet, here we are. Republicans are in control of both houses of Congress and the White House. And that makes our job clear. As the loyal opposition we will fight harder, we will fight longer and we will fight more passionately than ever for the rights of every human being in this country to be treated with respect and dignity. We will fight for economic opportunity, not just for some of our children, but for all of our children. We do not control the tools of government, but make no mistake, we know what we stand for, the sun will keep rising, and we will keep fighting—each day, every day, we will fight for the people of this country.

The time for ignoring the American people is over. It's time for us to come together to work on America's agenda. Democracy demands that we do so, and we are ready.

Print Citations

CMS: Warren, Elizabeth. "2016 Postelection Speech." Speech presented at the AFL-CIO Executive Council, Washington, DC, November, 2016. In *The Reference Shelf: Representative American Speeches 2016-2017*, edited by Betsy Maury, 133-137. Ipswich, MA: H.W. Wilson, 2017.

MLA: Warren, Elizabeth. "2016 Postelection Speech." AFL-CIO Executive Council. Washington, DC. November, 2016. Presentation. *The Reference Shelf: Representative American Speeches 2016-2017*. Ed. Betsy Maury. Ipswich: H.W. Wilson, 2017. 133-137. Print.

APA: Warren, E. (2017). 2016 postelection speech. [Presentation]. *Speech presented at the AFL-CIO Executive Council*. Washington, DC. In Betsy Maury (Ed.), *The reference shelf: Representative American speeches 2016-2017* (pp. 133-137). Ipswich, MA: H.W. Wilson. (Original work published 2016)

State of the State Address

By Jerry Brown

California Governor Jerry Brown delivers the California State of the State speech on January 24, focusing on climate change and delivers a harsh criticism of the Trump administration's "attack on science" and support of alternative facts in the nation's climate change debate. Brown further held that California would continue to support international and national efforts to limit fossil fuels and combat climate change whether or not such actions were supported by the Trump administration and held that the state of California would still adhere to the values of protecting and promoting diversity. Brown, who was elected governor in 2011, served as governor of the state between 1975 and 1983, at which time he was the youngest governor in the history of the state. After an unsuccessful bid for the Senate and Democratic presidential nomination, Brown served as mayor of Oakland (1999-2007) before winning an election for another gubernatorial term in 2011, thereby becoming both the state's 34th and 39th governor.

Thank you. Thank you for all that energy and enthusiasm. It is just what we need for the battle ahead. So keep it up and don't ever falter.

This is California, the sixth most powerful economy in the world. One out of every eight Americans lives right here and 27 percent—almost eleven million—were born in a foreign land.

When California does well, America does well. And when California hurts, America hurts.

As the English poet, John Donne, said almost 400 years ago: "No man is an island entire of itself; every man is a piece of the continent, a part of the main...And therefore never send to know for whom the bell tolls; it tolls for thee."

A few moments ago, I swore into office our new attorney general. Like so many others, he is the son of immigrants who saw California as a place where, through grit and determination, they could realize their dreams. And they are not alone, millions of Californians have come here from Mexico and a hundred other countries, making our state what it is today: vibrant, even turbulent, and a beacon of hope to the rest of the world.

We don't have a Statue of Liberty with its inscription: "Give me your tired, your poor, your huddled masses yearning to breathe free..." But we do have the Golden Gate and a spirit of adventure and openness that has welcomed—since the Gold Rush of 1848—one wave of immigration after another.

For myself, I feel privileged to stand before you as your governor, as did my father

---

Delivered on January 24, 2017 at the California State Capitol, Sacramento, CA.

almost sixty years ago. His mother, Ida, the youngest of eight children, was born in very modest circumstances, not very far from where we are gathered today. Her father arrived in California in 1852, having left from the Port of Hamburg, aboard a ship named *Perseverance*.

It is that spirit of perseverance and courage which built our state from the beginning. And it is that spirit which will get us through the great uncertainty and the difficulties ahead.

It is customary on an occasion like this to lay out a specific agenda for the year ahead. Six times before from this rostrum, I have done that, and in some detail. And, as I reread those proposals set forth in previous State of the State speeches, I was amazed to see how much we have accomplished together.

We have:

Increased—by tens of billions—support for our public schools and universities.

Provided health insurance to over five million more Californians.

Raised the minimum wage.

Reduced prison overcrowding and reformed our system of crime and punishment.

Made California a world leader in the fight against climate change.

Passed a water bond.

Built up a rainy day fund.

And closed a huge $27 billion deficit.

And during the last seven years, California has reduced the unemployment rate from 12.1 percent to 5.2 percent and created almost 2.5 million jobs. And that's not all.

But this morning it is hard for me to keep my thoughts just on California. The recent election and inauguration of a new President have shown deep divisions across America.

While no one knows what the new leaders will actually do, there are signs that are disturbing. We have seen the bald assertion of "alternative facts." We have heard the blatant attacks on science. Familiar signposts of our democracy—truth, civility, working together—have been obscured or swept aside.

But on Saturday, in cities across the country, we also witnessed a vast and inspiring fervor that is stirring in the land. Democracy doesn't come from the top; it starts and spreads in the hearts of the people. And in the hearts of Americans, our core principles are as strong as ever.

So as we reflect on the state of our state, we should do so in the broader context of our country and its challenges. We must prepare for uncertain times and reaffirm the basic principles that have made California the Great Exception that it is.

First, in California, immigrants are an integral part of who we are and what we've become. They have helped create the wealth and dynamism of this state from the very beginning.

I recognize that under the Constitution, federal law is supreme and that Washington determines immigration policy. But as a state we can and have had a role to play. California has enacted several protective measures for the undocumented: the

Trust Act, lawful driver's licenses, basic employment rights and non-discriminatory access to higher education.

We may be called upon to defend those laws and defend them we will. And let me be clear: we will defend everybody—every man, woman and child—who has come here for a better life and has contributed to the well-being of our state.

My second point relates to health care. More than any other state, California embraced the Affordable Care Act and over five million people now enjoy its benefits. But that coverage has come with tens of billions of federal dollars. Were any of that to be taken away, our state budget would be directly affected, possibly devastated. That is why I intend to join with other governors—and with you—to do everything we can to protect the health care of our people.

Third, our state is known the world over for the actions we have taken to encourage renewable energy and combat climate change.

Whatever they do in Washington, they can't change the facts. And these are the facts: the climate is changing, the temperatures are rising and so are the oceans. Natural habitats everywhere are under increasing stress. The world knows this.

One hundred and ninety-four countries signed the Paris Agreement to control greenhouse gases. Our own voluntary agreement to accomplish the same goal—the "Under Two M.O.U."—has 165 signatories, representing a billion people.

We cannot fall back and give in to the climate deniers. The science is clear. The danger is real.

We can do much on our own and we can join with others—other states and provinces and even countries, to stop the dangerous rise in climate pollution. And we will.

Fourth is infrastructure. This is a topic where the President has stated his firm intention to build and build big.

In his inaugural address, he said: "We will build new roads, and highways, and bridges, and airports, and tunnels, and railways all across our wonderful nation."

And in this, we can all work together—here in Sacramento and in Washington as well. We have roads and tunnels and railroads and even a dam that the President could help us with. And that will create good-paying American jobs.

As we face the hard journey ahead, we will have to summon, as Abraham Lincoln said, "the better angels of our nature." Above all else, we have to live in the truth.

We all have our opinions but for democracy to work, we have to trust each other. We have to strive to understand the facts and state them clearly as we argue our points of view. As Hugo Grotius, the famous Dutch jurist, said long ago, "even God cannot cause two times two not to make four."

When the science is clear or when our own eyes tell us that the seats in this chamber are filled or that the sun is shining, we must say so, not construct some alternate universe of non-facts that we find more pleasing.

Along with truth, we must practice civility. Although we have disagreed—often along party lines—we have generally been civil to one another and avoided the rancor of Washington. I urge you to go even further and look for new ways to work beyond party and act as Californians first.

Democrats are in the majority, but Republicans represent real Californians too. We went beyond party when we reformed workers' compensation, when we created a rainy day fund and when we passed the water bond.

Let's do that again and set an example for the rest of the country. And, in the process, we will earn the trust of the people of California.

And then there is perseverance. It is not an accident that the sailing ship that brought my great-grandfather to America was named *Perseverance*. That is exactly what it took to endure the dangerous and uncertain months at sea, sailing from Germany to America.

While we now face different challenges, make no mistake: the future is uncertain and dangers abound. Whether it's the threat to our budget, or to undocumented Californians, or to our efforts to combat climate change—or even more global threats such as a financial meltdown or a nuclear incident or terrorist attack—this is a time which calls out for courage and for perseverance. I promise you both.

But let's remember as well that after the perilous voyage, those who made it to America found boundless opportunity. And so will we.

Let me end in the immortal words of Woody Guthrie:

This land is your land, this land is my land

From California to the New York Island

From the Redwood Forest, to the Gulf Stream waters

This land was made for you and me...

Nobody living can ever stop me,

As I go walking that freedom highway;

Nobody living can ever make me turn back

This land was made for you and me.

California is not turning back. Not now, not ever.

Print Citations

CMS: Brown, Jerry. "State of the State Address." Speech presented at the California State Capitol, Sacramento, CA, January, 2017. In *The Reference Shelf: Representative American Speeches 2016-2017*, edited by Betsy Maury, 138-141. Ipswich, MA: H.W. Wilson, 2017.

MLA: Brown, Jerry. "State of the State Address." California State Capitol. Sacramento, CA. January, 2017. Presentation. *The Reference Shelf: Representative American Speeches 2016-2017*. Ed. Betsy Maury. Ipswich: H.W. Wilson, 2017. 138-141. Print.

APA: Brown, J. (2017). State of the state address. [Presentation]. *Speech presented at the California State Capitol*. Sacramento, CA. In Betsy Maury (Ed.), *The reference shelf: Representative American speeches 2016-2017* (pp. 138-141). Ipswich, MA: H.W. Wilson. (Original work published 2017)

Do Not Try to Divide Us

By Gloria Steinem

Feminist icon Gloria Steinem speaks at the January 21st Women's March on Wash-ington DC, which attracted more than 500,000 women and inspired women's rights marches held around the world on the same day. In her speech, Steinem focused on re-futing Donald Trump's claims to represent a populist majority and called upon women to fight against the continued threats to women's rights around the world. After working as a journalist for publications like the New Yorker, *and* Esquire, *Steinem gained a reputation for her investigative articles on women's rights issues. Steinem went on to found* Ms. *magazine and became one of the most respected feminist theorists of the era, seen by many as one of the key architects of the American feminist movement. The Women's March on Washington was organized as a response to the election of Donald Trump and attracted between 3 and 4.6 million in the United States, with as many as 2 million more gathered in sympathetic protests in 81 other nations.*

Friends, sisters and brothers, all of you who are before me today and in 370 marches in every state in this country and on six continents and those who will be commun-ing with us in one at 1 [p.m.] in a silent minute for equality in offices, in kitchens, in factories, in prisons, all over the world. I thank each of you, and I especially want to thank the hardworking visionary organizers of this women-led, inclusive march, one of whom managed to give birth while she was organizing this march. Who else can say that?

Thank you for understanding that sometimes we must put our bodies where our beliefs are. Sometimes pressing send is not enough. And this also unifies us with the many in this world who do not have computers or electricity or literacy, but do have the same hopes and the same dreams.

I think that because I and my beloved co-chairs, the Golden oldies right?—Harry Belafonte, Dolores Huerta, LaDonna Harris—all these great people, we may be the oldest marchers here today, so I've been thinking about the uses of a long life, and one of them is you remember when things were worse.

We remember the death of the future, with Martin Luther King, with Jack Ken-nedy, with Bobby Kennedy, with Malcolm X. Without those deaths for instance, Nixon would not have been elected, and there would not have been many of the wars that we had. Now, our great leaders like Barack Obama and Michelle Obama are still with us and remember how much we feared they might not be, and how much threat there was, in fact, on their lives. And they are with us.

Delivered on January 21, 2017 at the Women's March on Washington, Washington, DC.

And now, our honored Bernie Sanders is still with us. And not only with us but he's focusing on economic justice and achieving free universal college education in my state of New York. And now Hillary Clinton is alive and definitely not in jail. She who told the whole world that women's rights are human rights and human rights are women's rights. So crucial, when collectively violence against females in the world has produced a world in which for the first time there are fewer females than males.

I'm not trying to deny the danger that this day initiates. Trump and his handlers have found a fox for every chicken coop in Washington, and a Twitter finger must not become a trigger finger. Some very experienced doctors of the American Psychiatric Association have publicly written to warn us that, and I quote, "His widely reported symptoms of mental instability, including grandiosity, impulsivity, hypersensitivity to slights or criticisms, and an apparent inability to distinguish between fantasy and reality, lead us to question his fitness for the immense responsibilities of the office." Unquote.

This was on full display in his inaugural address yesterday. Everything that happened before him was a disaster. And everything that he would do would be fantastic, the best ever, miracles, and all the superlatives. He also said he was with the people. Indeed, he was the people. To paraphrase a famous quote, I just have to say, "I have met the people, and you are not them." We are the people.

Just this march in Washington today required 1,000 more buses than the entire Inauguration. A thousand more buses. And I was just talking with people from our many sister marches, including the one in Berlin, and they asked me to send a special message: "We in Berlin know that walls don't work."

And remember Poland where last month the government passed an anti-abortion law and six million women turned out in the streets and they had to change it. We are the people. We have people power and we will use it. All the power that you tried to eliminate. For instance, you tried to eliminate the Congressional Ethics Committee. You had to reinstate it, right? Because of people power. Because this, *this*, is the other side of the downside. This is an outpouring of energy and true democracy like I have never seen in my very long life. It is wide in age. It is deep in diversity. And remember the constitution does not begin with "I, the president." It begins with "We, the people."

So don't try to divide us. Do not try to divide us. If you force Muslims to register, we will all register as Muslims. I know that there are women here from corporations and media and all kinds of places that make it kind of risky for you to say what you care about, what you feel, and what you support. And there are women here, I know, who have survived a national and global sex industry that profiteers from body invasion. We are united here for bodily integrity. If you cannot control your body from the skin in, you cannot control it from the skin out, you cannot control your lives, our lives. And that means that the right to decide whether and when to give birth without government interference.

We are here and around the world for a deep democracy that says we will not be quiet, we will not be controlled, we will work for a world in which all countries are connected. God may be in the details, but the goddess is in connections. We are at one with each other, we are looking at each other, not up. No more asking daddy.

We are linked. We are not ranked. And this is a day that will change us forever because we are together. Each of us individually and collectively will never be the same again. When we elect a possible president we too often go home. We've elected an impossible president, we're never going home. We're staying together. And we're taking over. I thank you from the bottom of my heart. Make sure you introduce yourselves to each other and decide what we're gonna do tomorrow and tomorrow and tomorrow and we're never turning back. Thank you.

Print Citations

CMS: Steinem, Gloria. "Do Not Try to Divide Us." Speech presented at the Women's March on Washington, Washington, DC, January, 2017. In *The Reference Shelf: Representative American Speeches 2016-2017*, edited by Betsy Maury, 142-144. Ipswich, MA: H.W. Wilson, 2017.

MLA: Steinem, Gloria. "Do Not Try to Divide Us." The Women's March on Washington. Washington, DC. January, 2017. Presentation. *The Reference Shelf: Representative American Speeches 2016-2017*. Ed. Betsy Maury. Ipswich: H.W. Wilson, 2017. 142-144. Print.

APA: Steinem, G. (2017). Do not try to divide us. [Presentation]. *Speech presented at the Women's March on Washington*. Washington, DC. In Betsy Maury (Ed.), *The reference shelf: Representative American speeches 2016-2017* (pp. 142-144). Ipswich, MA: H.W. Wilson. (Original work published 2017)

Climate Statement

By Mike Bloomberg

Politician and businessman Mike Bloomberg, issues a speech on behalf of the 127 million Americans who signed the "We Are Still In" declaration condemning the Trump administration's stance on climate change and pledging to continue supporting the Paris Climate Accords agreement. Citing an "absence of leadership" from Washington, Bloomberg called on local and national leaders, citizens, and businesses to take proactive steps to ensure that the nation remained on track to meet climate change and emission reduction guidelines according to the 2015 Paris Climate Accords plan. Bloomberg was the 108th mayor of New York City from 2002 to 2013. He also founded the influential Bloomberg News company in 1990.

Open letter to the international community and parties to the Paris Agreement from U.S. state, local, and business leaders:

We, the undersigned mayors, county executives, governors, tribal leaders, college and university leaders, businesses, and investors are joining forces for the first time to declare that we will continue to support climate action to meet the Paris Agreement.

In December 2015 in Paris, world leaders signed the first global commitment to fight climate change. The landmark agreement succeeded where past attempts failed because it allowed each country to set its own emission reduction targets and adopt its own strategies for reaching them. In addition, nations—inspired by the actions of local and regional governments, along with businesses—came to recognize that fighting climate change brings significant economic and public health benefits.

The Trump administration's announcement undermines a key pillar in the fight against climate change and damages the world's ability to avoid the most dangerous and costly effects of climate change. Importantly, it is also out of step with what is happening in the United States.

In the U.S., it is local, tribal, and state governments, along with businesses, that are primarily responsible for the dramatic decrease in greenhouse gas emissions in recent years. Actions by each group will multiply and accelerate in the years ahead, no matter what policies Washington may adopt.

In the absence of leadership from Washington, states, cities, counties, tribes, colleges and universities, businesses and investors, representing a sizeable percentage of the U.S. economy will pursue ambitious climate goals, working together to

Delivered on June 5, 2017 in New York, NY.

take forceful action and to ensure that the U.S. remains a global leader in reducing emissions.

It is imperative that the world know that in the U.S., the actors that will provide the leadership necessary to meet our Paris commitment are found in city halls, state capitals, colleges and universities, investors and businesses. Together, we will remain actively engaged with the international community as part of the global effort to hold warming to well below 2°C and to accelerate the transition to a clean energy economy that will benefit our security, prosperity, and health.

Print Citations

CMS: Bloomberg, Mike. "Climate Statement." Statement presented in New York, New York, June, 2017. In *The Reference Shelf: Representative American Speeches 2016-2017*, edited by Betsy Maury, 145-146. Ipswich, MA: H.W. Wilson, 2017.

MLA: Bloomberg, Mike. "Climate Statement." New York, NY. June, 2017. Presentation. *The Reference Shelf: Representative American Speeches 2016-2017*. Ed. Betsy Maury. Ipswich: H.W. Wilson, 2017. 145-146. Print.

APA: Bloomberg, M. (2017). Climate statement. [Presentation]. New York, NY. In Betsy Maury (Ed.), *The reference shelf: Representative American speeches 2016-2017* (pp. 145-146). Ipswich, MA: H.W. Wilson. (Original work published 2017)

History Cannot Be Deleted Like Web Pages

By Angela Davis

Feminist and civil right activist Angela Davis gives a speech at the 2017 Women's March in Washington, DC, on January 21st. In her speech, Davis touched on issues including women's rights, the Native American protests at Standing Rock, the Black Lives Matter Movement, climate change, and income inequality. She focused her remarks on the concept of "resistance" against the forces of state violence, bigotry, xenophobia, sexism, and racism. Davis, a former professor at the University of California, Santa Cruz, became known for her feminist and black rights activism during the 1960s and was famous as one of the most prominent members of the American Communist Party as well as for her association with the Black Panther movement. The Women's March, or Women's March on Washington, was organized in response to the election of Donald Trump and attracted an estimated 500,000 women in Washington, DC, with between 3 and 4.6 million women joining in sympathetic marches around the nation and as many as 2 million participating in other gatherings in 81 nations around the world.

At a challenging moment in our history, let us remind ourselves that we the hundreds of thousands, the millions of women, trans-people, men and youth who are here at the Women's March, we represent the powerful forces of change that are determined to prevent the dying cultures of racism, hetero-patriarchy from rising again.

We recognize that we are collective agents of history and that history cannot be deleted like web pages. We know that we gather this afternoon on indigenous land and we follow the lead of the first peoples who despite massive genocidal violence have never relinquished the struggle for land, water, culture, their people. We especially salute today the Standing Rock Sioux.

The freedom struggles of black people that have shaped the very nature of this country's history cannot be deleted with the sweep of a hand. We cannot be made to forget that black lives do matter. This is a country anchored in slavery and colonialism, which means for better or for worse the very history of the United States is a history of immigration and enslavement. Spreading xenophobia, hurling accusations of murder and rape and building walls will not erase history.

No human being is illegal.

"The struggle to save the planet, to stop climate change, to guarantee the accessibility of water from the lands of the Standing Rock Sioux, to Flint, Michigan,

Delivered on January 21, 2017 at the Women's March on Washington, Washington, DC.

to the West Bank and Gaza. The struggle to save our flora and fauna, to save the air—this is ground zero of the struggle for social justice.

This is a women's march and this women's march represents the promise of feminism as against the pernicious powers of state violence. And inclusive and intersectional feminism that calls upon all of us to join the resistance to racism, to Islamophobia, to anti-Semitism, to misogyny, to capitalist exploitation.

Yes, we salute the fight for 15. We dedicate ourselves to collective resistance. Resistance to the billionaire mortgage profiteers and gentrifiers. Resistance to the health care privateers. Resistance to the attacks on Muslims and on immigrants. Resistance to attacks on disabled people. Resistance to state violence perpetrated by the police and through the prison industrial complex. Resistance to institutional and intimate gender violence, especially against trans women of color.

Women's rights are human rights all over the planet and that is why we say freedom and justice for Palestine. We celebrate the impending release of Chelsea Manning. And Oscar López Rivera. But we also say free Leonard Peltier. Free Mumia Abu-Jamal. Free Assata Shakur.

Over the next months and years we will be called upon to intensify our demands for social justice to become more militant in our defense of vulnerable populations. Those who still defend the supremacy of white male hetero-patriarchy had better watch out.

The next 1,459 days of the Trump administration will be 1,459 days of resistance: Resistance on the ground, resistance in the classrooms, resistance on the job, resistance in our art and in our music.

This is just the beginning and in the words of the inimitable Ella Baker, "We who believe in freedom cannot rest until it comes." Thank you.

Print Citations

CMS: Davis, Angela. "History Cannot Be Deleted Like Web Pages." Speech presented at the Women's March on Washington, Washington, DC, January, 2017. In *The Reference Shelf: Representative American Speeches 2016-2017*, edited by Betsy Maury, 147-148. Ipswich, MA: H.W. Wilson, 2017.

MLA: Davis, Angela. "History Cannot Be Deleted Like Web Pages." The Women's March on Washington. Washington, DC. January, 2017. *The Reference Shelf: Representative American Speeches 2016-2017*. Ed. Betsy Maury. Ipswich: H.W. Wilson, 2017. 147-148. Print.

APA: Davis, A. (2017). History cannot be deleted like web pages. [Presentation]. *Speech presented at the Women's March on Washington*. Washington, DC. In Betsy Maury (Ed.), *The reference shelf: Representative American speeches 2016-2017* (pp. 147-148). Ipswich, MA: H.W. Wilson. (Original work published 2017)

Bias is the Enemy of Science

By Adam Savage

Television celebrity Adam Savage delivers a speech at the first annual March for Science on April 22nd. Savage gives a passionate endorsement of science, the scientific method, and the scientific mindset as a way of solving complex problems and advancing human understanding about the world. He also warns against the insidious effects of bias when attempting to address or understand complex, emotional, or highly charged issues. Savage, best known as one of the primary stars of the hit, long-running television series MythBusters, is a former industrial designer and special effects expert. The March for Science, held on Earth Day 2017, was organized in reaction to the Trump administration's stance on climate change and attracted at least 1 million in cities around the world. The event's organizers have since announced plans to repeat the event in 2018.

Hello, San Francisco. I can't believe this crowd. Seriously, I can't believe that we have to come out. Now a speech from a guy with a high-school diploma.

I speak today not just to those who agree with me, to the choir, but also to those who don't. I'm assuming we begin from the same basic principles. We may differ in terms of the method, but I think we can agree on the goal: that we all want to leave a better world and life for our children, our loved ones, our communities. Science is the key way to achieve that.

If I'm going to talk about science, I want to define my terms. To begin with what is science, this morning the Internet described it to me as "the intellectual and practical activity encompassing the systematic study of the structure and behavior of the physical and natural world through observation and experiment."

It doesn't really roll off the tongue. How about this? Science is the systematic reduction of ignorance. Science is not an edifice or a citadel; it is a process. To riff off Robert Pirsig, "Science is not a thing. It is an event. It is a practice and most often this practice is done by scientists."

Claude Levi-Strauss said, "The scientist is not the person who gives the right answers, they're the one who asks the right questions." Science does not require a scientist in order to happen. It is in fact one of the oldest of human drives to explore. We are moved, we are driven, inspired to better understand our universe and ourselves.

We push ourselves to the edge of what is known and we seek to know more. We are, as a singular species—tinkerers, explorers, problem solvers. We are social, we are storytellers, we are question askers, we are scientists. You are all scientists.

Delivered on April 22, 2017 at the March for Science, San Francisco, CA.

Seriously, the last time you salted your food, you were testing, tasting, making assumptions, adding more salt when the first pinch wasn't enough. You weren't just seasoning; that was the scientific method making your food taste better.

All progress has been made using this method. Looking at what is in front of us, trying to understand it by guessing what will happen if a change is made, seeing how what actually happens when that change is made, rinse, repeat. Why are we marching today for science? Because science has an enemy. Our enemy is strong and it fights dirty. But science's enemy is not a person, a political party, an ideology, it is not a behavior, a budget or a law.

If science is about exploring and understanding our world, clearly then the enemy is our own proclivity as individuals and as communities to stay inside a bubble and see the world not as it is but how we wish it to be. This is called bias. Bias is the enemy of science. My dictionary says that bias, "implies an unreasoned and unfair distortion of judgment in favor of or against a person or a thing."

Bias is strong. It is in us, in our families, in our communities. It is in our institutions. It feels safe, but bias is very dangerous. It cannot only skew the results of a test, it can undermine our conclusions and the policies we make based upon those conclusions. It is imperative that each one of us confront our own personal as well as institutional bias and prejudice and to excise them in any way that we can.

A scientist knows this in their bones. This is why blind tests exist and double and triple, and I found out today, quadruple blind tests. It's because despite their commitment to the truth, a scientist knows that they can without even realizing it alter things toward a skewed or preferred result.

Mice have been used for generations in research, yet in only to 2014 a study indicated that the testosterone of male researchers could scare mice and alter their behavior. This cast doubt on thousands of published conclusions. But does this betray the weakness of science? No, it shows its strength, that science takes vigilance to ferret out the hidden mechanisms in order to better comprehend.

Gandhi says that "We must look the world in the face with calm and clear eyes even though the eyes of the world are bloodshot today." We have to be open and fearless and admit our mistakes and forgive ourselves and also to forgive the mistakes of others. Bias may be the enemy of science, but science is also the enemy of bias.

We can help science gain the upper hand. We can be part of the solution. We can witness institutional racism and bias and remove it. We demand policies based upon empirical evidence and consensus. We demand our laws to equally protect all of us and to use data to remove those that do not. We demand that our government acknowledge that global warming is happening and that we are the cause.

Look at your beautiful faces. Naomi Klein says, "To change everything, we need everyone." The hundreds of thousands of us on the streets in the United States and around the world are a confluence, a galaxy. We are a constituency. We are agents of change. More accurately, we are reagents. Each of us is a molecule, a precise geometry of atoms bonded together under unique rules and conditions. Individually on our own no single one of us can bring enough energy to an equation to accomplish something significant.

But when we band together, when we find our sisters and brothers, when we participate in our democracy, when we speak clearly to those in power from our hearts and with our votes, when we make our collective voices be heard, we can move worlds. So let us, all of us, molecules, reagents, scientists, humans, let us march to start a proper chain reaction. Let us bring about change and let's move this world.

Thank you.

Print Citations

CMS: Savage, Adam. "Bias Is the Enemy of Science." Speech presented at the March for Science, San Francisco, CA, April, 2017. In *The Reference Shelf: Representative American Speeches 2016-2017*, edited by Betsy Maury, 149-151. Ipswich, MA: H.W. Wilson, 2017.

MLA: Savage, Adam. "Bias Is the Enemy of Science." The March for Science. San Francisco, CA. April, 2017. Presentation. *The Reference Shelf: Representative American Speeches 2016-2017*. Ed. Betsy Maury. Ipswich: H.W. Wilson, 2017. 149-151. Print.

APA: Savage, A. (2017). Bias is the enemy of science. [Presentation]. *Speech presented at the March for Science*. San Francisco, CA. In Betsy Maury (Ed.), *The reference shelf: Representative American speeches 2016-2017* (pp. 149-151). Ipswich, MA: H.W. Wilson. (Original work published 2017)

Flake Announces Senate Future

By Jeff Flake

Republican Senator Jeff Flake announced his retirement on the Senate floor and used the opportunity to publicly level criticism at President Trump and his administration. Flake railed against "the personal attacks, the threats against principles, freedoms, and institutions, the flagrant disregard for truth or decency, the reckless provocations, most often for the pettiest and most personal reasons, reasons having nothing whatsoever to do with the fortunes of the people that we have all been elected to serve." Hailed by news outlets as "the most important speech of 2017," Flake spoke for 17 minutes about the need to change public discourse in Washington and specifically targeted the commander in chief for setting a poor example in his behavior. Flake spoke of the "reckless" leadership in the White House: "When such behavior emanates from the top of our government, it's something else: a danger to our democracy."

Mr. President, I rise today to address a matter that has been much on my mind, at a moment when it seems that our democracy is more defined by our discord and our dysfunction than it is by our values and our principles. Let me begin by noting a somewhat obvious point that these offices that we hold are not ours to hold indefinitely. We are not here simply to mark time. Sustained incumbency is certainly not the point of seeking office. And there are times when we must risk our careers in favor of our principles.

Now is such a time.

It must also be said that I rise today with no small measure of regret. Regret, because of the state of our disunion, regret because of the disrepair and destructiveness of our politics, regret because of the indecency of our discourse, regret because of the coarseness of our leadership, regret for the compromise of our moral authority, and by our—all of our—complicity in this alarming and dangerous state of affairs. It is time for our complicity and our accommodation of the unacceptable to end.

In this century, a new phrase has entered the language to describe the accommodation of a new and undesirable order—that phrase being "the new normal." But we must never adjust to the present coarseness of our national dialogue—with the tone set at the top.

We must never regard as "normal" the regular and casual undermining of our democratic norms and ideals. We must never meekly accept the daily sundering of our country—the personal attacks, the threats against principles, freedoms, and

---

Delivered on October 24, 2017 to the US Senate, Washington, DC.

institutions, the flagrant disregard for truth or decency, the reckless provocations, most often for the *pettiest* and most personal reasons, reasons having nothing whatsoever to do with the fortunes of the people that we have all been elected to serve.

None of these appalling features of our current politics should ever be regarded as normal. We must never allow ourselves to lapse into thinking that this is just the way things are now. If we simply become inured to this condition, thinking that this is just politics as usual, then heaven help us. Without fear of the consequences, and without consideration of the rules of what is politically safe or palatable, we must stop pretending that the degradation of our politics and the conduct of some in our executive branch are normal. They are not normal.

Reckless, outrageous, and undignified behavior has become excused and countenanced as "telling it like it is," when it is actually just reckless, outrageous, and undignified.

And when such behavior emanates from the top of our government, it is something else: It is dangerous to a democracy. Such behavior does not project strength—because our strength comes from our values. It instead projects a corruption of the *spirit*, and weakness.

It is often said that children are watching. Well, they are. And what are we going to do about that? When the next generation asks us, Why didn't you do something? Why didn't you speak up?—What are we going to say?

Mr. President, I rise today to say: Enough. We must dedicate ourselves to making sure that the anomalous never becomes normal. With respect and humility, I must say that we have fooled ourselves for long enough that a pivot to governing is right around the corner, a return to civility and stability right behind it. We know better than that. By now, we all know better than that.

Here, today, I stand to say that we would better serve the country and better fulfill our obligations under the Constitution by adhering to our Article 1 "old normal"—Mr. Madison's doctrine of the separation of powers. This genius innovation which affirms Madison's status as a true visionary and for which Madison argued in Federalist 51—held that the equal branches of our government would balance and counteract each other when necessary. "Ambition counteracts ambition," he wrote.

But what happens if ambition fails to counteract ambition? What happens if stability fails to assert itself in the face of chaos and instability? If decency fails to call out indecency? Were the shoe on the other foot, would we Republicans meekly accept such behavior on display from dominant Democrats? Of course not, and we would be wrong if we did.

When we remain silent and fail to act when we know that that silence and inaction is the wrong thing to do—because of political considerations, because we might make enemies, because we might alienate the base, because we might provoke a primary challenge, because ad infinitum, ad nauseam—when we succumb to those considerations in spite of what should be greater considerations and imperatives in defense of the institutions of our liberty, then we dishonor our principles and forsake our obligations. Those things are far more important than politics.

Now, I am aware that more politically savvy people than I caution against such talk. I am aware that a segment of my party believes that anything short of complete and unquestioning loyalty to a president who belongs to my party is unacceptable and suspect.

If I have been critical, it not because I relish criticizing the behavior of the president of the United States. If I have been critical, it is because I believe that it is my obligation to do so, as a matter of duty and conscience. The notion that one should stay silent as the norms and values that keep America strong *are* undermined and as the alliances and agreements that ensure the stability of the entire world are routinely threatened by the level of thought that goes into 140 characters—the notion that one should say and do nothing in the face of such mercurial behavior is *ahistoric* and, I believe, profoundly misguided.

A Republican president named Roosevelt had this to say about the president and a citizen's relationship to the office:

"The President is merely the most important among a large number of public servants. He should be supported or opposed exactly to the degree which is warranted by his good conduct or bad conduct, his efficiency or inefficiency in rendering loyal, able, and disinterested service to the nation as a whole. Therefore, it is absolutely necessary that there should be full *liberty* to tell the truth about his acts, and this means that it is exactly as necessary to blame him when he does wrong as to praise him when he does right. Any other attitude in an American citizen is both base and servile." President Roosevelt continued. "To announce that there must be no criticism of the President, or that we are to stand by the President, right or wrong, is not only unpatriotic and *servile*, but is morally treasonable to the American public."

Acting on conscience and principle is the manner in which we express our moral selves, and as such, loyalty to conscience and principle should supersede loyalty to any man or party. We can all be forgiven for failing in that measure from time to time. I certainly put myself at the top of the list of those who fall short in that regard. I am holier-than-none. But too often, we rush not to salvage principle but to forgive and excuse our failures so that we might accommodate them and go right on failing—until the accommodation itself becomes our principle.

In that way and over time, we can justify almost any behavior and sacrifice almost any principle. I'm afraid that is where we now find ourselves.

When a leader correctly identifies real hurt and insecurity in our country and instead of addressing it goes looking for somebody to blame, there is perhaps nothing more devastating to a pluralistic society. Leadership knows that most often a good place to start in assigning blame is to first look somewhat closer to home. Leadership knows where the buck stops. Humility helps. Character counts. Leadership does not knowingly encourage or feed ugly and debased appetites in us.

Leadership lives by the American creed: E Pluribus Unum. From many, one. American leadership looks to the world, and just as Lincoln did, sees the family of man. Humanity is not a zero-sum game. When we have been at our most prosperous, we have also been at our most principled. And when we do well, the rest of the world also does well.

These articles of civic faith have been central to the American identity for as long as we have all been alive. They are our birthright and our obligation. We must guard them jealously, and pass them on for as long as the calendar has days. To betray them, or to be unserious in their defense is a betrayal of the fundamental obligations of American leadership. And to behave as if they don't matter is simply not who we are.

Now, the efficacy of American leadership around the globe has come into question. When the United States emerged from World War II we contributed about half of the world's economic activity. It would have been easy to secure our dominance, keeping the countries that had been defeated or greatly weakened during the war in their place. We didn't do that. It would have been easy to focus inward. We resisted those impulses. Instead, we financed *reconstruction* of shattered countries and created international organizations and institutions that have helped provide security and foster prosperity around the world for more than 70 years.

Now, it seems that we, the architects of this visionary rules-based world order that has brought so much freedom and prosperity, are the ones most eager to abandon it.

The implications of this abandonment are profound. And the beneficiaries of this rather radical departure in the American approach to the world are the ideological enemies of our values. Despotism loves a vacuum. And our allies are now looking elsewhere for leadership. Why are they doing this? None of this is normal. And what do we as United States Senators have to say about it?

The principles that underlie our politics, the values of our founding, are too vital to our identity and to our survival to allow them to be compromised by the requirements of politics. Because politics can make us silent when we should speak, and silence can equal complicity.

I have children and grandchildren to answer to, and so, Mr. President, I will not be complicit.

I have decided that I will be better able to represent the people of Arizona and to better serve my country and my conscience by freeing myself from the political considerations that consume far too much bandwidth and would cause me to compromise far too many principles.

To that end, I am announcing today that my service in the Senate will conclude at the end of my term in early January 2019.

It is clear at this moment that a traditional conservative who believes in limited government and free markets, who is devoted to free trade, and who is pro-immigration, has a narrower and narrower path to *nomination* in the Republican party—the party that for so long has defined itself by belief in those things. It is also clear to me for the moment we have given in or given up on those core principles in favor of the more viscerally satisfying anger and resentment. To be clear, the anger and resentment that the people feel at the royal mess we have created are justified. But anger and resentment are not a governing philosophy.

There is an undeniable potency to a populist appeal—but mischaracterizing or misunderstanding our problems and giving in to the impulse to scapegoat and belittle threatens to turn us into a fearful, backward-looking people. In the case of the Republican party, those things also threaten to turn us into a fearful, backward-looking minority party.

We were not made great as a country by indulging or even exalting our worst impulses, turning against ourselves, glorying in the things which divide us, and calling fake things true and true things fake. And we did not become the beacon of freedom in the darkest corners of the world by flouting our institutions and failing to understand just how hard-won and vulnerable they are.

This spell will eventually break. That is my belief. We will return to ourselves once more, and I say the sooner the better. Because to have a healthy government we must have healthy and functioning parties. We must respect each other again in an atmosphere of shared facts and shared values, comity and good faith. We must argue our positions fervently, and never be afraid to compromise. We must assume the best of our fellow *man*, and always look for the good. Until that day comes, we must be unafraid to stand up and speak out as if our country depends on it. Because it does.

I plan to spend the remaining fourteen months of my *senate* term doing just that.

Mr. President, the graveyard is full of indispensable men and women—none of us here is indispensable. Nor were even the great figures from history who toiled at these very desks in this very chamber to shape this country that we have inherited. What is indispensable are the values that they consecrated in Philadelphia and in this place, values which have endured and will endure for so long as men and women wish to remain free. What is indispensable is what we do here in defense of those values. A political career doesn't mean much if we are complicit in undermining those values.

I thank my colleagues for indulging me here today, and will close by borrowing the words of President Lincoln, who knew more about healing enmity and preserving our founding values than any other American who has ever lived. His words from his first inaugural were a prayer in his time, and are no less so in ours: "We are not enemies, but friends. We must not be enemies. Though passion may have strained, it must not break our bonds of affection. The mystic chords of memory will swell when again touched, as surely they will be, by the better angels of our nature."

Thank you, Mr. President. I yield the floor.

Print Citations

CMS: Flake, Jeff. "Flake Announces Senate Future." Speech presented at the US Senate, Washington, DC, October, 2017. In *The Reference Shelf: Representative American Speeches 2016-2017*, edited by Betsy Maury, 152-157. Ipswich, MA: H.W. Wilson, 2017.

MLA: Flake, Jeff. "Flake Announces Senate Future." US Senate. Washington, DC. October, 2017. Presentation. *The Reference Shelf: Representative American Speeches 2016-2017*. Ed. Betsy Maury. Ipswich: H.W. Wilson, 2017. 152-157. Print.

APA: Flake, J. (2017). Flake announces Senate future. [Presentation]. *Speech presented at the US Senate*. Washington, DC. In Betsy Maury (Ed.), *The reference shelf: Representative American speeches 2016-2017* (pp. 152-157). Ipswich, MA: H.W. Wilson. (Original work published 2017)

5
Free Speech on Campus

A protester holds a sign during a demonstration outside of Zellerbach Hall on the U.C. Berkeley campus on September 14, 2017 in Berkeley, California. Police are out in force as protesters assemble where conservative political commentator Ben Shapiro is scheduled to speak.

Say No to Campus Thuggery

By Ben Shapiro

Daily Wire *editor-in-chief and former* Breitbart News *editor Ben Shapiro addresses a crowd at the University of California, Berkeley. Shapiro, an outspoken conservative political commentator attacked both political extremes on campus, the hard-left— as exemplified by Antifa—and the alt-right, though many of his controversial views aligned with the group that invited him, the Berkeley College Republicans. The speech titled, "Say No to Campus Thuggery," was also a call for Americans to see each other as individuals, rather than as members of various identity groups, and was also threaded with one of Shapiro's constant themes: the need for people to stop viewing themselves as victims and take control of their own lives.*

Thank you. Thank you so much. I only wish the administration had allowed us to fill up the rest of these seats, which we certainly would have.

One fan shouted out, "I love you, Ben!" Shapiro responded, "Love you right back!"

First of all, I have to thank Berkeley; I have to say, conservatives have done something amazing; they have achieved something incredible: if you look outside there is K-bar everywhere, they've built, basically these structures that keep Antifa from invading the premises. So that means that Berkeley has actually achieved building a wall before Donald Trump did.

Thank you all for being here, because obviously braving the idiots outside is not always easy: their speech is apparently violence, because my speech is violence, all speech is violence, so thank you for braving the slings and arrows of outrageous fortune by walking into a building. Congratulations to you.

Thanks to Fred Allen; thanks to Young America's Foundation, and the Berkeley College Republicans for their courage.

Thanks to the police; thank you to the police, who have done an amazing job.

These are the folks who stand between civilization and lawlessness. I saw the videos of business owners having to shutter up their windows today early; Bank of America blocking off its ATMs because they were afraid Antifa was going to break them, the only people who are standing between those ATMs and Antifa are the police, and all they get from the Left is a bunch of crap. That's all they get from the Left, but these are the heroes who stand between us and darkness, so thank them.

So I have a few other thank-you's: I want to say thank you to the morons who put up that sign across the way that says, "We say no to your white supremacist

---

Delivered on September 14, 2017 at the University of California, Berkeley, CA.

bullshit." I say thank you because I also say no to white supremacist bullshit. And if you stick around long enough in this speech, you will hear me do exactly that. The problem is I also say no to your identity-politics bullshit.

Thanks to Antifa, and the supposed anti-Fascist brigade, for exposing what the radical Left truly is; all of America is watching because you guys are so stupid. It's horrifying, I am grateful, and you can all go to hell, you pathetic, lying, stupid jack-asses. (applause)

The same goes for the mayor of this city, who has suggested that Antifa occasionally be given free rein over this city, and that conservatives should go home, because "we wouldn't want to provoke violence."

I do want to actually thank the administration for making the effort to put on this event tonight; there were a lot of obstacles, and I'll talk about the obstacles in a little bit, but they did attempt to make the effort, and they did unshackle the police to actually protect this. Thank you to the administration for doing that.

I saw a lot of headlines on the way here about how it was going to cost $600,000 in security for this event. And that is not due to me—I'm not the one out threatening to break windows; it's not due to you—you're here listening; it's due to the Antifa hard-Left morons who are out there breaking windows. And I do want to say one thing, which is that in a city as Left as Berkeley, if you're going to blame me for the $600,000 in spending on security, you're all Keynesians: think of all the jobs I just created.

Now, this lecture is titled, "Say No to Campus Thuggery." That's the title of the lecture because of Antifa and the wave of violence that has engulfed this campus since earlier this year. I spoke here last year, some of you may remember; I was here last year. I spoke in February 2016 here.

Nothing. It was a packed house; I had two security guards; that was it. No violence, no nothing, and now we are spending well into six figures so that I can say many of the same things.

It's utterly absurd. It's utterly absurd. But things have changed. Well, why have they changed?

It's because there's a pathetic new movement arising all over the country, from Sacramento to Berkeley to Dallas to Charlottesville. That movement says that speech is violence, and must be treated as such. This is groups like Refuse Fascism, (don't worry, we'll get to the alt-right later), this is groups like Refuse Fascism, which professes to promote protest, but has actually said that it won't rule out working with groups like Antifa.

Here is the poster that they put out earlier about me. I don't know who designs their posters, but guys, this is too many words. (laughter)

Bad logo and bad imagery, just poorly done.

They say on this that the problem isn't "campus thuggery." If you can't see this, it says, "No, Ben Shapiro, the problem is not campus thuggery. The problem is fascist intellectual thuggery in the service of the Trump/Pence fascist regime."

Well, to believe this you have to have your head so far up your ass you can actually see your own colon firsthand. (laughter)

Let's define a few terms: first of all, "Fascism intellectual thuggery." What actually is fascism? It's a term that gets thrown around a lot by people who have never read a book. Fascism is the phenomenon whereby people believe that they have the capacity to ram their beliefs down your throat at the point of a gun or say the point of a baton or by throwing Molotov cocktails. That's what fascism truly is. Fascism is more of a tactic than it is an ideology. It's sort of vague in terms of ideology; there are people on the Left who are fascist, people like Stalin, and then you've had people who are on the European Right, like Hitler, who was fascist, who was actually closer to the traditional American Left than he would be to the traditional American Right.

But I have been spending my entire career standing up against fascism, and the idea that an overreaching government that uses the power of the gun in order to compel people to do what they want.

Antifa is fascist; I am not a fascist.

And as far as the service to the Trump/Pence "fascist regime," first of all, I just want to note something: for all the talk about Trump and Pence being fascist, look at the protests outside: where is Orange Hitler shutting it down? He's nowhere to be found. This idea that we're living in a fascist country—we're actually living under a relatively ineffectual administration, if anything, but the idea that we're living in some sort of fascist dystopia is utterly absurd.

As far as the idea that I'm a white supremacist in service to Trump-Pence, couple problems there: one, as far as the service to Trump-Pence, again, I didn't vote for Trump, or Hillary; I didn't vote for either of them, actually, so this idea that I am somehow a servant of Trump is absurd and requires you to be functionally illiterate.

As far as the idea that I'm a white supremacist, you see the thing on the top of my head? (Shapiro bent forward so the audience could see his yarmulke.) This funny hat? It's called a yarmulke. White supremacists aren't that fond of it, which is why I was, according to the Anti-Defamation League, the number one recipient of white supremacist anti-Semitism on the internet among journalists in 2016.

But no, I'm a white supremacist now; because this is the way the Left works: if you don't agree with them, everyone is a white supremacist. You're a Nazi, Nazis should be punched, and therefore it's totally fine to stand outside and try to shut down events if you can get away with it. They're not getting away with it tonight because the police have been allowed to actually do their jobs. (applause)

So what is their specific objection to me? Well, according to this masterfully-done poster, it says, "Shapiro is coming to campus to spread ugly fascist views dressed up in slick-talking 'intellectual' garb."

I do like the "slick-talking." (laughter)

He continued quoting the flyer: "This is harmful! He, along with fascists of many stripes, have targeted Berkeley because reversing Berkeley's radical history would be a major advance for the consolidation of fascism on campuses everywhere and throughout society."

The reason I'm here—I've been asked this a lot—the reason that I am here is because fascism does *not* own this university. Because there are students who *do* want to hear differing views. Who *don't* want to be told that they can only hear one view. Who *don't* believe that the First Amendment should die under the jackboots and Birkenstocks of a bunch of anarchist, communist pieces of garbage. (applause)

But I don't just want to talk about the people who actually get violent, because I think that in a civil society this is one thing we should all agree on, and I've been pleased to see that even people like Nancy Pelosi have condemned Antifa; Nancy Pelosi, with whom I disagree on literally every issue it is possible to disagree on, including the proper use of Botox.

But she and I agree on this. We all agree that violence should be out-of-bounds, and if you're on the Left and you don't agree with that, let me suggest to you that you don't belong living in a civilized society, because a civilized society is based on the premise that the government has a monopoly on the legitimate use of force, as Max Weber put it, and the idea that you're supposed to violate that if you don't like what I'm saying makes you an uncivilized barbarian.

But it's not just that that I want to talk about; I want to talk about an ideology that goes a little bit deeper than that.

Antifa couldn't go anywhere without an ideology that runs broader than Antifa, without a group of people willing to look the other way. What is the view that undergirds Antifa? What is the view that undergirds the hard-Left, many of whom celebrate Antifa, or were doing so until it became politically unpalatable to do so?

It's a view that America is a terrible, horrible, no-good, very bad place.

Now the truth is that America is an incredible place. It's the greatest place in the history of the world. The freest, most prosperous country, the most tolerant country in the history of planet Earth. (applause)

This country is an amazing place full of opportunity. Nobody, by and large, cares enough about you to stop you from achieving your dreams. That includes you, people who are shouting out there in the audience. No one cares about you; get over yourselves. I don't care about you; no one cares about you; no one is trying to stop you because you're irrelevant to me. I have a wife and two children; I care about them. I don't care about you. You don't mean anything to me. (laughter)

That means, in a free country, if you fail, it's probably your own fault. If it is somebody else's fault, if somebody is actually trying to throw up obstacles in front of you in a way that is unjust and bigoted, point out the specific instance so we can all side with you. We all want to be on the same side. We all want to help out; when somebody is a racist and trying to stop you, we all want to sound off and stop that, too.

The idea, however, that America as a whole owns your failure when you can't point to specific problems, does not wash. It is you shifting the buck.

It's a waste of time and energy blaming your failures on "the system" unless you've got some evidence. But, unfortunately, on college campuses, and for the Left more broadly, there's been this notion that America is bad, and the reason that you fail is because America has historically been very bad. This is the identity politics of the Left. Because America is bad in that it targets you. America targets you, and we have an entire hierarchy of intersectionality that's been built by the Left to tell you whether your views are legitimate or not; the more victimized you are the more legitimate your views are.

So, the hierarchy goes something like this: the people whose views are most valuable and been most victimized. At the very top are people who are LGBT, and then you get black people, and then you get women, and then you get Hispanic people, and then you get Native Americans, and then you get Asians, and then you get Jews—Jews may be above Asians, maybe Jews—then Asians, and at the very, very bottom, you get straight white males. Those are the people who have nothing to say about anything because obviously they are the beneficiaries of this "white-privilege" system.

Now, the logic of intersectionality, because it suggests that the value of your opinion lies in your ethnic identity and your group identity, the idea is that if I attack your ideas, if I say that you have bad ideas, what I am really doing is attacking you personally; I'm really attacking your identity. I'm "aggressing" you. You might require counseling. (laughter)

This is the philosophy of microaggressions: my words are violence. Even the term "microaggression" suggests that it is an "aggression" against you; "microaggressions," I am "aggressing" you; it's an act of violence.

As NYU social psychologist Jonathan Haidt has said, "Microaggressions are small actions or word choices that seem on their face to have no malicious intent but that are thought of as a kind of violence nonetheless." The thing is, you don't actually have to intend to offend anyone to "microaggress" them; they just have to feel offended.

And the thing is that "microaggressions" are actual violence. This is why you see the dolts outside shouting that speech is violence, because they think that I am actually doing them violence when they don't hear me. But if they would hear me, then presumably I would be doing them violence and they would need counseling, and if they act with violence it's because it's in response.

And unfortunately, this university engages in precisely this sort of damaging attitude; so at the same time they are willing to allow the police to fight Antifa, they are fostering an attitude that says that certain types of speech are violence, which is the gas in the tank for groups like Antifa, it's the gas in the tank for the hard-Left.

Before my arrival, the university obviously put in place all sorts of security measures to stop people from getting violent, which is great. But they also put out a letter; and they put out a letter to all the students here, and here's what it said: it said that I was a threat, because they were going to offer "Support and counseling services for students, staff and faculty. We are deeply concerned about the impact some speakers may have on individuals' sense of safety and belonging."

He continued reading: "No one should be made to feel threatened or harassed simply because of who they are or what they believe," then pointed at himself, drawing laughter from the crowd.

He finished quoting, "For that reason, the following support services are being offered and encouraged."

And they offer employee support services, student support services. You see, I'm attacking your identity if we disagree about politics and you may require counseling. By the way, just a side note: if you require counseling because of this speech, let me suggest to you that it was a mistake for you to have foregone psychiatric treatment long ago. (applause)

I know, I'm super scary; look at me, I'm physically intimidating, as everyone knows. I understand; you're afraid I'm going to turn into the Hulk and ruin your life. But the truth is I think that you're big boys and girls and you can probably handle it. I assume you're not all a bunch of weaklings and pansies and snowflakes. That may not be a fair assumption, but I will assume it for the sake of this argument.

I assume you can handle disagreement. If, in fact, you cannot handle disagreement, you are making your life harder, and you are making your life worse, and you are making the country worse. You're driving political polarization by failing to engage on a level of discussion. As you know, we're going to do a Q&A after this, and I love taking questions. It's my favorite thing, and I have a rule which is if you disagree with me, you raise your hand and you go to the front of the line, because discussion makes the country better. (applause)

But you feeling insulted and then whining about it, and then suggesting that you're a victim, without evidence, and that I have victimized you because I won't accept your victimhood? This makes the country a worse place.

So I want to go briefly through a couple of the intersectional hierarchy groups, people who feel that they are victims in American society and explain why you are not, in fact, a victim; why you need to take control of your own life and become an adult.

So let's start with the idea that poor people in America are victimized. This is sort of the Bernie Sanders case: income inequality is the root of all evil. This is Antifa's case: that communism or anarchism would be a better solution then say, a free and civil society that's raised half the world out of abject poverty.

Income equality is not the big problem; nobody rich is making you poor. Bill Gates did not make you poor; Bill Gates provided you a product and if you bought it, that is your fault.

The upper middle class grew from 12% of Americans in 1979 to 30% as of 2014. That is a massive growth in the upper middle class. The rich are not making you poorer, they are paying your salary.

American income mobility, by the way, is just as strong as European countries with far more redistribution. Income mobility drops only when you drop out of high school or you have a baby out of wedlock. This is what makes you poor.

How about the idea that if you're black in America there's a white supremacist hierarchy that is keeping you down?

Now listen, you'd be a fool not to acknowledge, or a liar, not to acknowledge the history of racism in America. Everybody acknowledges that, if you have half a brain. Of course. Slavery, Jim Crow. Awful, evil treatment at the hands of awful, evil people. We all acknowledge this; we all acknowledge the collective sin of the

United States in promulgating this, and the individual sins, more importantly, of the people who actually promulgated this stuff. We all get that.

But that's not what we're talking about. Now we're talking about now. Because I wasn't born when Jim Crow was in place; I wasn't an adult when Jim Crow was in place. I know that I'm not a racist and I know I haven't acted in a racist manner, and I would bet you money that the people in this room haven't acted in a racist manner, that they haven't held slaves, or voted for Jim Crow. I will bet you money that is the case. (applause)

You cannot fix past injustices with current injustices. The only way to fix past injustices is with individual freedom. That's it.

The idea that black people in the United States are disproportionately poor because America is racist; that's just not true, at least not in terms of America's racism today keeping black people down. It's just not the case. If that were the case then you'd have to look at group income, and decide based on group income who's been victimized the most, and who the country was built for. By that standard, the country was built by Asians, because the racial group with the highest median income in the United States is Asians. The Constitution was not written by a bunch of people who speak Korean. Because the Constitution is a document of freedom, not a document of ethnicity.

So here are the three rules. You want to be rich in America; you want to do well in America? You want to put aside the whining about the system? Again, you point out to me an individual instance of racism, I will stand next to you and fight it, but if you whine about America? No good.

Okay. Here are the three rules that you need to fulfill as a person before you can start complaining about your life failures being the result of somebody else's actions. Number one, you need to finish high school. Number two: you need to get married before you have babies. Number three: You need to get a job.

That's it. You do those things you will not be permanently poor in the United States of America. (applause)

According to the Brookings Institute, 2% of Americans who followed these rules are in poverty. 75% have joined the middle class. What about racism? 71% of poor families with children are unmarried. The poverty rate among non-married white families was 22% in 2008; that same year the poverty rate among black married couples was less than 7%.

But what happened to racism? Why weren't those black married couples poorer than the single white moms? Because it doesn't have to do with color; it has to do with life decisions.

We can talk about differentials in crime, and where these statistics come from. The basic rule is: If you don't commit a crime, you're not going to be arrested for it. The police are not going around arresting black people for the fun of it. They're going around arresting criminals based on criminal reports, which is why the number of criminal reports, based on race, matches up exactly with the number of criminal arrests, based on race. If you don't report people for crime, it's hard for the police to know to pick them up.

How about women, this idea that women are vastly victimized in our society? Hillary Clinton is making beaucoup dollars off of this nonsense this week. As I tweeted earlier this week, this week we found out that a clown can emerge from the woods and scare half of Americans, and also "*It*" came out. (laughter, applause)

Hillary Clinton is going around whining about there's a glass ceiling, and she couldn't break through it, and it's all because of sexism, it's not because she was the world's worst candidate and a pretty appalling human being; no, it was because everybody is a sexist. Everybody is a sexist. We hear in this context very much about the "wage gap," the idea that women are paid significantly less than man, 72 cents on the dollar. That's absolute sheer nonsense, it is absolute nonsense. In 147 out of 150 of the biggest cities in America, women make 8% more than men do in their peer group. That wage gap is growing, not shrinking

At colleges, 55% of people in colleges are women; that gap is getting larger, not smaller; 58% of all graduate degrees go to women. The majority of voters are women. If we are living in a place where women are vastly victimized by men, I'd really like to see that place.

And as far as this idea that there's a vast rape epidemic going on on campus, every rape, as I've said a thousand times, every rape should be dealt with by the prosecution of the rapist, ending with their jailing, castration, or death. That's how I feel about rape. (applause)

But this nonsense statistic that's been presented that one in five women on college campuses is being raped is not true. It's just not true. The actual statistic, according to the Department of Justice, is something like one in every 58; obviously far too high, but not one in five. If it were one in five, by the way, if you're a woman at this campus, you should go to your parents and ask them what kind of nuts they are to send you in a war zone where you're likely to be raped.

How about the idea that gays and lesbians are really living under the boot of American society? In terms of income they certainly aren't; certainly not in terms of income: Women in lesbian couples make far more money than women in straight couples do. Men in gay couples make slightly less than men in straight couples, but same-sex couples with both partners in the labor force make $8,000 more per year than straight couples, and they are typically higher educated.

So that talks about the identity politics, this intersectional hierarchy of the Left.

But there's another group of people that engages in identity politics that I want to talk about now. And it's the battle between the identity politics of the Left and the identity politics of the so-called alt-right that is making the country a significantly worse place and it needs to stop now because it is utter and complete horrible bullshit. (applause)

The first thing to note: this notion that the alt-right is actually conservative is nonsense. Let me define what I mean by alt-right, because not everybody who likes Pepe memes or Harambe memes is a member of the alt-right. Not everybody that the Left says is alt-right is actually alt-right. The Left calls me alt-right, which is patently insane. You legitimately have to have a screw loose to call me alt-right; I spend half my career attacking the alt-right.

What is the alt-right? The alt-right are a group of people who believe that ideology and ethnicity are inextricably intertwined, just like the identity politics Left. On the identity politics Left, if you're a black person who is a leftist, you're a leftist because you're a black person. On the identity politics Right, Western civilization was not built by people with good ideas, it was built by people with white skin. And that means that people who don't have white skin cannot properly assimilate into Western civilization. This has no grounding in reality. The fact is that there are lots of white people in Britain before the Romans arrived, and they weren't living a civilized life, as we would currently call it, under Western civilization.

In fact, the people who—the Romans, when Italians were coming to the United States in the early part of the 20th century, there was tremendous discrimination against Italians because they weren't considered properly white. The definition of white moves around a lot, based on convenience. Sometimes Jews are white, sometimes Jews are not white; it sort of depends on what you're talking about. But according to the alt-right, because ideology and race are inextricably intertwined, they must have a white identity politics all their own. If there's a group of people who are fighting for the group identity politics of blacks or of women, or of gays and lesbians, then there has to be a white group that fights back on behalf of the white race.

As you may have noticed, I think all of this is disgusting. Western civilization is not built on race. There have been lots of countries all over Europe that were not particularly civilized and were quite white. Freedom, personal responsibility, separation of powers, God-given rights protected by a government elected with the consent of the governed—these are the values of Western civilization.

But the alt-right overtly rejects these ideas. They say the Constitution is outmoded, that it doesn't work. They say that government for white people is necessary and good, because you can't assimilate people into so-called "white culture." They hang out with neo-Nazis because a lot of them actually believe some of the same things neo-Nazis believe: white supremacy.

Let's be straight about this: this is, like 10,000 people across the country. This is not a million people; this is not ten million people; this is not 63 million people; this is not 200 million "deplorables." It's a very small select group of absolutely terrible people who believe absolutely terrible things.

But they're getting a lot of attention and coverage right now, because we live in a reactionary moment. A lot of the people are reacting to the identity politics of the Left by making nice with the alt-right. There's this weird notion on the Right that if you drink leftist tears that's enough. Drinking leftist tears is enough.

So if the alt-right ticks off the Left, they're fine. It's disgusting. It's disgusting. I have no other word for it. (applause)

It is not enough to stand against bad ideologies; you must also stand for a good ideology. You must stand for a good philosophy. You cannot stand with bad people just because you think those bad people make your enemies cry. The enemy of your enemy in a country where we're all supposed to be friends is not only bad strategy, it destroys the country wholesale. (applause)

So, how do we solve all this? We're on campus, and we're hearing the identity politics of the Left, and then you watch the news and you see the identity politics of the alt-right. How do you solve all of this?

Well, the way that you solve all of this, first of all, let's start with the campus thuggery, the way that you solve all of this is by letting the police do their jobs. Administrators need to let the police do their jobs. None of this would have gone anywhere if back in February, when Milo [Yiannopoulos], whom I significantly dislike, when Milo came to speak, if they had allowed the police to do their jobs, and arrest everyone who even hinted at violence. People who get violent should be arrested and they should spend time in jail, and the authorities have a responsibility to allow the police to do their jobs. (applause)

And this is not the fault of the cops; this is the fault of cowardly political actors, pusillanimous cowards who hide behind their desks every time some people on the Left whine a little bit.

The second thing that has to happen: you have to stop seeing everybody in America as an enemy who despises you based on identity. Again, they don't care about you; you're not that important a human. Not that many of us know each other; not that many of us care about each other; we care about our families; we care about our friends; and we certainly don't want to stop each other. We mostly want to be treated civilly, and we can all do that if we stop looking into each other's eyes and seeing a potential enemy instead of seeing somebody who's just a person, a person who probably doesn't care about you very much, and doesn't want to stop you and doesn't mind what you do. This is not difficult stuff.

And finally, stop seeing yourself as a victim, because in order to see everybody else as an enemy, which justifies your violence and hate against them, you have to see yourself as their victim.

Again: America is the greatest country in human history. You are not a victim. If you are a victim of something, you need to show me what you are a victim of and I will stand beside you. But do not blame the freest, most civil society in the history of planet Earth for your failures, because that's on you. (applause)

Now, was that so rough? Did we need $600,000 of security to hear all of that? I have a feeling that the majority of people protesting the speech have never heard of me. I'm not arrogant enough to believe that Antifa sits around watching Thug Life videos. (laughter)

If they did, I doubt they would be members of Antifa. (laughter)

But the idea that they're out there protesting, they're out there maybe getting violent, apparently four people were arrested for carrying weapons already; the idea that all that is happening is indicative of the fact that we have stopped seeing each other as individuals. We are all individuals. I'm an individual with a particular point of view. I am not a cardboard cutout for you to call a white supremacist; I'm not a cardboard cutout for you to call a Nazi; and neither is anybody else in this room.

Get to know people. Get to know their views. Discuss. Debate. That is what America is all about. (applause)

If we all do that, I do think that America can see a better day, because I think we're in a dark moment right now, but I think we can get to a brighter moment if we stop seeing each other as members of groups and identifying as members of groups, primarily, and instead see each other as individuals, made in God's image, one with equal value to another in God's eyes. If we do that, America will see a resurgence.

Thank you so much.

Print Citations

CMS: Shapiro, Ben. "Say No to Campus Thuggery." Speech presented at the University of California, Berkeley, CA, September, 2017. In *The Reference Shelf: Representative American Speeches 2016-2017*, edited by Betsy Maury, 161-171. Ipswich, MA: H.W. Wilson, 2017.

MLA: Shapiro, Ben. "Say No to Campus Thuggery." University of California. Berkeley, CA. September, 2017. Presentation. October, 2016. *The Reference Shelf: Representative American Speeches 2016-2017*. Ed. Betsy Maury. Ipswich: H.W. Wilson, 2017. 161-171. Print.

APA: Shapiro, B. (2017). Say no to campus thuggery. [Presentation]. Speech presented at the University of California. Berkeley, CA. In Betsy Maury (Ed.), *The reference shelf: Representative American speeches 2016-2017* (pp. 161-171). Ipswich, MA: H.W. Wilson. (Original work published 2017)

Statement on Truth-Seeking, Democracy, and Freedom of Thought and Expression

By Robert P. George and Cornel West

Robert P. George and Cornel West, two ideologically opposed academics jointly issue a statement on free speech on college campus. George, McCormick Professor of Jurisprudence and director of the James Madison Program in American Ideals and Institutions at Princeton University, is one of the country's most prominent conservative intellectuals. West, a professor of the practice of public philosophy and African and African-American studies at Harvard University, is a self-described "radical Democrat." George and West published a statement in support of "truth-seeking, democracy, and freedom of thought and expression." It's a politely worded denunciation of what the professors call "campus illiberalism," or the brand of thinking that led to this month's incident at Middlebury College, where students prevented an invited speaker from talking and a professor was attacked physically by some who were protesting the invitation.

The pursuit of knowledge and the maintenance of a free and democratic society require the cultivation and practice of the virtues of intellectual humility, openness of mind, and, above all, love of truth. These virtues will manifest themselves and be strengthened by one's willingness to listen attentively and respectfully to intelligent people who challenge one's beliefs and who represent causes one disagrees with and points of view one does not share.

That's why all of us should seek respectfully to engage with people who challenge our views. And we should oppose efforts to silence those with whom we disagree—especially on college and university campuses. As John Stuart Mill taught, a recognition of the possibility that we may be in error is a good reason to listen to and honestly consider—and not merely to tolerate grudgingly—points of view that we do not share, and even perspectives that we find shocking or scandalous. What's more, as Mill noted, even if one happens to be right about this or that disputed matter, seriously and respectfully engaging people who disagree will deepen one's understanding of the truth and sharpen one's ability to defend it.

None of us is infallible. Whether you are a person of the left, the right, or the center, there are reasonable people of goodwill who do not share your fundamental convictions. This does not mean that all opinions are equally valid or that all speakers are equally worth listening to. It certainly does not mean that there is no truth to be discovered. Nor does it mean that you are necessarily wrong. But they are not

Delivered on March 14, 2017 at Princeton University, Princeton, NJ.

necessarily wrong either. So someone who has not fallen into the idolatry of worshiping his or her own opinions and loving them above truth itself will want to listen to people who see things differently in order to learn what considerations—evidence, reasons, arguments—led them to a place different from where one happens, at least for now, to find oneself.

All of us should be willing—even eager—to engage with anyone who is prepared to do business in the currency of truth-seeking discourse by offering reasons, marshaling evidence, and making arguments. The more important the subject under discussion, the more willing we should be to listen and engage—especially if the person with whom we are in conversation will challenge our deeply held—even our most cherished and identity-forming—beliefs.

It is all-too-common these days for people to try to immunize from criticism opinions that happen to be dominant in their particular communities. Sometimes this is done by questioning the motives and thus stigmatizing those who dissent from prevailing opinions; or by disrupting their presentations; or by demanding that they be excluded from campus or, if they have already been invited, disinvited. Sometimes students and faculty members turn their backs on speakers whose opinions they don't like or simply walk out and refuse to listen to those whose convictions offend their values. Of course, the right to peacefully protest, including on campuses, is sacrosanct. But before exercising that right, each of us should ask: Might it not be better to listen respectfully and try to learn from a speaker with whom I disagree? Might it better serve the cause of truth-seeking to engage the speaker in frank civil discussion?

Our willingness to listen to and respectfully engage those with whom we disagree (especially about matters of profound importance) contributes vitally to the maintenance of a milieu in which people feel free to speak their minds, consider unpopular positions, and explore lines of argument that may undercut established ways of thinking. Such an ethos protects us against dogmatism and groupthink, both of which are toxic to the health of academic communities and to the functioning of democracies.

Print Citations

CMS: George, Robert P., and Cornel West. "Statement on Truth-Seeking, Democracy, and Freedom of Thought and Expression." Statement presented at Princeton University, Princeton, NJ, March, 2017. In *The Reference Shelf: Representative American Speeches 2016-2017*, edited by Betsy Maury, 172-174. Ipswich, MA: H.W. Wilson, 2017.

MLA: George, Robert P., and Cornel West. "Statement on Truth-Seeking, Democracy, and Freedom of Thought and Expression." Princeton University. Princeton, NJ. March, 2017. Presentation. *The Reference Shelf: Representative American Speeches 2016-2017*. Ed. Betsy Maury. Ipswich: H.W. Wilson, 2017. 172-174. Print.

APA: George, R.P., & C. West. (2017). Statement on truth-seeking, democracy, and freedom of thought and expression. [Presentation]. *Statement presented at Princeton University*. Princeton, NJ. In Betsy Maury (Ed.), *The reference shelf: Representative American speeches 2016-2017* (pp. 172-174). Ipswich, MA: H.W. Wilson. (Original work published 2017)

Free Inquiry on Campus: A Statement of Principles

By Middlebury College Faculty

Following the incident of March 2, 2017, when roughly 100 Middlebury College stu-dents prevented a controversial visiting speaker, Dr. Charles Murray, from communicat-ing with his audience on the campus, professors delivered this joint statement of core principles. During the widely publicized incident, a group of unidentified assailants mobbed the speaker, and one faculty member was seriously injured. The statement was intended to outline a code of conduct for public discourse on college campuses in a free society.

On March 2, 2017, roughly 100 of our 2500 students prevented a controversial visiting speaker, Dr. Charles Murray, from communicating with his audience on the campus of Middlebury College. Afterwards, a group of unidentified assailants mobbed the speaker, and one of our faculty members was seriously injured. In view of these unacceptable acts, we have produced this document stating core principles that seem to us unassailable in the context of higher education within a free society.

These principles are as follows:

- Genuine higher learning is possible only where free, reasoned, and civil speech and discussion are respected.

- Only through the contest of clashing viewpoints do we have any hope of re-placing mere opinion with knowledge.

- The incivility and coarseness that characterize so much of American politics and culture cannot justify a response of incivility and coarseness on the col-lege campus.

- The impossibility of attaining a perfectly egalitarian sphere of free discourse can never justify efforts to silence speech and debate.

- Exposure to controversial points of view does not constitute violence.

- Students have the right to challenge and to protest non-disruptively the views of their professors and guest speakers.

- A protest that prevents campus speakers from communicating with their au-dience is a coercive act.

Delivered on March 7, 2017 at Middlebury College, Middlebury, VT.

- No group of professors or students has the right to act as final arbiter of the opinions that students may entertain.

- No group of professors or students has the right to determine for the entire community that a question is closed for discussion.

- The purpose of college is not to make faculty or students comfortable in their opinions and prejudices.

- The purpose of education is not the promotion of any particular political or social agenda.

- The primary purpose of higher education is the cultivation of the mind, thus allowing for intelligence to do the hard work of assimilating and sorting information and drawing rational conclusions.

- A good education produces modesty with respect to our own intellectual powers and opinions as well as openness to considering contrary views.

- All our students possess the strength, in head and in heart, to consider and evaluate challenging opinions from every quarter.

- We are steadfast in our purpose to provide all current and future students an education on this model, and we encourage our colleagues at colleges across the country to do the same.

Print Citations

CMS: Middlebury College Faculty. "Free Inquiry on Campus: A Statement of Principles." Statement presented at Middlebury College, Middlebury, VT, March, 2017. In *The Reference Shelf: Representative American Speeches 2016-2017*, edited by Betsy Maury, 175-176. Ipswich, MA: H.W. Wilson, 2017.

MLA: Middlebury College Faculty. "Free Inquiry on Campus: A Statement of Principles." Middlebury College. Middlebury, VT, March, 2017. Presentation. *The Reference Shelf: Representative American Speeches 2016-2017*. Ed. Betsy Maury. Ipswich: H.W. Wilson, 2017. 175-176. Print.

APA: Middlebury College faculty. (2017). Free inquiry on campus: A statement of principles. [Presentation]. *Statement presented at Middlebury College*. Middlebury, VT. In Betsy Maury (Ed.), *The reference shelf: Representative American speeches 2016-2017* (pp. 175-176). Ipswich, MA: H.W. Wilson. (Original work published 2017)

The Importance of Free Speech on College Campuses

By Jeff Sessions

Jeff Sessions, Attorney General of the United States, gave a speech at Georgetown University Law Center stressing the importance of free speech on campus. More than 100 students and faculty members protested Sessions' speech, saying they were not allowed in to hear it, despite there being empty seats. Citing incidents at schools from Boise State to Middlebury College, Sessions said American universities are "transforming into an echo chamber of political correctness and homogeneous thought, a shelter for fragile egos." Sessions announced that the Justice Department "will enforce federal law, defend free speech and protect students' free expression from whatever end of the political spectrum it may come."

Thank you for that kind introduction. I am so pleased to be here at Georgetown Law and to be speaking at the Georgetown Center for the Constitution where the exchange of ideas is both welcomed and encouraged. Thank you, Professor Barnett for that introduction and for hosting me here with your students. And thank you students for letting me take part in this important conversation with you.

As you embark on another school year, you and hundreds of your peers across this campus will, we hope, continue the intellectual journey that is higher education. You will discover new areas of knowledge; you will engage in debates great and small; many of your views will be challenged and some changed. You will—if your institutions follow our nation's historic cultural and education traditions—pursue truth while growing in mind and spirit. In short, we hope you will take part in the right of every American: the free, robust, and sometimes contentious exchange of ideas.

As you exercise these rights, realize how precious, how rare, and how fragile they are. In most societies throughout history and in so many that I have had the opportunity to visit, such rights do not exist. In these places, openly criticizing the government or expressing unorthodox opinions could land you in jail or worse.

Let me tell you about one such example. It occurred one autumn when a few idealistic university students came together as a group to advocate for a deeply felt political creed. Wanting to recruit others to their cause, they staked out some ground on a campus walkway popular with students and approached them as they passed.

Delivered on September 26, 2017 at Georgetown University, Washington, DC.

They said things like: "Do you like freedom? Do you like liberty?" and then they offered to these passersby a document they revered and believed stood for these ideals: the U.S. Constitution. These young proselytizers for liberty did not block the walkway, did not disrupt surrounding activities, and did not use intimidation or violence to press their cause.

Nevertheless, a local government official labeled this behavior "provocative" and in violation of government policy. When the young people bravely refused to stop, citing their right to free speech, the local official had them arrested, handcuffed, and jailed.

This troubling incident could have occurred under any number of tyrannies where the bedrock American ideals of freedom of thought and speech have no foothold. But this incident happened right here in the United States, just last year, at a public college in Battle Creek, Michigan. A state official actually had students jailed for handing out copies of the United States Constitution.

Freedom of thought and speech on the American campus are under attack.

The American university was once the center of academic freedom—a place of robust debate, a forum for the competition of ideas. But it is transforming into an echo chamber of political correctness and homogenous thought, a shelter for fragile egos.

In 2017, the Foundation for Individual Rights in Education surveyed 450 colleges and universities across the country and found that 40 percent maintain speech codes that substantially infringe on constitutionally protected speech. Of the public colleges surveyed, which are bound by the First Amendment, fully one-third had written policies banning disfavored speech.

For example, at Boise State University in Idaho, the Student Code of Conduct prohibits "[c]onduct that a reasonable person would find offensive." At Clemson University in South Carolina, the Student Code of Conduct bans any verbal or physical act that creates an "offensive educational, work or living environment."

But who decides what is offensive and what is acceptable? The university is about the search for truth, not the imposition of truth by a government censor.

Speech and civility codes violate what the late Justice Antonin Scalia rightly called "the first axiom of the First Amendment," which is that, "as a general rule, the state has no power to ban speech on the basis of its content." In this great land, the government does not get to tell you what to think or what to say.

In addition to written speech codes, many colleges now deign to "tolerate" free speech only in certain, geographically limited, "free speech zones." For example, a student recently filed suit against Pierce College, a public school in southern California, alleging that it prohibited him from distributing Spanish-language copies of the U.S. Constitution outside the school's free speech zone.

The size of this free speech zone? 616 square feet—an area barely the size of a couple of college dorm rooms. These cramped zones are eerily similar to what the Supreme Court warned against in the seminal 1969 *Tinker v. Des Moines* case about student speech: "Freedom of expression would not truly exist if the right could be exercised only in an area that a benevolent government has provided as a safe haven."

College administrators also have silenced speech by permitting "the heckler's veto" to control who gets to speak and what messages are conveyed. In these instances, administrators discourage or prohibit speech if there is even a threat that it will be met with protest. In other words, the school favors the heckler's disruptive tactics over the speaker's First Amendment rights. These administrators seem to forget that, as the Supreme Court put it in *Watson v. City of Memphis* more than 50 years ago, "constitutional rights may not be denied simply because of hostility to their assertion or exercise."

This permissive attitude toward the heckler's veto has spawned a cottage industry of protestors who have quickly learned that school administrators will capitulate to their demands.

Protestors are now routinely shutting down speeches and debates across the country in an effort to silence voices that insufficiently conform with their views.

A frightening example occurred this year at Middlebury College. Student protestors violently shut down a debate between an invited speaker and one of the school's own professors. As soon as the event began, the protestors shouted for 20 minutes, preventing the debate from occurring.

When the debaters attempted to move to a private broadcasting location, the protestors—many in masks, a common tactic also used by the detestable Ku Klux Klan—pulled fire alarms, surrounded the speakers, and began physically assaulting them. In short, Middlebury students engaged in a violent riot to ensure that neither they nor their fellow students would hear speech they may have disagreed with.

Indeed, the crackdown on speech crosses creeds, races, issues, and religions. At Brown University, a speech to promote transgender rights was cancelled after students protested because a Jewish group cosponsored the lecture. Virginia Tech disinvited an African American speaker because he had written on race issues and they worried about protests disrupting the event.

This is not right. This is not in the great tradition of America. And, yet, school administrators bend to this behavior. In effect, they coddle it and encourage it.

Just over a week ago, after the Orwellian-named "anti-fascist" protestors had successfully shut down numerous campus speaker events in recent months with violent riots, Berkeley was reportedly forced to spend more than $600,000 and have an overwhelming police presence simply to prove that the mob was not in control of the campus.

In advance, the school offered "counseling" to any students or faculty whose "sense of safety or belonging" was threatened by a speech from Ben Shapiro—a 33-year-old Harvard trained lawyer who has been frequently targeted by anti-Semites for his Jewish faith and who vigorously condemns hate speech on both the left and right.

In the end, Mr. Shapiro spoke to a packed house. And to my knowledge, no one fainted, no one was unsafe. No one needed counseling.

Yet, after this small victory for free speech, a student speaking to a reporter said in reaction, "I don't think Berkeley should host any controversial speakers, on either side." That is, perhaps, the worst lesson to take away from this episode.

I know that the vast majority of students like you at the Constitution Center need no lecture on the dangers of government-imposed group think. But we have seen a rash of incidents often perpetrated by small groups of those students and professors unable or unwilling to defend their own beliefs in the public forum.

Unfortunately, their acts have been tolerated by administrators and shrugged off by other students. So let us directly address the question: Why should we worry that free speech is in retreat at our universities?

Of course, for publicly run institutions, the easy answer is that upholding free speech rights is not an option, but an unshakable requirement of the First Amendment. As Justice Robert Jackson once explained: "If there is a fixed star in our constitutional constellation, it is that no official, high or petty, can prescribe what shall be orthodox in politics, nationalism, religion, or other matters of opinion."

But even setting aside the law, the more fundamental issue is that the university is supposed to be the place where we train virtuous citizens. It is where the next generation of Americans are equipped to contribute to and live in a diverse and free society filled with many, often contrary, voices.

Our legal heritage, upon which the Founders crafted the Bill of Rights, taught that reason and knowledge produced the closest approximation to truth—and from truth may arise justice. But reason requires discourse and, frequently, argument. And that is why the free speech guarantee is found not just in the First Amendment, but also permeates our institutions, our traditions, and our Constitution.

The jury trial, the right to cross-examine witnesses, the Speech & Debate Clause, the very art and practice of lawyering—all of these are rooted in the idea that speech, reason, and confrontation are the very bedrock of a good society. In fact, these practices are designed to ascertain what is the truth. And from that truth, good policies and actions can be founded.

The Federalists against the Anti-federalists, Abraham Lincoln against Stephen Douglas, Dr. Martin Luther King Jr. against George Wallace. Indeed, it was the power of Dr. King's words that crushed segregation and overcame the violence of the segregationists. At so many times in our history as a people, it was speech—and still more speech—that led Americans to a more just, more perfect union.

The right to freely examine the moral and the immoral, the prudent and the foolish, the practical and the inefficient, and the right to argue for their merits or demerits remain indispensable for a healthy republic. This has been known since the beginning of our nation.

James Madison knew this when, as part of his protest against the Alien and Sedition Acts—the speech codes of his day—he said that the freedom of speech is "the only effectual guardian of every other right."

And, in a quote that I am reminded of daily in this job, Thomas Jefferson knew this when he said in words now chiseled in the stone of his memorial, "I swear upon the altar of God eternal hostility against every form of tyranny over the mind of man."

Soon you will be the professor, the university president, the Attorney General, and even the President of the United States. And you will have your own pressing issues to grapple with. But I promise you that no issue is better decided with less debate, indifference, and with voices unheard.

There are those who will say that certain speech isn't deserving of protection. They will say that some speech is hurtful—even hateful. They will point to the very speech and beliefs that we abhor as Americans. But the right of free speech does not exist only to protect the ideas upon which most agree at a given moment in time.

As Justice Brandeis eloquently stated in his 1927 concurrence in *Whitney v. California*: "If there be time to expose through discussion the falsehood and fallacies, to avert the evil by the processes of education, the remedy to be applied is more speech, not enforced silence."

And let me be clear that protecting free speech does not mean condoning violence like we saw recently in Charlottesville. Indeed, I call upon universities to stand up against those who would silence free expression by violence or other means on their campuses.

But a mature society can tell the difference between violence and unpopular speech, and a truly free society stands up—and speaks up—for cherished rights precisely when it is most difficult to do so.

As Justice Holmes once wrote: "If there is any principle of the Constitution that more imperatively calls for attachment than any other it is the principle of free thought—not free thought for those who agree with us but freedom for the thought that we hate." For the thought that we hate.

And we must do so on our campuses. University officials and faculty must defend free expression boldly and unequivocally. That means presidents, regents, trustees and alumni as well. A national recommitment to free speech on campus is long overdue. And action to ensure First Amendment rights is overdue.

Starting today, the Department of Justice will do its part in this struggle. We will enforce federal law, defend free speech, and protect students' free expression from whatever end of the political spectrum it may come. To that end, we are filing a Statement of Interest in a campus free speech case this week and we will be filing more in the weeks and months to come.

This month, we marked the 230th anniversary of our Constitution. This month, we also marked the 54th anniversary of the 16th Street Baptist Church bombing in Birmingham. Four little girls died that day as they changed into their choir robes because the Klan wanted to silence the voices fighting for civil rights. But their voices were not silenced.

Dr. Martin Luther King Jr. would call them "the martyred heroines of a holy crusade for freedom and human dignity," and I urge you to go back and read that eulogy and consider what it had to say to each of us. This is the true legacy of free speech that has been handed down to you. It was bought with a price. This is the heritage that you have been given and which you must protect.

So I am here today to ask you to be involved to make your voices heard—and to defend the rights of others to do the same.

For the last 241 years, we have staked a country on the principle that robust and even contentious debate is how we discover truth and resolve the most intractable problems before us.

Your generation will decide if this experiment in freedom will continue. Nothing less than the future of our Republic depends on it.

Print Citations

CMS: Sessions, Jeff. "The Importance of Free Speech on College Campuses." Speech presented at Georgetown University, Washington, DC, September, 2017. In *The Reference Shelf: Representative American Speeches 2016-2017*, edited by Betsy Maury, 177-182. Ipswich, MA: H.W. Wilson, 2017.

MLA: Sessions, Jeff. "The Importance of Free Speech on College Campuses." Georgetown University. Washington, DC. September, 2017. Presentation. *The Reference Shelf: Representative American Speeches 2016-2017*. Ed. Betsy Maury. Ipswich: H.W. Wilson, 2017. 177-182. Print.

APA: Sessions, J. (2017). The importance of free speech on college campuses. [Presentation]. *Speech presented at Georgetown University*. Washington, DC. In Betsy Maury (Ed.), *The reference shelf: Representative American speeches 2016-2017* (pp. 177-182). Ipswich, MA: H.W. Wilson. (Original work published 2017)

6
DREAMers and DACA

The Asian-American Dreamer rally outside Trump Tower in Manhattan on October 5, 2017 protests to defend the future of DACA, and in support of Asian-American DACA recipients who are being impacted by the dissolution of the DACA program under the Trump administration.

Keep the Door Open for Dreamers

By Joe Kennedy III

Speaking to his colleagues in the US House of Representatives, Senator Joe Kennedy III talks about the human face of immigrants protected under DACA and urges both President Trump and his colleagues to reconsider sending young DREAMers away. Joseph Patrick Kennedy serves as the U.S. Representative for Massachusetts's 4th congressional district, a position he has held since 2013.

Mr. Speaker, we all suffer when this country breaks its promises. But for our children, that cost compounds. They pay the interest on our inaction and inadequacy. They pick up the pieces of the precious things that we broke, the sacred resources we took for granted, the battles that we were too afraid to fight.

Time and again, by choice and by chance, they have not disappointed. Their broad shoulders carry twice as much twice as far. Their spines prove twice as sturdy as the adults meant to protect them.

American history is littered with the names of young men and women, and even boys and girls, forced to be heroes before their time: the patriots of D-day, memorialized in a statue called the Spirit of Youth in Normandy; 14-year-old Emmett Till, lynched by a lie; Addie Mae Collins, Cynthia Wesley, Carole Robertson, all 14, and Carol Denise McNair, 11, four choir girls lost at the 16th Street Baptist Church bombing in Alabama.

The Children's Crusade. Little boys and girls, kids, who dared defy Bull Connor's firehoses and attack dogs to be arrested and rearrested again and again as a Nation recoiled in horror. Nine African-American high school students from Little Rock marched into an all-White high school to prove that separate is not equal. Four college students from Kent State who gave their lives to a war-weary nation's plea for peace.

Thirteen-year-old Ryan White from Indiana who showed our Nation that an HIV diagnosis does not claim your dignity.

The record number of men and women under the age of 21 who showed up at military recruiting stations in 2001, signing up to serve a nation reeling from terror on its soil.

Nineteen-year-old Zach Walls who told us that love is love as he bravely defended his two moms before the Iowa State Legislature.

Seventeen-year-old Lila Perry from Missouri who withstood the sting of stigma by being true to herself and her gender identity.

Delivered on September 7, 2017 in the US House of Representatives, Washington, DC.

Thirty-one-year-old Alonso Guillen, a Texan who traveled 120 miles from safety into the heart of Hurricane Harvey's fury on a volunteer rescue mission, who gave his life so that others, strangers, might survive. His courage and sacrifice exemplify the best traits of our Nation. They place him squarely on the long list of young American heroes who have carried us toward a more perfect union.

But this week, President Trump slammed the door on 800,000 people like Alonso. DREAMers. Children raised in our neighborhoods, who run on our playgrounds, who pitch in our Little Leagues, who proudly march in 4th of July parades, who make lemonade stands, build snowmen, go to prom, and get summer jobs, who hit the books, who earn a living, who raise families of their own, who serve in our military, who give to this country just as much, just as faithfully as you or I.

Now, our President told them that they are not wanted, that he would rather see them in handcuffs, their families ripped apart, their futures in limbo, sent to be strangers in a strange land.

Mr. Speaker, sometimes this body has to make hard choices. Sometimes our solutions are complex. This is not one of those times. This one is easy. Our work comes down to a very simple question: What are we willing to ask our children to bear?

We have the power in this body to say: Not this, not again, that we will not ask the youngest among us to force our country's conscience to awake because of the burden that we, the adults in the room, place on their shoulders. We can do better. We can be braver. We can change the course of that history. We will not stand here and leave it for future generations to wonder why we allowed such harm to pass.

Print Citations

CMS: Kennedy III, Joe. "Keep the Door Open for DREAMers." Speech presented at the US House of Representatives, Washington, DC, September, 2017. In *The Reference Shelf: Representative American Speeches 2016-2017*, edited by Betsy Maury, 185-186. Ipswich, MA: H.W. Wilson, 2017.

MLA: Kennedy III, Joe. "Keep the Door Open for DREAMers." US House of Representatives. Washington, DC. September, 2017. Presentation. *The Reference Shelf: Representative American Speeches 2016-2017*. Ed. Betsy Maury. Ipswich: H.W. Wilson, 2017. 185-186. Print.

APA: Kennedy III, Joe. (2017). Keep the door open for DREAMers. [Presentation]. *Speech presented at the US House of Representatives*. Washington, DC. In Betsy Maury (Ed.), *The reference shelf: Representative American speeches 2016-2017* (pp. 185-186). Ipswich, MA: H.W. Wilson. (Original work published 2017)

We Cannot Admit Everyone

By Jeff Sessions

*President Trump's Attorney General Jeff Sessions announces that the current adminis-
tration will end the Deferred Action for Childhood Arrivals, or DACA program during
a widely viewed press conference. The policy, begun in 2012 was instituted by President
Obama after Congress repeatedly failed to pass the so-called DREAM Act that would
have created a path to citizenship for immigrants brought to the United States as children. In the speech the attorney general stresses the need to enforce immigration laws,
saying failing to do so in the past has "put our nation at risk of crime, violence and
even terrorism." Many Democrats criticized Sessions' speech as a mischaracterization
of the program charging that Sessions' description leaves a misleading impression about
DACA holders and the impact that the program has had on illegal immigration and
crime.*

Good morning. I am here today to announce that the program known as DACA that
was effectuated under the Obama Administration is being rescinded.

The DACA program was implemented in 2012 and essentially provided a legal
status for recipients for a renewable two-year term, work authorization and other
benefits, including participation in the social security program, to 800,000 mostly-
adult illegal aliens.

This policy was implemented unilaterally to great controversy and legal concern
after Congress rejected legislative proposals to extend similar benefits on numerous
occasions to this same group of illegal aliens.

In other words, the executive branch, through DACA, deliberately sought to
achieve what the legislative branch specifically refused to authorize on multiple
occasions. Such an open-ended circumvention of immigration laws was an unconstitutional exercise of authority by the Executive Branch.

The effect of this unilateral executive amnesty, among other things, contributed
to a surge of unaccompanied minors on the southern border that yielded terrible
humanitarian consequences. It also denied jobs to hundreds of thousands of Americans by allowing those same jobs to go to illegal aliens.

We inherited from our Founders—and have advanced—an unsurpassed legal
heritage, which is the foundation of our freedom, safety, and prosperity.

As the Attorney General, it is my duty to ensure that the laws of the United
States are enforced and that the Constitutional order is upheld.

Delivered on September 5, 2017 at the US Department of Justice, Washington, DC.

No greater good can be done for the overall health and well-being of our Republic, than preserving and strengthening the impartial rule of law. Societies where the rule of law is treasured are societies that tend to flourish and succeed.

Societies where the rule of law is subject to political whims and personal biases tend to become societies afflicted by corruption, poverty, and human suffering.

To have a lawful system of immigration that serves the national interest, we cannot admit everyone who would like to come here. That is an open border policy and the American people have rightly rejected it.

Therefore, the nation must set and enforce a limit on how many immigrants we admit each year and that means all can not be accepted.

This does not mean they are bad people or that our nation disrespects or demeans them in any way. It means we are properly enforcing our laws as Congress has passed them.

It is with these principles and duties in mind, and in light of imminent litigation, that we reviewed the Obama Administration's DACA policy.

Our collective wisdom is that the policy is vulnerable to the same legal and constitutional challenges that the courts recognized with respect to the DAPA program, which was enjoined on a nationwide basis in a decision affirmed by the Fifth Circuit.

The Fifth Circuit specifically concluded that DACA had not been implemented in a fashion that allowed sufficient discretion, and that DAPA was "foreclosed by Congress's careful plan."

In other words, it was inconsistent with the Constitution's separation of powers. That decision was affirmed by the Supreme Court by an equally divided vote.

If we were to keep the Obama Administration's executive amnesty policy, the likeliest outcome is that it would be enjoined just as was DAPA. The Department of Justice has advised the President and the Department of Homeland Security that DHS should begin an orderly, lawful wind down, including the cancellation of the memo that authorized this program.

Acting Secretary Duke has chosen, appropriately, to initiate a wind down process. This will enable DHS to conduct an orderly change and fulfill the desire of this administration to create a time period for Congress to act—should it so choose. We firmly believe this is the responsible path.

Simply put, if we are to further our goal of strengthening the constitutional order and the rule of law in America, the Department of Justice cannot defend this type of overreach.

George Washington University Law School Professor Jonathan Turley in testimony before the House Judiciary Committee was clear about the enormous constitutional infirmities raised by these policies.

He said: "In ordering this blanket exception, President Obama was nullifying part of a law that he simply disagreed with.....If a president can claim sweeping discretion to suspend key federal laws, the entire legislative process becomes little more than a pretense...The circumvention of the legislative process not only undermines the authority of this branch but destabilizes the tripartite system as a whole."

Ending the previous Administration's disrespect for the legislative process is an important first step. All immigration policies should serve the interests of the people of the United States—lawful immigrant and native born alike.

Congress should carefully and thoughtfully pursue the types of reforms that are right for the American people. Our nation is comprised of good and decent people who want their government's leaders to fulfill their promises and advance an immigration policy that serves the national interest.

We are a people of compassion and we are a people of law. But there is nothing compassionate about the failure to enforce immigration laws.

Enforcing the law saves lives, protects communities and taxpayers, and prevents human suffering. Failure to enforce the laws in the past has put our nation at risk of crime, violence and even terrorism.

The compassionate thing is to end the lawlessness, enforce our laws, and, if Congress chooses to make changes to those laws, to do so through the process set forth by our Founders in a way that advances the interest of the nation.

That is what the President has promised to do and has delivered to the American people.

Under President Trump's leadership, this administration has made great progress in the last few months toward establishing a lawful and constitutional immigration system. This makes us safer and more secure.

It will further economically the lives of millions who are struggling. And it will enable our country to more effectively teach new immigrants about our system of government and assimilate them to the cultural understandings that support it.

The substantial progress in reducing illegal immigration at our border seen in recent months is almost entirely the product of the leadership of President Trump and his inspired federal immigration officers. But the problem is not solved. And without more action, we could see illegality rise again rather than be eliminated.

As a candidate, and now in office, President Trump has offered specific ideas and legislative solutions that will protect American workers, increase wages and salaries, defend our national security, ensure the public safety, and increase the general well-being of the American people.

He has worked closely with many members of Congress, including in the introduction of the RAISE Act, which would produce enormous benefits for our country. This is how our democratic process works.

There are many powerful interest groups in this country and every one of them has a constitutional right to advocate their views and represent whomever they choose.

But the Department of Justice does not represent any narrow interest or any subset of the American people. We represent all of the American people and protect the integrity of our Constitution. That is our charge.

We at Department of Justice are proud and honored to work to advance this vision for America and to do our best each day to ensure the safety and security of the American people.

Thank you.

Print Citations

CMS: Sessions, Jeff. "We Cannot Admit Everyone." Speech presented at the US Department of Justice, Washington, DC, September, 2017. In *The Reference Shelf: Representative American Speeches 2016-2017*, edited by Betsy Maury, 187-190. Ipswich, MA: H.W. Wilson, 2017.

MLA: Sessions, Jeff. "We Cannot Admit Everyone." US Department of Justice. Washington, DC. September, 2017. Presentation. *The Reference Shelf: Representative American Speeches 2016-2017*. Ed. Betsy Maury. Ipswich: H.W. Wilson, 2017. 187-190. Print.

APA: Sessions, J. (2017). We cannot admit everyone. [Presentation]. *Speech presented at the US Department of Justice*. Washington, DC. In Betsy Maury (Ed.), *The reference shelf: Representative American speeches 2016-2017* (pp. 187-190). Ipswich, MA: H.W. Wilson. (Original work published 2017)

Statement on the Deferred Action on Childhood Arrivals (DACA)

By Barack Obama

Former President Barack Obama condemned the Trump administration's decision to rescind a policy that enabled undocumented immigrants brought to the United States as children to remain here with temporary permits. In a two-page Facebook post made on September 5, 2017, Obama vigorously disagreed with Trump's decision.

"Let's be clear: the action taken today isn't required legally. It's a political decision, and a moral question."

"Whatever concerns or complaints Americans may have about immigration in general, we shouldn't threaten the future of this group of young people who are here through no fault of their own, who pose no threat, who are not taking away anything from the rest of us," the post continues. Mr. Obama, who implemented Deferred Action on Childhood Arrivals (DACA) in 2012, said when he left office he would comment on Mr. Trump's actions at "certain moments where I think our core values may be at stake."

Mr. Obama's executive order deferred deportations for people who came to the United States undocumented as children. The Trump administration announced Tuesday that it would rescind DACA after giving Congress six months to figure out how to replace it.

Immigration can be a controversial topic. We all want safe, secure borders and a dynamic economy, and people of goodwill can have legitimate disagreements about how to fix our immigration system so that everybody plays by the rules.

But that's not what the action that the White House took today is about. This is about young people who grew up in America—kids who study in our schools, young adults who are starting careers, patriots who pledge allegiance to our flag. These Dreamers are Americans in their hearts, in their minds, in every single way but one: on paper. They were brought to this country by their parents, sometimes even as infants. They may not know a country besides ours. They may not even know a language besides English. They often have no idea they're undocumented until they apply for a job, or college, or a driver's license.

Over the years, politicians of both parties have worked together to write legislation that would have told these young people—our young people—that if your parents brought you here as a child, if you've been here a certain number of years,

Delivered on September, 5, 2017, Facebook.

and if you're willing to go to college or serve in our military, then you'll get a chance to stay and earn your citizenship. And for years while I was President, I asked Congress to send me such a bill.

That bill never came. And because it made no sense to expel talented, driven, patriotic young people from the only country they know solely because of the actions of their parents, my administration acted to lift the shadow of deportation from these young people, so that they could continue to contribute to our communities and our country. We did so based on the well-established legal principle of prosecutorial discretion, deployed by Democratic and Republican presidents alike, because our immigration enforcement agencies have limited resources, and it makes sense to focus those resources on those who come illegally to this country to do us harm. Deportations of criminals went up. Some 800,000 young people stepped forward, met rigorous requirements, and went through background checks. And America grew stronger as a result.

But today, that shadow has been cast over some of our best and brightest young people once again. To target these young people is wrong—because they have done nothing wrong. It is self-defeating—because they want to start new businesses, staff our labs, serve in our military, and otherwise contribute to the country we love. And it is cruel. What if our kid's science teacher, or our friendly neighbor turns out to be a Dreamer? Where are we supposed to send her? To a country she doesn't know or remember, with a language she may not even speak?

Let's be clear: the action taken today isn't required legally. It's a political decision, and a moral question. Whatever concerns or complaints Americans may have about immigration in general, we shouldn't threaten the future of this group of young people who are here through no fault of their own, who pose no threat, who are not taking away anything from the rest of us. They are that pitcher on our kid's softball team, that first responder who helps out his community after a disaster, that cadet in ROTC who wants nothing more than to wear the uniform of the country that gave him a chance. Kicking them out won't lower the unemployment rate, or lighten anyone's taxes, or raise anybody's wages.

It is precisely because this action is contrary to our spirit, and to common sense, that business leaders, faith leaders, economists, and Americans of all political stripes called on the administration not to do what it did today. And now that the White House has shifted its responsibility for these young people to Congress, it's up to Members of Congress to protect these young people and our future. I'm heartened by those who've suggested that they should. And I join my voice with the majority of Americans who hope they step up and do it with a sense of moral urgency that matches the urgency these young people feel.

Ultimately, this is about basic decency. This is about whether we are a people who kick hopeful young strivers out of America, or whether we treat them the way we'd want our own kids to be treated. It's about who we are as a people—and who we want to be.

What makes us American is not a question of what we look like, or where our names come from, or the way we pray. What makes us American is our fidelity to a set of ideals—that all of us are created equal; that all of us deserve the chance to make of our lives what we will; that all of us share an obligation to stand up, speak out, and secure our most cherished values for the next generation. That's how America has traveled this far. That's how, if we keep at it, we will ultimately reach that more perfect union.

Print Citations

CMS: Obama, Barack. "Statement on the Deferred Action on Childhood Arrivals (DACA)." Statement presented on Facebook. September, 2017. In *The Reference Shelf: Representative American Speeches 2016-2017*, edited by Betsy Maury, 191-193. Ipswich, MA: H.W. Wilson, 2017.

MLA: Obama, Barack. "Statement on the Deferred Action on Childhood Arrivals (DACA)." Facebook. September, 2017. Presentation. *The Reference Shelf: Representative American Speeches 2016-2017*. Ed. Betsy Maury. Ipswich: H.W. Wilson, 2017. 191-193. Print.

APA: Obama, B. (2017). Statement on the deferred action on childhood arrivals (DACA). [Presentation]. *Statement presented on Facebook.* In Betsy Maury (Ed.), *The reference shelf: Representative American speeches 2016-2017* (pp. 191-193). Ipswich, MA: H.W. Wilson. (Original work published 2017)

Index